Outcomes of High-Quality Clinical Practice in Teacher Education

A volume in
Advances in Teacher Education
Diane Yendol-Hoppey, *Series Editor*

Outcomes of High-Quality Clinical Practice in Teacher Education

edited by

David Hoppey
University of North Florida

Diane Yendol-Hoppey
University of North Florida

INFORMATION AGE PUBLISHING, INC.
Charlotte, NC • www.infoagepub.com

Library of Congress Cataloging-in-Publication Data

A CIP record for this book is available from the Library of Congress
http://www.loc.gov

ISBN: 978-1-64113-375-3 (Paperback)
        978-1-64113-376-0 (Hardcover)
        978-1-64113-377-7 (ebook)

We dedicate this book to all teacher educators who are working steadfast and often upstream to make clinical practice in teacher education a reality.

You inspire the field to move forward with your innovation, vision, passion, and commitment to making the world a better place for teacher candidates and PK–12 students.

CONTENTS

SECTION II

OUTCOMES OF NEW PRACTICES

SECTION III

OUTCOMES OF NEW COURSEWORK–FIELDWORK INTEGRATION

SECTION IV

OUTCOMES OF NEW PROGRAM CONFIGURATIONS

PREFACE

Today, teacher education is under attack. Multiple groups are questioning higher education's ability to prepare effective teachers (Cochran-Smith, 2005; Levine, 2007; National Council on Teacher Quality, 2013). Critics scrutinize program design, course syllabi, and point to the lack of real-life experiences that help teacher candidates connect theory to practice as reasons why graduates are underprepared for the reality of teaching in today's schools (Darling-Hammond, 2012; Zeichner, 2012). Simultaneously, teacher educators wrestle with developing innovative clinical models within their own universities where they often face the challenge of working within traditional university assignment and reward structures (Yendol-Hoppey, Hoppey, Morewood, Hayes, & Graham, 2013; Zeichner, 2010).

For decades, teacher educators have recognized the importance of clinical practice in teacher education. During the '80s and '90s the Holmes Partnership (1986, 1990, 1995) and the National Network for Educational Renewal (Goodlad, 1994) both called for creating a much stronger clinical component within teacher education that would require developing strong school-university partnerships. This reform effort asked teacher education programs to rethink the nature, quality, and intensity of teacher candidates' clinical experiences. Ideally, this rethinking would facilitate candidates' ability to bridge the theoretical and the practical throughout their preparation.

Over time there have been pockets of success with integrating quality partnership-based clinical practice in teacher education programs across the nation. However, profession-wide, teacher education programmatic

Outcomes of High-Quality Clinical Practice in Teacher Education, pages xi–xiv
Copyright © 2018 by Information Age Publishing
All rights of reproduction in any form reserved.

changes that reflected these goals never fully materialized. Recognizing that progress towards actualizing stronger clinical practice had stalled, the National Council for Accreditation of Teacher Education (NCATE, 2001) developed of a set of standards for defining and evaluating school-university partnerships. The discussion of these standards set the stage for the National Association of Professional Development Schools (NAPDS, 2008) to develop a list of nine essentials designed to provide a common understanding of quality clinical practice. In 2010, the NCATE Blue Ribbon Report continued the press for clinical practice by calling for teacher preparation programs to turn teacher education upside down and emphasize clinical learning (NCATE, 2010). In response to this recognition that clinical practice needed to take a more predominant place in teacher preparation, the Council for the Accreditation of Educator Preparation (CAEP) put in place a check on Colleges of Education's clinical efforts by requiring documentation of "effective partnerships and high-quality clinical practice with sufficient depth, breadth, diversity, coherence, and duration to ensure that candidates demonstrate their developing effectiveness and positive impact on all students' learning and development" (2015; http://caepnet.org/standards/standard-2). Finally, in 2016 the American Association of Colleges for Teacher Education (AACTE) convened the Clinical Practice Commission, comprised of representation from a wide group of educational organizations and institutional types, to provide a report focused on how to strengthen clinical practice within teacher education programs. This report, entitled *A Pivot Toward Clinical Practice, Its Lexicon, and Renewing the Profession of Teaching* (AACTE, 2018), reflects the beginning of a multiphased process that aims to strengthen clinical practice across the nation.

It is important to note though that, to date, much of the literature on clinically intensive teacher preparation has been conceptual and theoretical in nature. Though the idea of clinical practice in teacher education is not new, research on the outcomes of clinically intensive teacher education is in its infancy. We have many descriptions of clinically practice including illustrations of school–university partnerships and teacher residency programs but still too little empirical evidence. Therefore, the objective of this book is to share emerging research related to a variety of innovative clinical practices, roles, and models that teacher educators can use as they seek to embed clinical practice within their own programs. The book is intended to stimulate the thinking of faculty navigating the challenges of designing, implementing, and studying clinically intensive teacher education. That said, this book moves beyond the conceptual design of programs and seeks to make visible the intricacies and complexities associated with clinically intensive teacher education practices through empirical study.

In combination, these chapters also showcase emerging research designs that focus on the outcomes associated with a wide-range of stakeholders including teacher candidates, in-service teachers, university faculty and student learning. The research shared within this book provides teacher educators ideas for establishing research agendas, gathering data, and studying outcomes of their programs. Therefore, this book challenges teacher educators to participate in not only engaging in clinical practice but also beginning to think more systematically and intentionally about how they can establish a collective and collaborative research agenda that uses data to inform the future of clinically intensive teacher education.

David Hoppey and **Diane Yendol-Hoppey**
University of North Florida

REFERENCES

American Association of Colleges of Teacher Education. (2018). *A pivot toward clinical practice, its lexicon, and the renewal of educator preparation.* Retrieved from https://aacte.org/professional-development-and-events/clinical-practice -commission-press-conference

Cochran-Smith, M. (2005). Teacher education and the outcomes trap. *Journal of Teacher Education, 56*(5), 411–417.

Council for the Accreditation of Educator Preparation. (2015). *Accreditation standards.* Retrieved from http://caepnet.org/standards/standard-2

Darling-Hammond, L. (2012). *Powerful teacher education: Lessons from exemplary programs.* San Francisco, CA: Jossey-Bass.

Goodlad, J. I. (1994). The national network for educational renewal. *The Phi Delta Kappan, 75*(8), 632–638.

Holmes Group. (1986). *Tomorrow's teachers: A report of the Holmes Group.* East Lansing, MI: Author.

Holmes Group. (1990). *Tomorrow's schools: Principles for the design of professional development schools.* East Lansing, MI: Author.

Holmes Group. (1995). *Tomorrow's Schools of Education.* East Lansing, MI: Author.

Levine, A. (2007). Executive summary: Educating school teachers. *Essays in Perspective, 1*(Winter), 1–12.

National Association of Professional Development Schools. (2008). *What it means to be a professional development school.* Retrieved from www.napds.org

National Council for the Accreditation of Teacher Education. (2001). *Standards for professional development schools.* Retrieved from www.ncate.org/~/media/ Files/caep/accreditation.../ncate-standards-2008.pdf?la=en

National Council for the Accreditation of Teacher Education. (2010). *Transforming teacher education through clinical practice: A national strategy to prepare effective teachers. A report of the Blue Ribbon Panel on Clinical Preparation and Partnership for Improved Student Learning.* Washington, DC: Author. Retrieved from caepnet .org/~/media/Files/caep/accreditation-resources/blue-ribbon-panel.pdf

National Council on Teacher Quality. (2013). *Teacher prep review: A review of the nation's teacher preparation programs.* Washington, DC: Author. Retrieved from https://www.nctq.org/review/home

Yendol-Hoppey, D., Hoppey, D., Morewood, A., Hayes, S., & Graham, M. (2013). Micropolitical and identity challenges influencing new faculty participation in teacher education reform: When will we learn? *Teachers College Record, 115*(7), 1–31.

Zeichner, K. (2010). Rethinking the connections between campus courses and field experiences in college- and university-based teacher education. *Journal of Teacher Education, 61*(1–2), 89–99.

Zeichner, K. (2012). The turn once again toward practice-based teacher education. *Journal of Teacher Education, 63*(5), 376–382.

ACKNOWLEDGMENTS

We want to recognize the many colleagues who have influenced this work and collaborated with us on designing, implementation, monitoring, and researching high quality clinically based teacher education practices and programs over the years. Our higher education journey has been taken place across many settings—the Pennsylvania State University, the University of Florida, West Virginia University, the University of South Florida and the University of North Florida. At each stop on our journey we have been blessed to work with dedicated and knowledgeable colleagues in programs with high quality clinical practices. This includes university faculty and administrators, school district leaders, school principals, in-service teachers, pre-service teacher candidates, and doctoral students that make a difference. These relationship and what we learned in each of these contexts continue to influence our work today. We are grateful to:

- The invaluable mentorship of Nancy Dana, Jim Nolan, and James McLeskey. We continually try to pay it forward in our work with the next generation of teacher education scholars.
- The many school based leaders and teacher leaders who embrace and model the pivotal role school-based teacher educators play in clinical practice. We are particularly grateful to Jim Brandenburg, Kevin Berry, Lacy Reed, Darby Delane, Anne Copeland, Caroline Scott, Craig Butz, Paula Renfro, Pat Willis, and Sonita Young.
- Our current and former teacher candidates who continue to be the lifeblood of the profession. Your infectious energy and enthusiasm

Outcomes of High-Quality Clinical Practice in Teacher Education, pages xv–xvi
Copyright © 2018 by Information Age Publishing
All rights of reproduction in any form reserved.

to improve outcomes for all students is inspiring. We look forward to you taking the lead as future school-based teacher educators.

- Our current and former doctoral students who challenge us to think outside the box and seek ways to solve the persistent dilemmas that impact the teaching profession. It is an honor to work with you on the front lines as we collectively develop, implement, and study high quality clinically based teacher education programs and practices.

- Our former colleagues at the University of South Florida who served with us on Educator Preparation Committee including David Allsopp, Ilene Berson, Michael Berson, Bill Black, Becci Burns, Paula Cate, Ann Cranston-Gingras, Barbara Cruz, Robert Dedrick, Darlene DeMarie, Danielle Dennis, Betsy Doone, Cheryl Ellerbrock, Allen Feldman, Sara Flory, Bea Green, Stacy Hahn, Sophia Han, Kris Hogarty, Angie Hooser, Jennifer Jacobs, Joan Kaywell, Sarah Kiefer, Jeany McCarthy, Audra Parker, Barbara Shircliffe, Jason Jude Smith, Phil Smith, Mike Stewart, Vasti Torres, Darren Towne, Steven Thornton, Katie Tricarico, Eugenia Vomvordi-Ivanovic, and Sarah van Ingen. This committee engaged in many courageous conversations that served as the catalyst for developing the clinical practices heuristic shared in this book.

- We must recognize our current colleagues in the College of Education and Human Services at the University of North Florida who are engaged in this important work now. We truly appreciate your vision for delivering and studying the outcomes of high quality clinically based teacher education programs. The benefits of this complex and challenging work will be felt for generations.

- Lastly, we would like to express our appreciation to Amanda Laukitis, Samantha Kwiatkowski, and Caran Mullins who generously supported this work by gathering information, editing chapters, and assembling the book. Without your efforts, this book would have not gone to press.

CHAPTER 1

DEFINING HIGH QUALITY CLINICAL PRACTICE IN TEACHER EDUCATION

Diane Yendol-Hoppey and David Hoppey
University of North Florida

ABSTRACT

In this introductory chapter we (a) define high quality clinical practice in teacher education to build an understanding of a continuum of clinical models; (b) provide an overview of why researching outcomes of clinical practice in teacher education is important; (c) highlight the need for programmatic change and conducting engaged scholarship; (d) share a heuristic that organizes clinical practices into six overarching areas that help program faculty plan, structure, and enact high quality clinical teacher education programs; (e) discuss how the book is organized and summarize each chapter briefly; and (f) conclude with some guiding questions to consider as you read the research in this book.

High quality clinical teacher education practice is an approach to teacher preparation that began decades ago. Over the course of many years, organizations have continued to call upon teacher preparation programs to

Outcomes of High-Quality Clinical Practice in Teacher Education, pages 1–14
Copyright © 2018 by Information Age Publishing

1

integrate practice with PK–12 students throughout the teacher preparation program (AACTE, 2018; Holmes Group, 1986, 1990, 1995; NCATE, 2010). Although pockets of clinically intensive educator preparation programs exist, today we continue to witness the implementation of teacher preparation efforts that vary substantially in their commitment to teacher candidate learning within the context of practice and throughout the preparation program. This has been most recently noted within the American Association of Colleges of Teacher Education (AACTE) Clinical Practice Commission's statement: *A Pivot Toward Clinical Practice, Its Lexicon, and Renewing the Profession of Teaching:*

> Unfortunately, since the publication of the Blue Ribbon Panel report, reform and reinvention efforts have largely been scattered and with some haphazard attempts by programs and universities grappling with the idea of immersing teacher preparation in clinical practice. A unified professional structure with a shared understanding of clinical practice has yet to develop in teacher preparation. (2018, p. 3)

Given that the blue ribbon panel's report was almost a decade ago, what are the "haphazard models" that have emerged?

TODAY'S HAPHAZARD CONTINUUM
OF TEACHER EDUCATION

In order to depict what high quality clinical practice in teacher education is and is not, we can offer a continuum of teacher preparation configurations reflecting five distinct approaches (Yendol-Hoppey, 2013). These models include: clinically limited, clinically accompanied, clinically intensive, clinically centered, and a clinical-only model.

First, *clinically limited* teacher preparation refers to programs that require little to no opportunities for practicing teaching. These often exist in the context of alternative preparation. For example, in Florida the Educator Preparation Institute (EPI) program pathway, a competency-based approach to teacher certification, allows the institution to determine the hours of clinical practice. In some cases, as few as 50 hours are provided candidates to observe, practice, or refine practice. A second model, *clinically accompanied* teacher education refers to programs that may include multiple field experiences but do not systematically and intentionally couple or align theory and research with practice opportunities for professional learning. These programs often have little university-based teacher educator involvement in the field and the classroom teacher does not possess a conceptual understanding of the teacher preparation program coursework. This typically leaves the teacher candidate responsible for independently negotiating the clinical space as well as independently making the connections between the coursework and the field. Given the complexity of classrooms today, teacher candidates need much more support then this as they learn to teach.

Unlike the clinically limited and accompanied-models, *clinically intensive* teacher education provides teacher candidates the opportunity to practice teaching throughout the program receiving high quality mentoring from school-based teacher educators coupled with coaching from university-based teacher educators. The intent of a clinically intensive program is to systematically and intentionally link coursework and fieldwork so that teacher candidates can experience, with support, the interplay between thinking about teaching and practicing teaching. The link encourages teacher educators to plan clinical tasks with school-based partners that link coursework to student learning.

Much less frequently occurring is *clinically centered* teacher preparation. Clinically centered teacher preparation systematically and intentionally begins with the learning needs of the PK–12 students within a particular school context. The teacher candidates' tasks are then designed with specific attention to these student needs. This approach is like working from the inside out and requires transforming the way teacher educators plan their curriculum and subsequent instruction. The idea of being clinically centered requires teacher educators to place PK–12 students at the forefront as they design their syllabus so that the syllabus addresses the classroom, school, and community issues and dilemmas present. The assumption embedded in a clinically centered program is that teacher candidates will learn to teach within a complex and uncertain context by developing a reflective practice and professional educator dispositions to solve problems of practice. This situates the school at the center of the teacher education program and requires programs to restructure and repurpose across the traditional school and higher education boundaries. To do this, teacher educators have to "be there" to understand the school context and the learners' needs.

These clinically intensive and clinically centered structures not only pay attention to how long teacher candidates learn in the field but more importantly *what kind of learning* happens in the field. Like a teaching hospital, the clinically intensive and clinically centered models point to the importance of systematically and intentionally building professional knowledge and practice by linking the PK–12 classroom and school to the coursework. This continuum was expanded upon by Dennis et al. (2017) as they described the ontological and epistemological differences related to learning to teach within each of the models.

In addition to these four models, alternative pathways have also emerged to address the mounting teacher shortage. These alternative pathways typically use a clinical-only model of teacher preparation. This model is most visible when districts do not have a pool of credentialed teachers to hire from and, as a result, are forced to hire uncertified teachers without substantial formal preparation. This group of teachers relies on support for learning to teach from those who work within the schools where they work or other nonprofit organizations. This demand places a tremendous burden on school administrators and other teachers in the school to develop the requisite professional knowledge. Providing this extra level of support to noncertified teachers is particularly challenging in underperforming schools where the same educators are called upon to give their full attention to facilitating the learning of PK–12 students. Preparing individuals to teach through a *clinically only* model is highly concerning in low performing schools where high levels of teacher turnover occur and the teachers are often the least qualified and/or experienced.

Today, the most recent report by the AACTE Clinical Practice Commission (2018) offers a set of proclamations and tenets that once again provide guidance to teacher educators interested in advancing clinical preparation. The report defines clinical practice in teacher education as a preparation pathway that requires teacher candidates to work for an extended period in authentic educational settings to engage in the pedagogical work of the profession of teaching. This book is written for and by individuals who are interested in the design, implementation, and/or study of clinical practice within the clinically intensive and clinically centered models of teacher education.

WHO WROTE THESE CHAPTERS AND WHY ARE THESE AUTHORS SPECIAL?

We believe that the chapters within this book are written by courageous individuals who think about, engage in, and study the clinical practices within their context. They study what they do. They are courageous because they have made time within their already demanding work lives as teacher educators to engage with partners, each other, and their students to deepen and integrate the clinical components of their programs. Then they have studied the work to better understand the impact. Similar to preparing medical professionals, clinical practice in teacher education requires the complex and time intensive work of supporting teacher candidate ability to link theory, research, and practice as well as ongoing inquiry into identifying high impact pedagogical practices that support teacher candidate learning.

As described above teacher preparation models have run the gamut across decades. The gold standard for teacher preparation requires programs to make high quality clinical practices the norm rather than the exception. Actualizing these calls will likely require teacher educators to develop a "shared understanding of clinical practice" (AACTE, 2018, p. 3). This book brings together the work of teacher educators who share the fundamental commitment to clinical practice and understanding the outcomes of these efforts. The chapters within this book reflect the research of university teacher education faculty who also engaged in sustained collegial conversations with public school partners in order to create and document specific moves towards systematically embedding clinical practice into the fabric of their programs.

HOW CAN WE RECOGNIZE ENGAGEMENT AND ENGAGED RESEARCH?

Understanding impact and outcomes requires nurturing a particular type of teacher educator who engages in sustained collegial work with public school partners. These teacher educators often employ research opportunities that are consistent with Boyer's (1990, 1996) *Engaged Scholarship*. Many of the authors within this book utilized Engaged Scholarship as a research stance to enhance their teacher education program. Specifically, Boyer (1990) defined Engaged Scholarship as blending: (a) the *scholarship of discovery*, which contributes to the search for new knowledge through collaborative inquiry; (b) the *scholarship of integration*, which makes connections across contexts and disciplines, places specialized knowledge in larger contexts, and advances knowledge through synthesis; (c) the *scholarship of application* through which scholars ask how knowledge can be applied to educational dilemmas, address school needs, as well as test, inspire, and challenge theory; and (d) the *scholarship of teaching*, which includes working with partners to create, transform, and extend knowledge of teaching beyond the university walls.

Opportunities for engaged scholarship strengthen important teacher education reform efforts. This type of research, when applied to developing clinical practice in teacher preparation, is multifaceted, time-intensive, and characterized by episodic bursts of progress that typically necessitates participants to cross disciplinary as well as institutional borders. Engaged scholarship requires an openness to exploring new knowledge bases, awareness of political savviness, and extraordinarily navigation skills. Teacher educators who conduct Engaged Scholarship have the potential to provide critical and uniquely relevant contributions to the empirical literature related to clinical practice (e.g., The Holmes Group, National Network for Educational Renewal, National Association of Professional Development Schools). In this book, we recognize engaged work as an important approach to scholarship in professional education.

WHAT KIND OF CHANGE IS NEEDED?

Sometimes we hear the question, how many clinical hours are enough? We are certain from this book that this is the wrong question. Moving forward with systemic efforts to include more clinical practice in teacher education programs cannot be actualized without deep changes in how we shape the learning experiences for candidates in the field. The types of innovations discussed within the chapters of this book require teacher educators to move beyond adding more hours or making first order changes that focus on incrementally tweaking roles, practices, coursework, and programs. These innovations required second order change (Cuban, 2001) that require teacher educators and their school partners to think differently about the roles they play, the way they work with one another, the way resources are used, and the expertise they must develop. Second order change requires that universities and their school partners view the preparation and retention of new teachers as a shared responsibility. Shared responsibility requires university and school partners to rethink structures and build upon the research related to job-embedded professional learning.

While we have recognized the authors' engaged scholarship and their efforts to contribute new ways of thinking about roles, practices, coursework–fieldwork configurations, and program configurations, we would be remiss if we did not emphasize that these shifts require a unique kind of teacher educator. First, the authors of these chapters had to be willing to let go of tradition and reconceptualize their work as teacher educators to place at the forefront practice-based learning. Alan Tom (1997) argued decades ago that shifts in faculty identity would be essential in order to actualize the goals of high quality clinical practice. This shift often required the authors to let go of traditional practices and long-standing identities related to their work. They demonstrated the disposition to innovate. Furthermore, these authors needed to understand and draw upon the empirical literature related to supporting learning through practice. Once the innovation was defined, they identified the time and space to enact these innovations by securing support from many stakeholders as well as navigating the tricky and messy work of implementing change. Upon building and implementing the innovation, the authors of these chapters studied the innovations to try and "get it right."

A HEURISTIC FOR UNDERSTANDING CLINICAL PRACTICES IN TEACHER EDUCATION

So why have so many teacher education programs failed to enact and sustain high quality clinical practices in their programs? Even after 25 years, there have still been "too many spectators and not enough players" (Holmes Group, 1995, p. 92) in enacting high quality clinical practice. One reason we have only achieved pockets of success is that as a field we have not operationalized the practices needed to enact high quality clinical practice.

To begin operationalizing these practices, we offer a heuristic (Yendol-Hoppey et al., 2017). The heuristic was constructed by synthesizing the experiences of a group of approximately 20 teacher education faculty who defined themselves as teacher educators at the University of South Florida. The group met monthly to discuss their teacher education work and this heuristic, which is presented as a framework comprised of six different clinical practices, emerged from their discussion. This heuristic provides a framework for thinking about operationalizing clinical practice in teacher preparation programs.

To investigate *what* university-based teacher educators might do to strengthen clinical practice, the inquiry group used a year-long, collaborative process to collect, develop, and negotiate stakeholder perspectives that resulted in a set of clinical practices. The resulting framework includes six complementary types of practices: (a) clinical evaluation practices that focus on quality assurance; (b) clinical coaching practices which focus on supporting performance and program coherence; (c) partnership practices which focus on creating a culture of shared responsibility for teacher education; (d) methods course practices which focus on ensuring a strong course-to-field experience connection; (e) leadership practices that focus on facilitating the development, implementation, and sustainability of clinical practices; and (f) research practices that include studying impact on teacher candidate and PK–12 student learning. Each of these six practices would be enacted using a set of contextually sensitive routines (see Table 1.1).

The studies shared within this book fall within the practices defined by this heuristic. By specifying and organizing routines within each of these clinical practices in a way that demonstrates the complexity of the work, colleges of education can rethink the traditional structures that compromise actualization of second-order change. These structures might include making shifts to work assignments, tenure and promotion criteria, and the nature of research.

HOW IS THIS BOOK ORGANIZED?

This book focuses on identifying the outcomes of *high quality clinical practice* in teacher education. The book is organized into four sections: (a) the outcome of new roles, (b) the outcome of new practices, (c) the outcome of new coursework/fieldwork configurations, and (d) the outcome of new program configurations.

TABLE 1.1   Clinical Practices for University- and School-Based Teacher Educators

Clinical Evaluation Practices *Assessing Candidate Quality*	Clinical Coaching Practices *Supporting and Strengthening Candidate Performance*	Partnership Practices *Facilitating SBTE[a] & UBTE[b] Shared Responsibility for Teacher Education*	Methods and Foundation Course Practices *Creating Strong Course-to-Field and Field-to-Course Connection*	Educator Preparation Leadership Practices *Overseeing Clinically Intensive Programs*	Research Practices *Engaging in Teacher Education Research Practices*
• Conduct UBTE evaluations • Conduct SBTE evaluations • Review Candidate self evaluation • Conduct evaluation conference(s) with candidate and SBTE • When necessary collaborate as triad[c] to create and support a plan for continual improvement • Review professional standards concerns and participate in student initiated grievance processes	• Conduct observations to gather evidence for shared inquiry into candidate practice • Implement a range of signature pedagogies that focus on supporting candidate learning (e.g., inquiry, clinical supervision, content coaching, PLCs, teaching rounds, co-teaching) • Identify goals with candidate • Conduct coaching pre and post conferences with candidate and, when appropriate triad	• Establish a culture of shared responsibility for educator • Co-construct a shared understanding of candidate field experience expectations • Communicate regularly across stakeholders • Share feedback regarding coursework and fieldwork • Provide professional development support to strengthen learning of both UBTE & SBTE • Collaborate with stakeholders to	• Understand the clinical context including: curriculum, resources, and common pedagogical (core) practices • Work with school partners to design and revise curriculum and performance tasks • Facilitate candidate development of ability to negotiate curriculum and instructional tensions between course and field • Assure candidate understanding of the content needed for application of	• Bring together all faculty involved to develop program coherence • Facilitate on-going self-study • Collect, review, analyze, and share program related data • Collaborate with department chair on scheduling and staffing arrangement (including across departments) • Assure UBTE & SBTE credentials (e.g., effective, recency, relevancy) • Oversee professional standards	• Studying Teacher Education Program & Practices (e.g., evaluation, coaching; partnerships, course instruction, leadership) • Conducting Program Evaluation • Valuing a wide-range of paradigmatic (e.g., translational, applied, engaged scholarship) and methodological approaches (e.g., including self-study, action research) • Collaborative scholarship

(continued)

TABLE 1.1 Clinical Practices for University- and School-Based Teacher Educators (continued)					
Clinical Evaluation Practices *Assessing Candidate Quality*	**Clinical Coaching Practices** *Supporting and Strengthening Candidate Performance*	**Partnership Practices** *Facilitating SBTE[a] & UBTE[b] Shared Responsibility for Teacher Education*	**Methods and Foundation Course Practices** *Creating Strong Course-to-Field and Field-to-Course Connection*	**Educator Preparation Leadership Practices** *Overseeing Clinically Intensive Programs*	**Research Practices** *Engaging in Teacher Education Research Practices*
• Conduct additional evaluations if educator candidate is on action plan • Maintain evaluation records and submit identified components as critical tasks • Write letters of recommendation for potential employers for candidates	• Maintain on-going communication related to candidate's growth • Plan and teach seminars designed to link theory and practice • Problem solve • Maintain regular contact with other program UBTE & SBTE to enhance coherence • Develop an understanding of course content that should be "performed" • Attend supervisory meetings	• problem solve • Create communication tools • Co-select placements • Engage in collaborative curriculum building, co-teaching, and research • Participate in ongoing partnership assessment	knowledge • Develop SBTE and UBTE knowledge of subject-specific course instruction • Provide representations of practice, opportunities, deconstruction of practice, and opportunities for approximations of practice within course • Integrate coursework with field work through linked assignments • Participate in program coherence meetings	concerns and student grievances • Maintain evaluation records • Develop and implement program orientations each fall • Work with school partners to identifying partnership schools/placements for practicums and final internships • Recruit new partnership teachers for mentor training • Coordinate fingerprinting • Collaborate with advising	• Educator preparation grant writing activities

(continued)

TABLE 1.1 Clinical Practices for University- and School-Based Teacher Educators (continued)

Clinical Evaluation Practices *Assessing Candidate Quality*	Clinical Coaching Practices *Supporting and Strengthening Candidate Performance*	Partnership Practices *Facilitating SBTE[a] & UBTE[b] Shared Responsibility for Teacher Education*	Methods and Foundation Course Practices *Creating Strong Course-to-Field and Field-to-Course Connection*	Educator Preparation Leadership Practices *Overseeing Clinically Intensive Programs*	Research Practices *Engaging in Teacher Education Research Practices*
	• Conduct regular informal visits with candidates to support candidate learning		• Faculty Course Leads provide leadership across sections (e.g., adjuncts) • Revise and update syllabi, which may include preparing undergraduate/graduate program committee	• Collaborate with enrollment services on recruiting efforts	

a SBTE- School-based Teacher Educator
b UBTE- University-based Teacher Educator (Course/Field)
c Triad- SBTE, UBTE, teacher candidate

Section I includes two examples of the unique role configurations that support the implementation and sustainability of clinical practice in teacher education. For example, in Chapter 2, "Understanding Mentoring Practices in a Professional Development School Partnership: Collaborating With the Professional Development Associate," Mark and Nolan investigate the role of the mentor teacher as teacher educator by examining mentoring from the mentor's perspective. This case study explored the self-reported practices of mentors in the PDS context to understand how these practices developed and changed over time. Findings suggested a specific mentoring practice that has not been previously discussed in the literature, collaborating with the university supervisor to expand a framework for effective mentoring of teacher candidates.

New roles are also identified as critical in the study presented in Chapter 3. This study, entitled "The Site Coordinator Role in a Clinically Rich Teacher Education Program" by DeBiase, Butler, Khan, and Dyer, studied a teacher preparation program that increased the clinical intensity through the induction of a new full time faculty position known as the site coordinator. Site coordinators fulfill distinct roles and provide extensive supervision and coaching, playing a significant role in the preparedness of program graduates. They found that program graduate retention rates have surpassed that of the national average.

Although new roles are important to implementing change, in Section II, a variety of new practices are identified that support clinical practice. As noted above, high quality clinical practice not only emphasizes more time in the clinical setting but, even more important, how that time is used. Chapter 4 presents a study by Rodgers, Vescio, Burns, and Gibbs, entitled "The Role of Preservice Teacher Coaching in Clinically Rich Teacher Education." This study examined teacher candidates' learning as they participated in coaching cycles. Their work distinguished the practice of using coaching cycles from the more traditional use of observation for evaluative purposes. They found that coaching fostered a type of individualized, job-embedded support that led to change in interns' daily teaching, elicited collaboration and communication that benefited intern growth, and supported learning of the skills and dispositions necessary to intern success.

In the study presented in Chapter 5, entitled "Creating Spaces for Becoming: Interrogating the Voices That Arise in Clinical Practice," Hayes and Bolyard investigated how a professional learning community emerged as a practice that creates spaces for dialogue that helped teacher candidates recognize the dilemmas of their practice, interrogate and problematize what they experienced and believed, and explore multiple possibilities for their future actions. They found that teacher candidates began to problematize the status quo and challenge the sacred stories of their classrooms/school. However, these teacher candidates struggled to negotiate the tensions among the historical, social, and political discourses in which they practiced. This study demonstrates the importance of re-visioning the traditional seminar courses as professional learning communities in which all stakeholders might engage in questioning *what is* in order to imagine possibilities for *what might be.*

A final example of a new practice is offered in Chapter 6. The Brady and Miller study entitled "Curriculum-Based VAM: An Alternative to Traditional VAM in Clinically Rich Teacher Education" offers a rich description of the evaluation context teacher preparation programs face today. They describe the current educational evaluation climate and discuss consequences of the VAM effort. The authors then offer a curriculum-based, action research alternative VAM approach for clinical practice in teacher education. The chapter highlights the results of their teacher preparation program's efforts to incorporate an alternative, action-research focused VAM.

Section III included examples of new coursework-fieldwork integration. In Chapter 7, "'We Need to be Prepared!': Teacher Candidates' Third Learning Space With University ELLs," Amos investigated the impact of regular interactions with English language learners enrolled in a university's ESL program on teacher candidates. In order to increase this contact, a clinical experience was designed in conjunction with a university ESL program that offers ESL classes to non-native international students who wish to improve their English language skills. This research investigated the impact of the clinical experience and found that third spaces provided the participants with opportunities to make their own assumptions problematic, inquire into the relationships between academic and practical knowledge, and discover new findings on their own. The findings indicate that the feedback teacher candidates receive from university instructors as they work within these third spaces play an important role to candidate success.

In Chapter 8, entitled "Fostering a Civic Ethos: Teacher Candidates as Effective Citizens in an Urban PDS, Special Education Context," Reed and Gray describe how to use the PDS model to create coursework–fieldwork integration related to service learning. The service learning component connects academic content to community experiences and uses critical reflection as a means to promote learning. This chapter shares the impact of a service learning experience within a middle school special education context on teacher candidates becoming civically engaged learners.

A final example of coursework-fieldwork integration can be found in Chapter 9. In this chapter, "Understanding Teacher Candidates' Perspectives of Learning to Teach During an Innovative Summer Practicum," Hoppey, Allsopp, Riley, Frier, and Hahn investigated how teacher candidates come to understand, develop, and construct meanings from the daily events and interactions within an alternative summer practicum experience that is tightly coupled with a methods course. They provide insight into the impact of tightly coupling coursework with rich clinical experiences as an important component of effective teacher preparation.

The final section of the book, Section IV, offers two examples of new program configuration. In Chapter 10, "Restructuring Teacher Preparation With Culturally Relevant Principles: A Best Practice for Clinically Rich Teacher Preparation and 21st Century Learners," Underwood, Dickinson, and Cantu studied a restructured teacher preparation program designed to prepare teacher candidates to address the growing needs of diverse classrooms. The teacher in residence program demonstrates how academic success can be achieved when the conventional model of teacher preparation is restructured with anti-racist teacher preparation strategies, which include innovative field experiences in highly diverse classrooms, reformed course work and professional development to include comprehensive instruction on culturally responsive pedagogy, and on-going personal reflections, while at the same time working directly with diverse students. This chapter provides an overview of the program including an in-depth analysis of the use of critical autobiography for capturing teacher candidate development.

In Chapter 11, entitled "Perceptions of Preparedness: Reflections of Deaf Education Program Graduates," Kilpatrick, Headrick-Hall, and Wolbers articulate that the roles and responsibilities for which deaf education teacher preparation programs are preparing graduates are changing. This study shares the findings of a qualitative interview study of graduates of one redesigned deaf education program and provides suggestions for the future design.

Finally, in Chapter 12, Burns offers her unique synthesis as she looks across the chapters to discuss a core set of principles as well as provide direction for the future. She raises enduring questions that the field needs to grapple with as we move forward in developing, implementing, and studying clinical practice.

What Questions Might You Consider as You Explore the Chapters?

As you explore each chapter within this book, consider the following questions. These questions are intended to help programs envision the possibilities for clinical practices and provide ideas for studying outcomes of these efforts.

1. To what extent has your program engaged in shifts, such as these described in the book, toward assuring clinical practice is central to your teacher education program(s)?
2. What new roles, practices, course configurations, or program configurations have you developed that should be studied within your

context *or* might you develop and study within your context? What will it take for you to engage in this research?

3. Is your program engaged in second-order change? How have you shifted the nature of roles, practices, course configuration, and program configurations? What evidence do you have that your own program is simultaneously shifting the nature of roles, practices, course configuration, and program configurations to create high quality clinical practice?

REFERENCES

American Association of Colleges of Teacher Education. (2018). *A pivot toward clinical practice, its lexicon, and renewing the profession of teaching.* Retrieved from https://aacte.org/professional-development-and-events/clinical-practice-commission-press-conference

Boyer, E. L. (1990). *Scholarship reconsidered: Priorities of the professoriate.* New York, NY: Carnegie Foundation for the Advancement of Teaching.

Boyer, E. L. (1996). The scholarship of engagement. *Journal of Public Outreach, 1*(1), 11–20.

Cuban, L. (2001). *How can I fix it? Finding solutions and managing dilemmas.* New York, NY: Teachers College Press.

Dennis, D., Burns, R. W., Tricarico, K., van Ingen, S., Jacobs, J., & Davis, J. (2017). Problematizing clinical education: What is our future? In R. Flessner & D. R. Lecklider (Eds.), *The power of clinical preparation in teacher education* (pp. 1–20). New York, NY: Rowman & Littlefield.

Holmes Group. (1986). *Tomorrow's teachers.* East Lansing, MI: Author.

Holmes Group. (1990). *Tomorrow's schools: Principles for the design of professional development schools.* East Lansing, MI: Author.

Holmes Group. (1995). *Tomorrow's Schools of Education.* East Lansing, MI: Author.

National Council for the Accreditation of Teacher Education. (2010). *Transforming teacher education through clinical practice: A national strategy to prepare effective teachers.* Retrieved from http://www.highered.nysed.gov/pdf/NCATECR.pdf

Tom, A. R. (1997). *Redesigning teacher education.* Albany: State University of New York Press.

Yendol-Hoppey, D. (2013, November). *Teacher education in the United States: Possibilities and problems.* Invited Keynote at ISATT 2013 Conference, Uberaba, Brazil.

Yendol-Hoppey, D., Hoppey, D., Jacobs, J., Burns, R. W., Allsopp, D., & Ellerbrock, C. (2017, March). *Defining university-based clinically rich teacher education practices and understanding the implications for university-based teacher educators.* Presentation at the meeting of American Association of Colleges of Teacher Education, Tampa FL.

SECTION I

OUTCOME OF NEW ROLES

CHAPTER 2

UNDERSTANDING MENTORING PRACTICES IN A PROFESSIONAL DEVELOPMENT SCHOOL PARTNERSHIP

Collaborating With the Professional Development Associate

Kelly M. Mark
State College Area School District

James F. Nolan
Penn State University

ABSTRACT

As many teacher education programs have moved towards more clinically-centered preparation, the role of the mentor teacher as teacher educator has taken on increasing importance. Unfortunately empirical studies that exam-

Outcomes of High-Quality Clinical Practice in Teacher Education, pages 17–37

ine mentoring from the mentor's perspective are relatively rare. This qualitative study reports the findings of research conducted with four mentors in a professional development school (PDS) teacher preparation context. This instrumental case study with phenomenological underpinnings sought to answer the following research questions: (a) What are the self-reported mentoring practices of mentors in the PDS context? (b) Why do mentors engage in these practices? (c) How have these practices developed and changed over time? Data gathered through the methods of semi-structured interviews and classroom observations were analyzed using open coding to create narrative profiles of each mentor. In addition, cross-case analysis was utilized to identify similarities and differences across the practices of the four mentors. This paper reports on one specific mentoring practice that has not been discussed in the literature: collaborating with the university supervisor. This practice was also used to support and expand Yendol-Hoppey and Dana's (2007) framework for effective mentoring in order to provide illustrations of the domains for effective mentoring of preservice teachers.

In a climate in which teacher preparation is under great scrutiny and there is a call for more intense, high quality clinically-based teacher education, the role of mentor teacher during clinical experiences has taken on new meaning and implies greater responsibilities for those who choose to take on that role (Zeichner & Bier, 2015). The mentor has the potential to greatly influence not only how the novice teaches but also what the novice thinks and believes about teaching; therefore, the mentor and the field placement experience are important elements in teacher preparation (Clarke & Jarvis-Selinger, 2005; Franke & Dahlgren, 1996). In order for teacher education programs to best support or facilitate their work, it seems urgent to try to understand how mentors engage in the practice of mentoring as well as the development of the beliefs that inform their practices (Clarke, Triggs, & Nielsen, 2014). With greater understanding about the expertise of these professionals, we are able to identify professional development opportunities that have potential to improve teacher education practices.

While mentors have not been viewed historically as teacher educators, more recently mentors are, in fact, becoming recognized as teacher educators (Feiman-Nemser, 1998; Nolan & Parks, 2010). Based on the potential impact, positive or negative, they have on preservice teachers it is hard to argue against that view. The amount of time that a preservice teacher spends with a mentor teacher is typically greater than the amount of time spent with any other single teacher educator.

Mentors working with elementary preservice teachers have complex roles in the classroom. Not only are they responsible for educating the students in their classroom, the teacher part of the role, they also are responsible for educating the preservice teacher about teaching elementary students, arguably the teacher educator part of the role. Some researchers argue that mentors may not see themselves as teacher educators due to the traditional epistemology of teacher education, where knowledge is located at the university, and a culture of teaching as isolating (Feiman-Nemser, 1998). However, with a growing number of studies indicating that mentors can be thoughtful and effective classroom-based teacher educators (Awaya et al., 2003; Feiman-Nemser & Parker, 1993; Nolan & Parks, 2010; Parker-Katz & Bay, 2007; Yendol-Hoppey & Dana, 2007), it is imperative to learn about their practices to potentially improve mentoring for all.

EDUCATIVE MENTORING

Educative mentoring has roots in Dewey's (1938) concept of educative experiences, which are experiences that promote future growth and lead to richer subsequent experiences. According to Dewey, the educator is responsible for arranging physical and social conditions so that learners have growth-producing experiences. The learner interacts with her or his own environment in ways that result in growth (Feiman-Nemser, 2001; Schwille, 2008; Yendol-Hoppey & Dana, 2007). Feiman-Nemser (2001), who first contrasted this concept with a more traditional supervisory approach to mentoring, describes educative mentoring in following way:

> Educative mentoring rests on an explicit vision of good teaching and an understanding of teacher learning. Mentors who share this orientation attend to beginning teachers' present concerns, questions, and purposes without losing sight of long-term goals for teacher development. They interact with novices in ways that foster an inquiry stance. They cultivate skills and habits that enable novices to learn in and from their practice. They use their knowledge and expertise to assess the direction novices are heading and to create opportunities and conditions that support meaningful teacher learning in the service of student learning. (p. 18)

Educative mentoring is about being responsive to the needs of the preservice teacher and providing him or her with appropriate challenges and long-term learning opportunities in deep and personal ways. Yendol-Hoppey and Dana (2007) conceptualize the content of educative mentoring in their book, *The Reflective Educator's Guide to Mentoring*. They write, "Educative mentoring is a complicated act, as it entails simultaneously attending to three components: 1) creating an educative mentoring context; 2) guiding a mentee's professional knowledge development; and 3) cultivating the dispositions of a successful educator" (p. 15). The three domains that these authors describe serve as a framework for understanding the practices of mentors. Figure 2.1 depicts Yendol-Hoppey and Dana's conception of Educative Mentoring using un-shaded boxes. However, this study

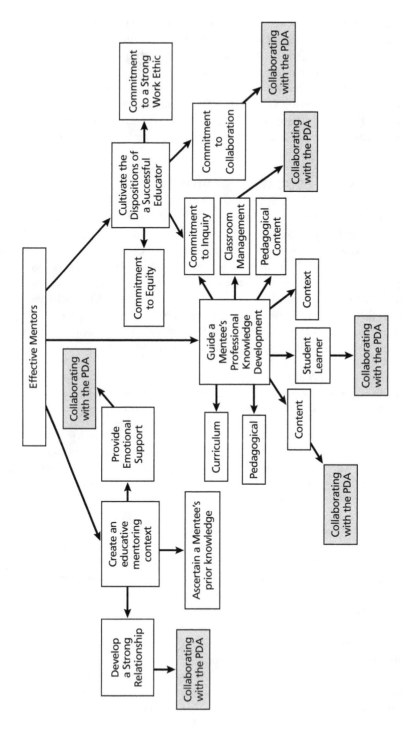

Figure 2.1 Adapted framework for effective mentors including collaborating with the PDA. *Note:* White boxes were identified as educative mentoring by Yendol-Hoppey and Dana while the grey boxes are concepts that have been added as a result of this study.

adds an important educative mentoring practice previously absent from the literature to the framework, *collaborating with the university supervisor*. These practices are illustrated in the shaded boxes.

PURPOSE OF THE STUDY

This paper addresses one key, but relatively unexplored mentoring practice that was identified through a larger study examining mentoring practices within a professional development school (PDS) context. In addition to examining mentors' current practices, this study looked at the development of their mentoring practices over time. Three primary research questions were addressed in the study:

1. What are the self-reported mentoring practices of mentors in a PDS context?
2. Why do the mentors engage in these practices?
3. How have these practices developed and changed over time?

While several practices emerged from this study, this chapter identifies and describes one particular practice in which all four mentors engaged, collaborating with the university supervisor, who in this context is referred to as the professional development associate (PDA).

Context

Darling-Hammond (2014) identified three context related components she believed were critical for programs to achieve high-quality teacher preparation: coherence and integration, explicit links between theory and practice, and new partnerships with schools. This study was situated in a "highly developed" elementary PDS partnership between Central State University and the Sunshine Valley School District.

This PDS program, designed collaboratively by teams of mentor teachers, school administrators, and university faculty, encompasses the final year of a 4-year undergraduate teacher preparation program for elementary candidates. This extended clinical experience, developed with collaboration from all stakeholders, allows interns to experience explicit connections between their coursework and their elementary students. Over the years, the partnership gradually grew from 14 interns in two schools to more than 50 interns and mentors in all 8 elementary schools in the district. In contrast to many PDS partnerships in which each school is viewed as a separate PDS, this PDS is viewed as one community, distributed across all of the district's elementary schools. To emphasize the unity of one PDS, a variety of structures encourage collaboration and interaction across all school sites.

The PDS that exists between Central State University and the Sunshine Valley School District is an exemplary PDS that has won numerous national awards (e.g., Association of Teacher Educators, Holmes Partnership; National Association for Professional Development Schools). The mission of this elementary PDS collaborative, which both encompasses and extends the mission of each partner, is expressed by its four goals: (a) enhance the educational experiences of all learners; (b) ensure high quality induction into the profession for new teachers; (c) engage in furthering our own professional growth as teachers and teacher educators; and (d) educate the next generation of teacher educators (Nolan et al., 2009).

Mentors and Professional Development Associates

When the partnership was initially established, a deliberate decision was made to change the terminology that had been used traditionally to refer to the triad roles in the student teaching relationship. The change in name was intended to symbolize important change in roles and expectations. Thus, student teachers became "interns." Cooperating teachers became "mentors," and student teaching supervisors became "professional development associates" (PDA). While the mentor and PDA engage in similar functions when working with interns, they are viewed as distinctly different roles in the partnership.

The PDA role resembles that of a supervisor in a traditional student teaching experience. However, there are significant differences. PDAs come from a variety of roles including tenure track faculty, graduate assistants, retired elementary educators, and reassigned elementary teachers who leave their classrooms for 2 to 3 years to serve as PDAs before returning to the classroom. The PDA is expected to get to know the elementary students well and to work with them when appropriate, to engage in a variety of supervisory activities with the intern, and to share expertise with the mentor as well as to benefit from the mentor's expertise. Due to the expanded role expectations, the PDA is encouraged to spend at least 2 hours per week in each classroom. The supervision load of a PDA varies significantly. For some (reassigned teachers) being a PDA is a full-time role. For others (faculty, GAs) serving as a PDA makes up only a portion of the individual's total responsibilities. Because roles vary, a PDA may supervise as few as four interns or as many as twelve.

The model of teaching that is advocated in this PDS context is a co-teaching model in which both the intern and mentor are typically engaged in working directly with students (Badiali & Titus, 2011). The pacing of this scaffolded approach to planning and teaching is dependent on the needs of the particular intern and enables the preservice teachers to "grow 'roots' on their practice" (Darling-Hammond, 2014, p. 551). Over the course of the year, interns develop at their own pace, and have opportunities to develop their teaching practices on a deeper level in many subject areas. This responsive model is representative of the policy call for clinically based teacher preparation (Zeichner & Bier, 2015).

METHODS

Participants

Four current PDS mentors were invited to participate in the study through a process of purposive sampling. In order to broadly explore mentoring practices, participants were selected who represented variety in years of teaching experience, experience as a mentor within the PDS partnership, gender, and elementary school. Two of the mentors were considered veteran mentors due to mentoring more than 10 years and two were considered novice mentors because they had mentored for 5 years. To provide additional contrasting data, each of the participants represented different elementary schools within the PDS context, and one of the novice mentors selected was the only male mentor in the PDS at the time of the study. In addition, two of the mentors participated as interns in the same PDS context when they were preservice teachers, while two did not.

Data Collection and Analysis

This research is a collective case study with phenomenological underpinnings in order to understand mentoring practices from the mentor's point of view. Interviews were the primary source of data for this study. Three semi-structured interviews were conducted with the mentors. The first life history interview was modeled after Seidman's (2013) approach to phenomenological interviewing. The second interview was crafted to begin to understand mentoring practices over time with different interns and PDAs and utilized photo elicitation to aid the mentor in providing details about each experience (Banks, 2001). The third interview, an espoused platform conference, was conducted to access the mentors' espoused beliefs about mentoring to make their implicit beliefs explicit (Nolan & Hoover, 2008). Additionally, weekly ongoing conversations took place with each mentor based on field notes and photographs taken from classroom observations of their mentoring practices in action. Open coding was used to create individual profiles for each participant, however the full profiles are not included in this chapter. Once the four profiles were created, a cross-case analysis of the four mentors was conducted to identify similarities and differences across them. Additionally, Yendol-Hoppey and Dana's (2007) conceptual framework for educative mentoring was used to identify mentoring practices that supported or contributed to the framework (see Figure 2.1). This analysis led to the identification and description of four mentoring practices including the specific mentoring practice discussed in this chapter, *collaborating with the PDA*. The first author played the role of observer for the study while the second author served as a critical friend.

FINDINGS

Collaborating With the Professional Development Associate

In contrast to the vast majority of studies, which have looked at mentoring from the viewpoint of university researchers, this study was designed to capture the mentor's own perspective about mentoring practices. Thus, it is not entirely surprising that one of the key practices identified by all four mentors, collaborating with the PDA, has not been previously recognized in the literature as an important mentoring practice.

The practice of collaborating with the PDA was often used to directly support and benefit the intern teacher candidate. However, it was also quite evident that the intern was not the sole beneficiary of mentor-PDA collaboration. In some cases, the individual who seemed to benefit most directly from the collaboration was the mentor. This occurred most often when the collaboration took the form of the PDA supporting the mentor as s/he interacted with the intern. This was especially important in situations where the intern was struggling in one way or another. Less frequent, but still beneficial for the mentor, was the collaboration that directly supported the mentor as she engaged in teaching elementary students. All four mentors (Rebecca, Tara, Amy, and Mike) engaged in the practice of collaborating with the PDA, but there were similarities and differences in what this practice looked like across the mentors.

Rebecca
Rebecca is a veteran third grade teacher and a veteran mentor in the PDS collaboration between Sunshine Valley School District and Central State University. Rebecca utilized her PDAs to support her as a mentor and a classroom teacher. As a mentor, she described receiving support from her PDA during challenging times with her interns, as well as learning how to mentor in order

to provide feedback to her intern. She also utilized the PDA to support her interns. Finally, as a classroom teacher, she described how she used the PDA's expertise in her classroom to support elementary students.

During Rebecca's most recent year of mentoring, she described working with her PDA to strategize how to best support Amanda, a struggling intern. In this example, Rebecca received mentor support from her PDA:

> The PDA has been very supportive and I have really appreciated that. Yes, we did spend significant time talking about it. I'd text her and say, "Hey I really need to be with you. We need to brainstorm. Can we meet? She's falling apart at this point. I need some help. I need help being able to articulate with her, what do you suggest?" (Interview 4, lines 87–91)

Rebecca needed to talk with her PDA about Amanda's struggles prior to helping Amanda. The PDA became a sounding board for Rebecca to vent about her frustrations and solicit ideas for how to best support the intern.

In addition to receiving mentor support from her PDA, Rebecca, also described learning how to mentor from her PDAs, specifically in regards to providing feedback. Rebecca admired Dan's abilities to provide feedback to the interns and strived to provide feedback in the same way. Dan was an experienced university professor who also served as a PDA. He had many years of supervisory experience with preservice teachers. He served as a model for gradually releasing the responsibility of evaluation from himself to the intern. For example, Rebecca commented, "He does that so gradually and so slowly you really have to just pay attention because at the end he's not really telling them anything, they're naming it all and he does that so skillfully" (Interview 2, lines 474–476).

Over the years, Rebecca has mentored a number of interns, including some who have struggled in different ways and she has always collaborated with her PDA to support her interns. Christina, Bobby, Lisa, and Amanda, were four interns who experienced different struggles during their internships. Through interview transcripts, the language of "we" was often used when describing her work with the different PDAs assigned to her over the years. With her first intern, Christina, Rebecca describes working with her PDA, Dan, to differentiate expectations:

> I had an intern that was very strong in many ways, but she also had just some real difficulties completing things on time and getting things in and it took a lot of support to get her to complete things and to really encourage her because she would get anxious. Dan was the PDA and we worked together to really encourage her and give her extra support so she could complete some of the tasks some of the kind of things she needed to get done on a regular basis. (Interview 4, lines 4 –7).

Examples also occurred during the years Rebecca worked with Bobby and Lisa with Josh as her PDA. Josh was a retired elementary teacher who worked as an adjunct faculty member in this PDS context. In the year Bobby was her intern, Josh was sensitive to Bobby's family and financial needs. Like Rebecca and Dan, Rebecca and Josh adjusted deadlines and responsibilities in order for Bobby to be successful with coursework and classroom assignments, and found resources to help him with his financial needs.

These examples illustrate how Rebecca collaborated with her PDAs to best support her interns who have struggled in different ways over the years. She reflected about the positive experiences she had when working with her PDA to meet her interns' needs:

> But the PDAs have always been really great and flexible. I can see that that wouldn't be the case sometimes but I was really lucky I think that I had PDAs that really had that same sense of feeling that we really need to differentiate here. But I also think that that's part of the philosophy; my take on the philosophy of the PDS is that the reason we have this full year program is because we have so many differences and people that need different things and this gives them that opportunity to actually go through that full year and be able to be successful. How do we help people be successful? It's not going to be the same for everyone. (Interview 4, lines 91–98).

Finally, Rebecca collaborated with her PDA in her classroom to support content and student learning while simultaneously supporting her intern. In her experience, Rebecca has worked with two PDAs, who had particular content expertise in mathematics. These PDAs have worked with Rebecca and her interns to plan and teach math units:

> I've had PDAs that were experts in math to help them [interns]. I loved working with Katherine. I liked having her because she was so helpful with math and I tried to utilize her expertise and gifts and asked her to help plan math units with them and model, she would model lessons once a week so that felt neat to me to be able to utilize her expertise in doing that. (Interview 2, lines 504–510).

It is important to distinguish that Rebecca did not collaborate with the PDA to learn about math instruction herself in this example, but as a way to support her students and her intern. Rebecca volunteered to mentor in the PDS program because she wanted another teacher in her classroom. She recognized the expertise her PDAs had and worked with them as teachers, as well. In the example of working with Katherine to plan and model math lessons in her classroom, Rebecca had the opportunity to have two additional teachers in her classroom, her intern and her PDA to enhance the educational experiences of all learners; in particular, Rebecca's third grade students.

Tara

Tara is a veteran third grade teacher and a veteran mentor in the PDS collaboration between Sunshine Valley School District and Central State University. Tara participated as an intern in the PDS program for her undergraduate student teaching experience at Central State. She is currently teaching and mentoring in the same district where she completed her internship. Tara described collaborating with her PDA for mentor support and intern support. She identified working with her PDA during a struggling time with an intern. She also relied on her PDA to provide feedback to her intern when teaching responsibilities did not allow Tara to sit down immediately and debrief with her intern.

When Tara worked with her first intern, she experienced struggles related to her intern's lack of preparation for teaching content. She recounted how supportive her PDA, George, was in helping her navigate that struggle. George was a reassigned elementary teacher from the Sunshine Valley School District.

> We tried different things. George was great. He was a fantastic PDA all around. Hugely supportive. He sometimes said some of the hard stuff that I wasn't able to say or he said it in a different way, but he was also very understanding. (Interview 2, lines 108–110)

Tara did not feel alone when she needed to have tough conversations with her intern. She genuinely appreciated when George was able to communicate things to her intern that were difficult for Tara to say. She collaborated with the PDA as a source of mentor support during this challenging time. While the PDAs are present week to week, often seeing their interns for at least 2 hours per week, PDAs are not "living with" the intern on a daily basis as the mentors do. George's willingness to have hard conversations with Tara's intern may have relieved Tara of experiencing hurt feelings from her intern in the classroom the very next day. Collaborating with the PDA in this way can help to develop or preserve a relationship between the intern and the mentor. The PDA was willing to sacrifice his relationship with the intern temporarily in order to support the mentor.

One of Tara's beliefs about effective mentoring was to provide specific feedback and to conduct systematic observations, but she struggled with the challenging time constraints in the school day. One solution to this problem was for Tara to collaborate with her PDA as a resource to provide feedback to her intern during these challenging times, which supported both Tara and the intern. After her intern was finished teaching a lesson, Tara sometimes did not have time to debrief with an intern because she may be teaching the next lesson. In these circumstances, Tara appreciated when the PDA could debrief the lesson with her intern so feedback could be provided in a timely manner:

> I think something that's been really helpful that's happened in the last few years, is when a lesson is taught and you have a few minutes to take someone out and decompress that whole lesson because I don't have time until much later to talk about a lesson. If Allison has just taught something, I really appreciate when the PDA can take the intern right away and talk about that lesson. Sometimes I don't get to it until after school, sometimes I don't get to it until the day after that. It could take awhile. (Interview 2, lines 545–550)

Tara's collaboration with the PDA included both mentor and intern support.

Amy

Amy is a novice fourth grade teacher and a novice mentor in the PDS collaboration between Sunshine Valley School District and Central State University. Amy participated as an intern in the PDS program for her undergraduate student teaching experience at Central State. She is currently teaching and mentoring in the same district where she completed her internship.

Amy described collaborating with her PDA in both different and similar ways from Rebecca and Tara. As a new mentor, she identified instances of learning from her PDA, alongside her intern, about classroom teaching. Additionally, she learned about mentoring from her PDA. She also described receiving mentor support and intern support from her PDA when she worked with struggling interns.

Amy described being vulnerable with her intern in order to develop a trusting relationship. For example, she recounted learning effective teaching strategies from her first PDA, Margaret, a veteran reassigned teacher within the school district. Amy was able to use Margaret's expertise to help herself and her intern develop knowledge about their students. As a new teacher and mentor, Amy learned teaching strategies from utilizing Margaret's expertise in her classroom by having her model reading lessons. Margaret had taught second grade for many years in the district and her knowledge of primary learners was valuable to both Amy and her intern:

> There was one particular time Margaret had given Ashley feedback on her lesson about the kids fiddling with the table and stuff on the table. She told Ashley to not teach reading at a table, and that blew my mind. [I thought], Oh my, that's how I have my classroom set up, that's how everyone else in this school has their classroom set up. So Margaret showed us how to put the chairs in the same shape as the table, but without the table, and then there is nothing for the kids to touch and they weren't on the floor, so they weren't rolling and doing all those things. (Interview 2, lines 68–76)

In addition to learning about effective teaching strategies from her PDA, Amy described what she also learned about effective mentoring strategies. During Amy's first year as a mentor, Margaret modeled how she valued making time and space for thoughtful reflection. Margaret would always take Amy's intern aside after a teaching experience to debrief the lesson and allow space for reflection. "It was something she valued which taught me to value that as well. They need a chance to talk it out" (Interview 2, lines 292–293).

In addition to working with Margaret, Amy specifically recalled working with her PDA Josh, who supported her intern Brianne in trying her ideas in the classroom, and taught Amy about mentoring:

> Josh was very supportive in letting her try things and reflect on her own teaching and I guess I had learned this from Josh, when Josh had been my PDA. He would always say, "One, kids can smell fear, and two, kids are the most forgiving creatures on the planet." So you can't mess them up. Josh very much felt that way and as long as you are kind and respectful to children, then it doesn't matter what else you do. So letting Brianne "fail," it wasn't so much letting her fail as much as it was letting her really see what she was getting herself into. (Interview 2, lines 382–388)

Josh was the impetus for supporting Brianne in trying new ideas in the classroom. More than that, Amy learned about what allowing her interns to "fail" actually meant for her mentoring.

In addition to learning from her PDA as both a classroom teacher and mentor, Amy described collaborating with her PDA for both mentor and intern support when her intern was struggling. Amy struggled to develop a trusting relationship with her intern, Michelle. When she spoke about working with her PDA to problem solve this situation, Amy often used the term "we" language in her interview when referring to her mentor-PDA partnership:

> The PDA and I kept strategizing, "well how about we go this route?" so we tried things like maybe if we keep a communication log, maybe if I write it down for you, you can take home what the expectations are, maybe we start a Google Doc so you can see all the questions written down so when you go home you can have them. So we tried different interventions to support her and try to scaffold her own reflection. (Interview 4, lines 27–31)

Amy did not have to navigate these types of struggles on her own. She was able to receive support for her mentoring by strategizing one on one with her PDA to brainstorm strategies for supporting her intern in being successful. These examples of collaborating with the PDA illustrate how Amy both learned from her PDA as a teacher and mentor and how she worked with her PDA to support struggling interns.

Mike

Mike is a veteran fourth grade teacher and novice mentor in the PDS collaboration between Sunshine Valley School District and Central State University. Mike described how he utilized his PDA as a resource for learning about his teaching. When he was a brand new mentor in the PDS, Mike did not collaborate with his PDA in this manner. Over time, however, he recognized the wealth of expertise his PDAs had, and began to seek out their feedback about his teaching:

> I felt like when Dan was my PDA especially I felt like I wanted to tap into him as a resource for myself and since he was in there watching me teach so much why not ask for his feedback? I would often seek feedback when Dan was around. I didn't do that as much with Joan and I definitely did not do that much with Jessica because I was definitely new to the whole thing. Even with Joan and now with Iris who was Justine's PDA and is my current intern's PDA, I definitely have started to ask them their thoughts and kind of use them as a resource for my own teaching. I mean they are going to be in here as much as they are, and they see me teach, they must have thoughts about it. So why not figure out what their thoughts are because these are people that have a wealth of experience that should be drawn from. (Interview 2, lines 266–275)

Mike collaborated with the PDA in order to receive feedback about his classroom teaching versus learning new ideas for teaching, receiving support as a mentor, or receiving support for his interns. He is unlike the other three mentors because according to Mike, he had not experienced a struggling intern during his years as a mentor, which would explain why he did not have examples of collaborating with the PDA for support.

Looking Across the Four Mentors

All four mentors in this study collaborated with the PDA as a resource in some way. Across the four mentors, there were similarities and differences among the ways in which they utilized the PDAs. Sometimes, the mentor learned mentoring techniques from the PDA. In other cases, the mentor learned strategies related to teaching. There are other examples when the mentor received support from the PDA when working with struggling interns. The following section describes those similarities and differences in how the mentor, as both a mentor and teacher, collaborated with the PDA.

Resource to Support Their Mentoring

Three of the four mentors described how they used their PDA as a resource to support their mentoring in two ways. Rebecca, Tara, and Amy all collaborated with their PDA for mentor support during times with struggling interns. Whether they needed to vent, brainstorm strategies, or needed the PDA to have hard conversations, they all described receiving mentor support during those difficult times. When asked to describe a particular struggle with an intern, these mentors used "we" in their language without hesitation to indicate they were not in the struggle alone. As a result, this practice allowed these mentors to be able to create an educative mentoring context by providing emotional support to the intern and developing a strong relationship with the intern. Having a third person to relieve the mentor of navigating struggles on their own was a common use of the PDA among Rebecca, Tara, and Amy. Providing this type of support to the mentor requires that the PDA sees supporting the mentor as an important part of the work and also requires that the PDA be able to provide the emotional support that both the mentor and intern need. In addition, the PDA needs to be skilled at having difficult, emotionally intense conversations.

Second, these mentors described how they used their PDA as a resource to learn about mentoring. Both Rebecca and Amy described instances when they used their PDA as a resource to learn how to mentor. For example, Rebecca talked about the manner in which Dan provided feedback to her intern and how there was a gradual release of responsibility from him providing feedback to the intern reflecting about her teaching. Rebecca admired that process and tried to enact it herself as a mentor. Amy learned from Margaret about valuing reflection as an important component of providing feedback to interns. Watching Margaret provide time for interns to talk about their teaching consistently taught Amy to value that as well. Josh also taught Amy about allowing her interns to "fail" and what that meant for her mentoring. In order for PDAs to provide this type of support, they must be willing to have the mentor participate in and/or observe interactions between the PDA and the intern and must also be willing to have conversations with the mentor where they lay out the beliefs and knowledge that underlie their interactions with interns.

Working as a Team to Support Struggling Interns

Rebecca, Tara, and Amy all used their PDA to support their interns. When navigating different strategies for struggling interns, the mentor and PDA worked as a team to implement strategies to support the intern. In addition to using their PDA to navigate struggles with different interns over the years, Tara talked about using her PDA as a resource to support her interns by providing feedback. When Tara was unable to provide timely feedback to her intern following a teaching episode, she appreciated when her PDA would debrief with her intern, providing immediate feedback. This feedback provided support to both the intern and to Tara since it created an opportunity for the intern to get immediate feedback, something that Tara believed as a mentor was important. Rebecca also used the PDA to support her intern in planning for instruction by collaborating with the PDA to utilize her teaching expertise. PDAs who wish to collaborate with mentors in this arena must be knowledgeable about preservice teacher development, must be disposed to differentiate instruction to enhance intern learning, must be skilled observers of instruction, and possess excellent conferencing skills.

Strengthening Their Classroom Teaching to Support Student Learning

Data from the mentors indicated that mentors also use their PDA as a resource for their classroom teaching to support student learning. They did not solely view PDAs as resources for mentoring, but as resources for their own teaching. Rebecca described this practice when speaking about her years working with Katherine and utilizing her math expertise in the classroom. Katherine would model and teach math lessons in order to support the math instruction for the students in the classroom. Amy also described using her PDA as a resource to learn teaching strategies that impacted her classroom teaching and her students. As a new teacher and mentor in the school district, Amy and her intern would watch the PDA, Margaret, model and teach reading lessons. Amy received professional development from the PDA that impacted her classroom teaching strategies in addition to her mentoring.

Resource to Provide Feedback on Teaching Performance

Mike utilized the PDA differently from the other three mentors. He described using his PDAs as a resource to evaluate and enhance his own teaching performance. Mike did not necessarily have PDAs teach in his classroom, nor did he describe new teaching strategies that he learned from his PDAs. He did, however, share that as he became a more seasoned mentor, he sought feedback about his own teaching performance from PDAs whom he felt had valuable expertise to share. Again, he did not perceive any significant struggles with the interns he had mentored which may explain his limited use of the PDA.

In order for PDAs to collaborate with mentors concerning the teaching practices that they observe in the mentor's class, as Mike, Rebecca, and Amy referenced, the PDA must be knowledgeable about instructional practices, must develop a positive relationship with the mentor and must have a workload that allows spending time in the classroom observing when the mentor is teaching. In addition, it is advantageous if the PDA understands and has the skills and dispositions to participate in co-planning and co-teaching.

CONNECTIONS TO MENTORING
CONCEPTUAL FRAMEWORK

There are many connections between collaborating with the PDA and Yendol-Hoppey and Dana's (2007) components of effective mentors. It is important to remember that their framework focuses more directly on mentoring beginning, inservice teachers, while this study focused on mentoring preservice teachers. The following section summarizes how collaborating with the PDA is illustrated within the components of the effective mentoring framework.

Create an Educative Mentoring Context

Yendol-Hoppey and Dana (2007) identify three descriptors to create an educative mentoring context: (a) develop a strong relationship, (b) ascertain a mentee's prior knowledge, and (c) provide emotional support. Examples of mentors collaborating with the PDA in this study illustrate the first and third of these descriptors.

Collaborating with the PDA develops a strong triad relationship. Interns spend an entire school year in their mentor's classroom, and many have likened the relationship to one of being "married" for the school year. Collaborating with the PDA revealed more than one member of the "marriage." Tara collaborated with the PDA in a way that prevented her from having to have hard conversations with her intern that may have resulted in hurt feelings for the intern. The PDA was a crucial piece of Tara's mentoring in order to develop a strong relationship with her intern, which is the first descriptor for creating and educative mentoring context. Her PDA was willing to be the "bad guy" and shoulder the burden for Tara by being the communicator in the relationship.

Provide emotional support is the other descriptor illustrated by collaborating with the PDA in order to create an educative mentoring context. Like much of the research on mentor roles, emotional support connects with many of them. The data from this study showed that at times, mentors collaborated with the PDA to provide emotional support to the interns. For example, Tara, Amy, and Rebecca all described times when they worked with an intern who struggled for some reason or another. In each of their experiences, they recalled collaborating with the PDA in order to support the needs of the intern. Often, the mentor and PDA worked together to brainstorm strategies or ideas for how to best support the intern. The mentors were not left alone in these situations to figure it out for themselves. While certainly, mentors are likely providing emotional support on a daily basis when PDAs cannot be present, when serious issues arose, they were able to collaborate with someone else who also wanted the intern to succeed. In recounting these experiences, mentors often used the language of "we" when detailing these events. It was clear they felt they had a partner to work with towards the same goal for the intern.

Guide a Mentee's Professional Knowledge Development

The second component of Yendol-Hoppey and Dana's effective mentoring is guiding a mentee's professional knowledge development. The authors describe seven different types of knowledge within this component: curriculum, pedagogical, content, student learner, context, pedagogical content, and classroom management. Rebecca certainly utilized the mathematical content knowledge expertise of her PDAs to support her interns, and arguably many of the other types of knowledge. Amy's examples of working with Margaret, the veteran primary teacher, to learn alongside her intern about teaching first grade, were illustrations of guiding the mentee's knowledge in the areas of student learners and classroom management. The PDA is a critical piece of mentoring in the framework. To rely on one person to attend to all seven of the knowledge bases is an overwhelming task. Mentors in the PDS context were able to share the responsibility for developing knowledge of content, student-learners, and classroom management with the intern's PDA.

Cultivate the Dispositions of a Successful Educator

Commitment to Collaboration was illustrated through collaborating with the PDA. According to Yendol-Hoppey and Dana, "Novice teachers need to learn how to collaborate within their work environment so that they can contribute to ongoing improvement in their professional practice" (2007, p. 26). Mentors are able to model this commitment with this practice and provide a foundation for their interns to take with them into their first years of teaching. When the triad works together to support a struggling intern, or support the classroom of students, interns are seeing examples in action of how to utilize colleagues outside of their immediate classroom walls to support them as professionals. According to Yendol-Hoppey and Dana, "To address the needs of an increasingly diverse population, teachers must possess the sophisticated skills to support each other, facilitate learning, and problem solve together" (p. 26). The ways that mentors collaborate with the PDA may expose interns to the possibilities for collaboration and lay the foundation for collaboration with their colleagues in the future.

Collaborating with the PDA is a prevalent practice across this study and the mentoring framework. We believe this speaks to the powerful impact the PDAs have on mentors' practices. Mentors and PDAs could use this framework together to think about how to best support the interns they work with each year. The illustrations of the mentoring practice in this study, collaborating with the PDA, can influence how those charged with supervision tasks can support mentor teachers. At times the PDA can support the mentor in educative mentoring, while at times the PDA and mentor may engage in educative mentoring together.

CONCLUSION

This study found collaborating with the PDA was a significant and widespread practice of these mentors. Not only were the PDAs useful in supporting the interns, but they also supported the mentors as well as the students in the classrooms. Collaborating with the PDA benefitted the mentors (a) as they learned how to mentor, (b) by providing them support as they mentored, (c) by helping them learn about their teaching, and (d) by providing feedback about teaching. The PDA and mentor practice benefitted the interns as they collaboratively provided support and differentiation for difficult situations, providing feedback in a timely manner, and supporting interns with planning and teaching. This study demonstrates that educative mentoring occurs by expanding beyond the dyadic relationship between mentor and student teacher. Educative practices occur when the mentor and PDA embrace the triad relationship and work together to strengthen intern and teacher learning.

The literature reviewed as the foundation for this study in regards to mentoring practices, roles and responsibilities, and knowledge does not mention the supervisor as a part of those components. By including the mentor practice of collaboration with the PDA, as illustrated in this PDS, mentors and supervisors of undergraduate preservice teachers may begin to envision their work together as a triad team versus two separate dyadic relationships, mentor-intern and supervisor-intern. This finding largely impacts the research on mentoring practices as it may encourage teacher education programs to closely consider how to utilize their supervision resources in order to achieve a more fully functioning triad relationship in non-PDS contexts.

A study conducted by Burns (2012) that focused on the viewpoint and practices of the PDA in a PDS triad found a similar result in terms of PDA practice. In Burns' research, the PDS supervisors also conceptualized their role to include providing support to mentor teachers. Additional studies that examine the concept of mentor-university supervisor collaboration could be helpful in delineating the types of relationships, knowledge, skills and dispositions that are required to make this kind of collaboration more widespread in clinical experiences. Including the voices of the PDAs and/or interns in conjunction with the mentors would allow teacher educators to look at this practice among the different members of the triad. The PDAs who have worked with these four mentors over the years have impacted their mentoring practice. Although student teacher supervisors in all contexts should be invigorated by the findings of this study, supervisors in more traditional context may experience frustration as they are often not the ones who make decisions about how much time they are able to spend with their student teachers. Supervisors are often limited in the ways they can support mentors without the opportunity to develop a detailed understandings of mentor teachers' work (Clarke et al., 2014). Without significant, dedicated time with the mentor, it is very difficult to achieve the kind of presence a PDA is able to achieve in the PDS context. It seems that any movement teacher preparation contexts can make towards resourcing and enacting a closer supervisor–mentor relationship may have real benefits for all three triad members.

REFERENCES

Awaya, A., McEwan, H., Heyler, D., Linsky, S., Lum, D., & Wakukawa, P. (2003). Mentoring as a journey. *Teaching and Teacher Education, 19*(1), 45–56.

Badiali, B. J., & Titus, N. E. (2011). Co-teaching: Enhancing student learning through mentor-intern partnerships. *School University Partnerships, 4*(2), 74–79.

Banks, M. (2001). *Visual methods in social research.* Thousand Oaks, CA: SAGE.

Burns, R. W. (2012). *Conceptualizing supervision in the professional development school context: A case analysis* (Doctoral dissertation). Retrieved from https://etda.libraries.psu.edu/files/final_submissions/7142

Clarke, A., & Jarvis-Selinger, S. (2005). What the teaching perspectives of cooperating teachers tell us about their advisory practices. *Teaching and Teacher Education, 21*(1), 65–78.

Clarke, A., Triggs, V., & Nielsen, W. (2014). Cooperating teacher participation in teacher education: A review of the literature. *Review of Educational Research, 84*(2), 163–202.

Darling-Hammond, L. (2014). Strengthening clinical preparation: The holy grail of teacher education. *Peabody Journal of Education, 89*(4), 547–561.

Dewey, J. (1938). *Experience and education.* The Kappa Delta Pi Lecture Series. New York, NY: Touchstone.

Feiman-Nemser, S. (1998). Teachers as teacher educators. *European Journal of Teacher Education, 21*(1) 63–74.

Feiman-Nemser, S. (2001). Helping novices learn to teach: Lessons from an exemplary support teacher. *Journal of Teacher Education, 52*(1), 17–30.

Feiman-Nemser, S., & Parker, M. B. (1993). Mentoring in context: A comparison of two U.S. programs for beginning teachers. *International Journal of Educational Research, 19*(8), 699–718.

Franke, A., & Dahlgren, L. (1996). Conceptions of mentoring: An empirical study of conceptions of mentoring during the school-based teacher education. *Teaching and Teacher Education, 12*(6), 627–641.

Nolan, J., Badiali, B., Zembal-Saul, C., Burns, R., McDonough, M., Wheland, M.,... & Queeney, D. (2009). The Penn State-State College elementary professional development school collaborative: A profile. *School-University Partnerships, 3*(2), 19–30.

Nolan, J., & Parks, K. (2010, May). *Mentors as teacher educators: Unpacking the thinking and practices of veteran mentors in the PDS context.* Paper presented at the annual meeting of the American Educational Research Association, Denver, CO.

Nolan, J. F., & Hoover, L. A. (2008). *Teacher supervision and evaluation: Theory into practice.* Hoboken, NJ: Wiley.

Parker-Katz, M., & Bay, M. (2007). Conceptualizing mentor knowledge: Learning from the insiders. *Teaching and Teacher Education, 24*(5), 1259–1269.

Schwille, S. (2008). The professional practice of mentoring. *American Journal of Education, 115*(November), 139–167.

Seidman, I. (2013). *Interviewing as qualitative research* (4th ed.). New York, NY: Teachers College Press.

Yendol-Hoppey, D., & Dana, N. (2007). *The reflective educator's guide to mentoring: Strengthening practice through knowledge, story, and metaphor.* Thousand Oaks, CA: Corwin Press.

Zeichner, K., & Bier, M. (2015). Opportunities and pitfalls in the turn toward clinical experience in US teacher education. In E. R. Hollins (Ed.), *Rethinking field experiences in pre-service teacher preparation: Meeting new challenges for accountability* (pp. 20–46). New York, NY: Routledge.

CHAPTER 3

THE SITE COORDINATOR ROLE IN A CLINICALLY RICH TEACHER EDUCATION PROGRAM

Jessica A. DeBiase, William (Will) A. Butler, Ruhi Khan, and Penelope A. Dyer
Arizona State University

ABSTRACT

Teacher quality and retention in the United States are persistent issues that are detrimental to student achievement and the learning environment. The Arizona State University Mary Lou Fulton Teachers College recognized its role in addressing these issues from a teacher preparation program perspective. As a result, the Teachers College redesigned its program and increased the clinical intensity of the program through the induction of a new full time faculty position known as the site coordinator. Site coordinators fulfill distinct roles and provide extensive supervision and coaching, playing a significant role in the preparedness of program graduates. Recent findings show that program graduate retention rates have surpassed that of the national average. The implications of these findings hold promise for other teacher preparation programs, state education agencies, school districts and most importantly, student learning.

Outcomes of High-Quality Clinical Practice in Teacher Education, pages 39–59
Copyright © 2018 by Information Age Publishing

For some time, the student teaching component of teacher preparation has been held in low regard, particularly when supervision falls primarily on adjunct or retired faculty and there is a lack of training for cooperating mentor teachers. (Rodgers & Keil, 2007). Consequently, new teachers often enter the field ill prepared and more likely to leave the profession. Compounding these issues, research from the McCaffrey, Koretz, Lockwood, and Hamilton (2004) shows teacher quality being consistently identified as the most important school based factor in student achievement and teacher retention as an important factor in determining a school's learning environment (McLaurin, Smith, & Smillie, 2009). Clinically rich teacher preparation programs positively impact both of these areas by aligning with current research regarding high quality supervision.

The Mary Lou Fulton Teachers College at Arizona State University recognized its responsibility related to strengthening clinical practice within teacher preparation by engaging in a process of transformation. This transformation led to the creation of full time clinical, nontenure track faculty positions that provide extensive and consistent supervision. The supervision emphasizes three key activities: (a) coaching by focusing on lesson planning and implementation that is continuous throughout the student teaching experience, (b) using a fair measure to grade each teacher candidates' teaching performance, and (c) working closely with cooperating teachers (Rodgers & Keil, 2007). In their roles, the clinical faculty are responsible for course instruction and supervision within the field. They provide teacher candidates extensive and consistent support for lesson planning and implementation that is continuous throughout the clinical experience, using a fair measure to assess each teacher candidates' teaching performance, and working closely with cooperating teachers (Rodgers & Keil, 2007). In their roles, the clinical faculty are responsible for course instruction and field based supervision.

Success of the revamped program is evident in that 92% of Mary Lou Fulton Teachers College teacher candidates who graduated from the 2012, 2013, and 2014 cohorts have been retained (Mary Lou Fulton Teachers College, Teacher Preparation Research and Evaluation Project, 2015), which is higher than the national retention rate (Ingersoll, Merrill, & Stuckey, 2014; U.S. Department of Education, National Center for Education Statistics, 2012). Retention and other data at the Mary Lou Fulton Teachers College is provided by the Teacher Preparation Research and Evaluation Project or T-Prep, a department within the Teachers College that examines research questions by collecting, tracking, analyzing, and disseminating data.

ITEACHAZ TEACHER PREPARATION PROGRAM

iTeachAZ, the undergraduate teacher preparation program designed by Mary Lou Fulton Teachers College, began in 2010 with a pilot of 30 students in three school districts. In the Fall of 2011, the college expanded iTeachAZ to include 436 students in 189 schools across 28 districts with an estimated 68% of participating schools being Title I and 23% classified as rural or suburban (Mary Lou Fulton Teachers College, Teacher Preparation Research and Evaluation Project, 2015). Teachers College administrators, faculty, and school district partners worked together to revamp the teacher preparation program by reducing the number of theoretical education courses offered, increasing the number of content area courses taken by education majors, and doubling the amount of time students spend engaging in clinically rich components, thus completing 150 hours of classroom internships during the first two semesters of the education program and a full year (i.e., over 1,500 hours) clinical residency during the last two semesters. Being one of the largest teacher preparation programs in the country, the Teachers College at ASU is one of the first colleges of education in the country to offer a residency program at the undergraduate level to this scale and to completely revamp the education curriculum to be more responsive to the needs of prekindergarten through 12th grade students in Arizona and across the country. By May 2015, 1,934 students had enrolled in the iTeachAZ program in undergraduate and some graduate programs spanning elementary, early childhood, secondary, bilingual, and special education, which equates to approximately 484 teacher candidates per school year (Mary Lou Fulton Teachers College, Teacher Preparation Research and Evaluation Project, 2015). Approximately, one-third of the student graduates are teachers of color. This is over 10% more than both the state and national average.

Hallmarked by its senior year residency component, iTeachAZ affords teacher candidates a full year clinical experience and placement in cohorts with approximately 20–25 members in participating school districts. Teacher candidates begin their residency when new district in-service teachers report for duty, which typically precedes the official start of classes based on the ASU academic calendar. Therefore, teacher candidates experience a full range of professional responsibilities and the rhythm of the full school year through co-teaching opportunities with a mentor teacher. The teacher candidates in the iTeachAZ program have a model for opening the school year and closing the school year, something that many student teachers do not experience. This provides a comprehensive experience that helps teacher candidates make an informed decision about whether or not teaching is a field in which they can succeed. Once they complete the program, teacher candidates can become certified in elementary education, early childhood, bilingual education, secondary education, and special education along with the passing of associated teacher educator exams.

The Site Coordinator Role

Each teacher candidate cohort is supervised by a full-time clinically embedded faculty member, also known as a site coordinator. The mission of the site coordinator is to:

> Participate in the preparation of teacher candidates so they enter the teaching profession as highly effective and reflective practitioners, provide hands-on support and development for all stakeholders that results in a positive, lasting impact on student achievement, maintain a positive working relationship with district and school level personnel, maximize the expertise of mentor teachers by facilitating ongoing training and support, and develop additional personal and professional leadership skills as a manager, facilitator, mentor, and clinically embedded instructor. (Mary Lou Fulton Teachers College, n.d., p. 2)

Site coordinators at the Mary Lou Fulton Teachers College are a diverse group, but have all been prepared to use specific supervision models and/or rubrics: *Teaching Skills, Knowledge, and Responsibilities Performance Standards Rubric,* also referred to as the TAP Instructional rubric (National Institute for Excellence in Teaching, 2013), cognitive coaching (http://www.thinkingcollaborative .com/), emotional intelligence (http://www.6seconds.org/2010/01/27/ the-six-seconds-eq-model/h), and co-teaching (Friend, 2007).

Site coordinators serve the program by fulfilling three distinct roles: Administrator, instructor, and coach. As administrators, site coordinators serve as liaisons between the local school district (administrators, mentor teachers, and P–12 students) and the College (teacher candidates, faculty, and staff) ensuring that the programming is serving all stakeholders at the highest level and performs various tasks in support of the district partnership, teacher candidate preparedness and ultimately, P–12 students. As instructors, site coordinators provide clinically embedded coursework with attention to pedagogy and professionalism skills taught in district locations. As coaches, site coordinators provide frequent and focused feedback to teacher candidates throughout the program by conducting walkthroughs and performance assessments, modeling use of data, having crucial conversations, and engaging with the student support process when necessary. The site coordinator works closely with the mentor to collaborate and align areas for improvement.

To ensure the fidelity of these practices across site coordinators, a site review process has been used. The purpose of the site review is to determine to what degree site coordinators are implementing key components with fidelity and generate data-based evidence that indicates equitable,

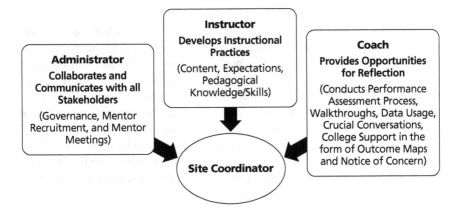

Figure 3.1 Site coordinator roles.

high-quality iTeachAZ program implementation across cohorts. When differences in practices are present, site coordinators receive professional development in these areas to promote the quality of practices within each of the aforementioned roles. The remainder of the chapter will discuss each of these three roles (Figure 3.1).

Site Coordinator as Administrator

In the iTeachAZ program, site coordinators acquaint their cohorts of teacher candidates first through a "meet and greet" session held during the last few weeks of the teacher candidate's junior year and as an opportunity for the district personnel to introduce themselves to the rising seniors. This involvement and openness demonstrates each site coordinator's strong relationship with the district, which supports building trust (Range, Duncan, & Hvidston, 2013). Beyond this initial introduction, site coordinators are also charged with facilitating governance meetings, mentor recruitment, and hosting mentor meetings.

Governance. Taylor (2008) notes the relationship between stakeholders on the university side and the school side as being historically viewed as separate and unequal. Site coordinators bridge the divide between the university and districts by facilitating quarterly governance meetings. Using the concept of shared governance, stakeholders can make decisions efficient and prioritize the actions of each party (Stensaker & Vabo, 2013). This benefit was echoed by Kocolowski's (2010) finding that shared leadership structures are an attempt for all stakeholders to move forward with a singular goal. For iTeachAZ, the goal is teacher candidate preparation and P–12 student achievement.

Quarterly governance meetings, which are facilitated and chaired by the site-coordinator, are attended by district administration including superintendents, assistant superintendents, directors, human resources representatives, building principals, community stakeholders, and university staff and faculty. The meetings provide a way for teacher candidate performance data, including cohort averages in instructional competencies and professionalism scores, co-teaching trends, reports from mentor teachers, and college initiatives to be shared with the district. Second, quarterly governance meetings allow a district to share pertinent district initiatives and collaborate in filling employment openings. It is not uncommon for arrangements to be made by district partners in which a job fair is held specifically for iTeachAZ candidates. This level of commitment is indicative of not only their support for the program but in the success of iTeachAZ teacher candidates in their senior year.

Mentor Recruiting and Mentor Meetings

Site Coordinators also find and recruit quality mentors by working with the district and school administrators. Site coordinators and district partners use mentor selection criteria established by the Teachers College and ensure that potential mentors are meeting district teaching expectations and requirements specified by the state department of education (Sallis, 2002). To participate as an iTeachAZ mentor, all mentors must complete a 4-hour online training module outlining the components of iTeachAZ.

In addition, site coordinators further promote sufficient mentor preparation by holding a meeting at the beginning of the semester to reinforce expectations; they also conduct monthly mentor meetings to provide support in coaching, and share data related to teacher candidate performance. The mentor meetings are often used as a medium for mentors to ask questions and collaborate with fellow iTeachAZ mentors. Veteran mentors are sometimes accommodated with online meetings or alternative all day Saturday training. The support provides mentors the means to employ effective mentoring strategies provided by a program of mentor preparation (Hobson, Ashby, Malderez, & Tomlinson, 2008) and not revert to their own teacher preparation experience instead of utilizing what the college requires (Ambrosetti, 2014). Mentor quality is enhanced by the trainings provided by site coordinators. One mentor reported, "the monthly meetings with the supervisors were very handy as far as continuing to up our skills and then mentoring" (Mary Lou Fulton Teachers College, Teacher Preparation Research and Evaluation Project, 2015, p. 3).

Given that mentors come to the program with varying levels of experience and expertise in coaching, topics covered are derived from the specific needs of the teacher candidates and differentiated based on each teacher candidate's performance results with a focus on immediate implementation. For example, a coaching strategy such as whisper coaching may be modeled for all mentor teachers, however, the application of the strategy will be differentiated according to their teacher candidate's needs. Site coordinators follow up with mentors via phone or email to determine effectiveness of coaching strategies applied and may also support the mentors in the classroom during implementation. One mentor said:

> Our site coordinator has been fantastic. I can't remember who else said it, but has been such a resource to go to and a real support system when things maybe haven't been going so well or when I have a question that—and I haven't had too many that weren't covered in the trainings, but when I do she has been someone who seems like she's constantly available and always can offer more solutions than maybe what I thought of. (Mary Lou Fulton Teachers College, Teacher Preparation Research and Evaluation Project, 2015, p. 3).

The relationship between the mentor and the site coordinator is vital to the long-term success of the teacher candidate. In addition to the site coordinator serving as an administrator, he/she is responsible for pedagogical knowledge shared during course instruction.

Site Coordinator as Instructor

Site coordinators also serve as instructors. They teach three courses in addition to supervising a cohort of teacher candidates per semester. All site coordinators teach the student teaching course, which ranges from 4 to 8 credits, taken in two semesters over the senior year residency. Alongside the utilization of a student teaching course, three additional aspects strengthen the iTeachAZ teacher preparation program. First, courses/meetings for the teacher candidates and mentors are held at the P–12 district sites which promotes strong relationships between the site coordinator and the district. Second, site coordinators use teacher candidate performance data to inform topics in the teacher education course and in the mentor trainings, thus allowing the instruction to be relevant and timely throughout the school year. Third, coursework is clinically embedded within the school districts so that faculty are able to embed what is realistic instructionally within the schools rather than what is traditionally dictated by the "ivory tower" of the university. Within these structures, the site coordinator facilitates the connection and exploration of program content, instructional and professionalism expectations, and pedagogical knowledge and skills.

Program content. Students enrolled in the elementary, early childhood, bilingual, secondary, and special education programs complete four semesters in the iTeachAZ program. In the first and second semesters, students complete anywhere from 12 to 17 credit hours in coursework depending on program area. For all programs and in both terms, students take a clinical field experience course which introduces lesson planning templates, co-teaching models, specific instructional competencies, and professionalism expectations and complete a minimum of 75 field experience hours in an internship placement. During the senior year, residency students typically attend one full day of coursework and complete field work in the school placement for 4 days a week. Students take three to four courses ranging from 12 to 16 credits, one of which is known as the student teaching course. The student teaching course was designed to connect instructional strategies within content areas with the classroom practicum component and focuses heavily on instruction of eight domains (instructional plans, standards and objectives, presenting instructional content, activities and materials, academic feedback, managing student behavior, knowledge of students, and teacher content knowledge) from the TAP Instructional Rubric (National Institute for Excellence in Teaching, 2013) and the Mary Lou Fulton Teachers College Professionalism Rubric including four domains: showing professionalism, growing and developing professionally, maintaining accurate records, and home–school communication. These instructional and professionalism expectations are reinforced to teacher candidates and shared with mentor teachers by use of a "welcome week" training organized by each site coordinator, where mentor teachers at the school site meet with the teacher candidates for the first time.

Each site coordinator teaches the student teaching course and ensures the content and assignments are clinically embedded. Teacher candidates practice direct and inquiry lesson planning, learn best practices in formative and summative assessment, and understand how to backwards plan instruction using student assessment data. The knowledge about using assessment results for backwards planning is applied directly to unit and lesson planning and measured directly in the classroom as the teacher candidates instruct. The course also addresses how to plan and deliver culturally responsive teaching to plan for academic success, cultural competence, and critical consciousness through the view of socially just practices. Finally, teacher candidates learn to create effective resumes and cover letters, and explore interviewing techniques that assist them in job hunting. District human resources experts and site principals offer practical techniques and tips using a mock interviewing process, which supports the collaborative effort to meet employment needs in participating school districts.

Course assignments are structured so that teacher candidates must apply knowledge directly in their classrooms and are aligned to teacher candidates' progression of teaching responsibilities. With the support of their site coordinator, teacher candidates must continually analyze their own practice and make adjustments that ensure progress in their teaching. The final student achievement showcase assignment requires teacher candidates to analyze student achievement data and reflect on effective and ineffective teaching practices implemented during unit plans of instruction. Teacher candidates present during public forums held for mentor teachers, faculty, and district administrators. Site coordinators review candidates' impact, as well as their ability to reflect upon their impact on student learning, during these public presentations. Every aspect of iTeachAZ is designed to provide teacher candidates the knowledge, skills, and dispositions they need to make an immediate impact on student achievement.

Instructional and Professionalism Expectations

Teacher candidates are formally observed and evaluated four times per year (two times per semester) by their site coordinator using the TAP Instructional Rubric (National Institute for Excellence in Teaching, 2013). Each of the indicators on the rubric is scored from 1 to 5, with 1 indicating unsatisfactory performance, 3 indicating proficient performance, and 5 indicating exemplary performance. Teacher candidates must earn a score of a 2 in each of the eight TAP indicators by the end of the first semester of the senior year residency to achieve a passing grade in the student teaching course and a score of a 3 by the end of the second semester. For dual certification programs, teacher candidates must demonstrate proficiency in each of the eight TAP indicators for each certification area they are seeking. During the first year of implementation, 28 trained and certified site coordinators completed almost 2,500 teaching performance assessments using the TAP Instructional Rubric (National Institute for Excellence in Teaching, 2013).

Additionally, teacher candidates must apply knowledge and skills in showing professionalism, growing and developing professionally, and maintaining accurate records and show emerging skill levels in the area of home–school communication consistently over the course of the year. Failure to achieve these benchmarks results in a failing grade in the student teaching course. Mentor teachers provide feedback on instructional competencies and professionalism bi-weekly via the completion of mentor progress reports and collaborate frequently with the site coordinator on their teacher candidate's progress. Site coordinators acknowledge each mentor teachers' input when formally assessing using both rubrics.

Pedagogical content knowledge. Pedagogical content knowledge (PCK) is embedded within each student teaching course session and modeled by site coordinators. As Shulman (1986) suggests, PCK includes not only the subject matter but also knowledge of the best ways of developing the subject to make it understandable to students. Shulman (1986) further states that the study of misconceptions and how that affects subsequent learning is vital to developing PCK. Based on the assumption that the activation and building of student background knowledge is essential to the learning process, the student teaching courses provide guidance in a wide range of instructional strategies that can be used to teach different subject areas by first activating background knowledge, redirecting misconceptions, and providing authentic activities that will help build new learning. Educational research also indicates that task authenticity and task expectations must be integrated in courses to ensure high student teacher performance (Allen, 2011). Within the program field-based courses, the teacher candidates are given authentic activities that can be applied directly in their P–12 classrooms. For example, site coordinators teach and model academic feedback by demonstrating how to formulate responses to student answers based on PCK about typical student background knowledge and possible misconceptions. Teacher candidates are given the opportunity to script feedback to correct misconceptions or reinforce accurate knowledge for an upcoming lesson in their own P–12 classroom and practice with their peers during the student teaching course. They then implement the lesson with their P–12 students and later reflect on how the preplanned academic feedback impacted student performance.

Site Coordinator as Coach

Site coordinators serve as experts who encourage accurate and sustained implementation of new practices learned in coursework (Kretlow & Bartholomew, 2010) and choose appropriate strategies (modeling, observing, and engaging in dialog) to meet the different kinds of learning teacher candidates are experiencing (Knight, 2007). At the end of each semester, teacher candidates provide feedback regarding the site coordinator on these skills. For example, a teacher candidate commented, "Dr. X has always provided anything we needed to better understand any of the X rubric and how we can better our instruction. She has also provided assistance with not just issues in school but emotional as well, which is something we all appreciated a lot" (Mary Lou Fulton Teachers College Teacher Candidate, personal communication, May 15, 2016). An additional comment states, "Dr. X has always kept a reflective attitude and thanks to that and her efforts, we have become reflective ourselves. She has always provided relevant and useful feedback which I can always use to better my instruction" (Mary Lou Fulton Teachers College Teacher Candidate, personal communication, May 15, 2016). Site coordinators strive to provide feedback, opportunities for self-reflection, and offer support through an explicit performance assessment process, completing walkthroughs, using data to make programmatic decisions, and provide targeted support, having crucial conversations and using the college's student support process.

Coaching via walkthroughs. Site coordinators recognize coaching as a process of growth and learning and provide specific feedback based on the tracking of progression (Marzano and Simms, 2013). The site coordinator also has to rely on the mentor teacher for coaching since the mentor is with the teacher candidate more often. Site coordinators facilitate mentor meetings on a monthly basis during which one component is always being instructed and practicing a coaching method. This coaching need is derived by data from conducting walkthroughs a minimum of four times each semester, or eight times a year. The site coordinator makes unscheduled, random visits to the classroom in which the mentor and teacher candidate continue to be engaged in the class. The teacher candidate and mentor can then access these data points via an online tracking system. Teacher candidates have an opportunity to reflect upon the lesson and follow up with the site coordinator. Mentor teachers use walkthrough data along with their own observations to provide on-the-spot coaching for the teacher candidates.

These 10–15 minute informal, unannounced observations document co-teaching models currently implemented by the teacher candidate and the mentor teacher at the time of the observation as well as the areas of refinement and reinforcement during a snapshot in time. One teacher candidate stated during a post-interview that, "It was nice to have somebody constantly checking up on what you were doing. Kind of giving you advice in that way" (Mary Lou Fulton Teachers College, Teacher Preparation Research and Evaluation Project, 2015, p. 1). Site coordinators observe teacher candidates implementing practices learned, collect evidence, and provide descriptive feedback to identify an area of reinforcement, an area of refinement, and support learning using individual coaching opportunities (Kretlow & Bartholomew, 2010). Table 3.1 shows samples from evidence collected during a walkthrough and next steps for the teacher candidate to implement in order to ensure student engagement. This feedback

TABLE 3.1   Walkthrough Evidence and Next Steps

Evidence	Next Steps
The teacher candidate has the students read portions of the textbook using the popcorn reading strategy to help students grasp the concepts presented in social studies. The teacher candidate asks questions and only some students raise their hand to respond. Not all students raise their hands to answer the questions.	Consider using activities that promote student engagement. How can you have students glean the same information from the text while more than just a few students are participating? An option may be to have groups create a poster that shows information students have learned and then engaging in a gallery walk. This type of activity provides opportunities for all students to engage in the learning process.
Students were engaged in an experiment on static electricity; teacher candidate called students attention and demonstrated static electricity by rubbing balloon on her hair and, while hovering over a pile of shredded paper, made the paper rise to meet the balloon. The directions were to observe and record the observations but not all students did so and several had questions after about their expectations.	Have mentor teacher script your directions from the moment you seek the kids' attention to the point where they are expected to work; observe the mentor as she provides direction to see how she implements attention grabber and how to ensure students understood the direction.

is viewable to all three parties involved—the site coordinator, the mentor, and the teacher candidate.

While this feedback is entered into a system to be stored so that all the parties can see it, on the spot coaching can also occur during walkthroughs. This could be something as simple as a note for the teacher candidate to review or it could be a whisper coaching opportunity from the site coordinator. For instance, during an observation, the site coordinator notices that the teacher candidate provides a correct answer after the student gives the incorrect answer and the teacher candidate moves on. The site coordinator may whisper to the teacher candidate that they go back and reask or retest the student to make sure that they retain the correct information. The site coordinator can also have a conversation with the mentor and provide suggestions that the mentor can use to support the teacher candidate.

There is a fine line between providing feedback to the teacher-candidate and giving the mentor a task to complete. In the above example, even though the mentor can see the feedback as well, the responsibility is put on the teacher-candidate for follow up but the "next steps" allows the mentor to also facilitate that discussion. If further development is needed, the site coordinator may model the strategy during course time or work collaboratively with the mentor teacher to support the teacher candidate in implementation, affording the teacher candidate multiple opportunities to practice newly learned strategies with real students and receive individualized feedback (Kretlow & Bartholomew, 2010). Alternatively, if application of a strategy is effective, a site coordinator will encourage continued use, resulting in implementation of the practice at an increasing level during future instruction.

Ingersoll, Merrill, and May (2014) contend that practice teaching opportunities and feedback within new teachers' pedagogical preparation are factors that impact teacher retention. Ingersoll, Merrill, and May (2014) noted that teacher candidates with these elements in their program were less likely to leave teaching after their first year of employment. In a 2015 interview with former teacher candidates, one in-service teacher pointed out that having that constant feedback helped in her current practice. She stated, "Having those with my principal it's an easy conversation because I'm used to that dialogue" (Mary Lou Fulton Teachers College, Teacher Preparation Research and Evaluation Project, 2015, p. 1). Another stated, "the program has done wonders for my transition to my first year, preparing me, the expectations" (Mary Lou Fulton Teachers College, Teacher Preparation Research and Evaluation Project, 2015, p. 3).

Coaching via performance assessment process. Coupled with formative assessment measures, site coordinators conduct four formal observations per year, known as the performance assessment. The performance assessment process is shown in Figure 3.2. Teacher candidates plan a lesson based on

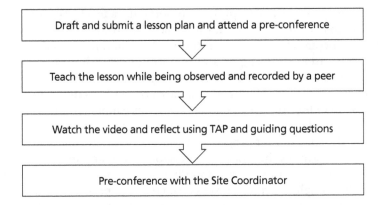

Figure 3.2 Performance assessment process.

state standards and student need as demonstrated in the assessment data; site coordinators pre-conference, observe and evaluate teacher candidates using the TAP Instructional Rubric (National Institute for Excellence in Teaching, 2013), and conduct a post-conference within 24–48 hours after the observation to afford teacher candidates time to reflect on the video-taped lesson. During the post conference, site coordinators use elements of cognitive coaching (Thinking Collaborative, 2016) by asking open ended questions and promoting reflection based on observed evidence through listening, probing for deeper meaning and being nonjudgmental, a critical skill for building a foundation of trust. A former student notes "... our site coordinator would watch us; we would always have a post conference with them and have a discussion about what went well, what would you change, what would you do... What did you think about this aspect of your lesson..." (Mary Lou Fulton Teachers College, Teacher Preparation Research and Evaluation Project, 2015, p. 1). In conjunction with high levels of reflection, teacher candidates examine the impact of instruction on student learning by reviewing and categorizing student work as "falls far below," "approaches," "meets," and "exceeds" to determine if the students have met the objective. This evidence along with the evidence collected during the observation determines the teacher candidates' abilities to meet the proficiency in the eight TAP Instructional Rubric indicators assessed (National Institute for Excellence in Teaching, 2013).

Coaching via Bi-Weekly Performance Data

In addition to collecting data from walkthroughs and performance assessments, data is gathered from mentor teachers via a bi-weekly progress report enabling mentors to share and document co-teaching approaches, an area of reinforcement and refinement in both instruction and professionalism, and attendance. By reviewing progress report data, a teacher candidate can see which co-teaching approaches have been used more heavily and the instructional competencies and professionalism knowledge and skills that appear to be areas of strengths and opportunities for improvement over time. For example, a teacher candidate might notice that managing student behavior has been identified as an area of reinforcement three times over the span of four progress reports. At the same time, he/she may notice that instructional planning has been identified as an area of refinement two times over the span of four progress reports. The teacher candidate can use this data to inform his/her own strategies for growth and improvement.

At multiple points in year, site coordinators compile all data from completed walkthroughs, performance assessments, and progress reports to get an overall trend analysis and use this data to formulate individual interventions and plan classroom instruction and mentor meetings. Site coordinators often model use of data in their classroom instruction to show teacher candidates how to backwards plan as well as highlight evidence to enhance the teacher candidates' instructional skills. Teacher candidates benefitted from the triangulated data as it provided a model of how data can be used to drive overall instruction (Creswell & Miller, 2010). One teacher candidate noted:

> My site coordinator was phenomenal and she was crazy about student data. Data, data, data, data, data. At the time, we would roll our eyes like, "All right [sic], we're talking about data again," but it is crucial. The farther we got into the year, the more we saw it. The more control that we had, it was like, "Oh, I really need this to decide what I'm going to teach." I do, I feel like I came into this like, "All right, I know I have to get data before I can just start teaching," so that was nice. (Mary Lou Fulton Teachers College, Teacher Preparation Research and Evaluation Project, 2015, p. 3)

Coaching via crucial conversations and student support process. Sometimes, teacher candidates are not successful in demonstrating sufficient knowledge and skills to demonstrate required competencies in the TAP Instructional Rubric (National Institute for Excellence in Teaching, 2013) and/or the Mary Lou Fulton Teachers College Professionalism Rubric. In this case, crucial conversations are needed. These conversations promote the realistic and holistic teacher candidate development and support teacher candidates in meeting benchmarks/performance gates to ensure the quality of teachers entering the profession. Site coordinators must also assist mentors in holding conversations that are evidence based; this practice is supported by Edwards-Groves' (2014) study indicating that when mentors are reminded of how to structure their conversations with their mentees that the meetings and conversations are more productive.

If having the crucial conversation does not prove successful, a site coordinator may choose to complete an *outcome map*. The underlying purpose of

TABLE 3.2 **Number of Supporting Our Students (SOS) Cases and Retention**					
Year	Number of SOS Forms Submitted	Number of Students Changed to a Non-Certification Program	Number of Students Who Left ASU	Number of Students Dismissed From Program	Retention of iTeachAZ Students
2012	85	21	12	11	86.6%
2013	103	29	11	10	89.6%
2014	133	22	7	6	91.5%
2015	201	19	5	5	92.7%
2016	212	24	4	3	93.3%

Note: Adapted from *ASU President's Award for Innovation Application,* by Mitchell, Cocchiarella, Harris & Ludlow, 2016.

the outcome map is to document and clearly outline the actions, knowledge, and skills that are required for the teacher candidate to successfully improve his/her instructional performance or professionalism. The action steps listed on the outcome map are time bound to promote close monitoring by all parties, and agreed upon by the teacher candidate. In the event that a teacher candidate has been unsuccessful in meeting the desired outcome(s) outlined in the outcome map, the faculty member submits a n*otice of concern,* flagging the teacher candidate as requiring a higher level of support from the college. The teacher candidate meets with a member of the advising team and is provided options, which are based on individual circumstance or need. Interventions may range from university-wide supports taking the forms of financial assistance, counseling opportunities, or degree changes to more targeted strategies focused on accountability for academic expectations, professionalism standards, or proficiency in instructional practice. Depending on the situation, teacher candidates might be able to continue in the program with support, switch to educational studies (a degree that does not lead to certification), or may decide not to pursue the field of teaching. Table 3.2 demonstrates the impact of the supporting our students (SOS) process on the retention of iTeachAZ teacher candidates in the iTeachAZ program. Table 3.2 represents the number of student support cases submitted and the impact of the process on retaining iTeachAZ students in the program.

MEASURES OF PROGRAM SUCCESS

The iTeachAZ program evaluation data offers various measures of program success and demonstrates the connection to practices within the site coordinator roles. Teacher candidates are leaving the program prepared for the teaching field. This claim is made and evidenced by the demonstrated proficiency levels in instructional competencies and professionalism of teacher candidates, and by graduation and employment rates. In serving the iTeachAZ program, site coordinators ensure that all teacher candidates are proficient in both instructional practices and professionalism using the performance assessment process with the end goal of producing high quality teachers. Table 3.3 provides average scores for the final performance assessment for all teacher candidates concluding their senior year residency and illustrates proficiency (a score of 3) in all areas. The performance assessment process, described earlier, allows for self-reflection by the teacher candidate, thus increasing performance as a preservice teacher and assisting with the transition to becoming an in-service teacher.

Teacher candidate preparedness is also evident in graduation and employment rates. For the 2012, 2013, and 2014 cohorts, iTeachAZ had a graduation rate of 99%, 99%, and 97% respectively, with 96% certifying in Arizona; additionally, 80% of iTeachAZ graduates are employed in an iTeachAZ partnering school district and 70% of graduates teach in Title I schools (Mary Lou Fulton Teachers College, Teacher Preparation Research and Evaluation Project, 2015). The iTeachAZ program has not only demonstrated encouraging employment rates post-graduation, but it has also produced high quality teachers and begun to pave the way in tackling the teacher retention issue. In 2002, the National Center for Educational Statistics reported that at the 5-year mark, 54% of new teachers were still teaching (Freedman & Appleman, 2009). New statistics from a 2012 survey conducted by the

TABLE 3.3   Spring 2016 Final Performance Assessment Averages for 364 Teacher Candidates

TAP Indicator	Score	Professionalism Indicator	Score
Instructional Plans	3.25	A.1 Professional Relationships	3.46
Managing Student Behavior	3.30	A.2 Fulfilling Professional Responsibilities	3.40
Standards & Objectives	3.21	B.1 Content Knowledge	3.34
Presenting Instructional Content	3.32	B.2 Professional Growth	3.30
Activities & Materials	3.45	C.1 General Record Keeping	3.18
Academic Feedback	3.23	C.2 Student Progress	3.18
Teacher Content Knowledge	3.33	D.1 Communicates Program Information to Parents	2.57
Teacher Knowledge of Students	3.35	D.2 Communicates Student Performance to Parents	2.58
		D.3 Resources for Students	2.54
Overall Performance	3.30	Overall Performance	3.06

National Center for Educational Statistics estimate that closer to 70% of new teachers are staying for at least 5 years (Hanna & Pennington, 2015). At the Mary Lou Fulton Teachers College, Year 1–3 retention data is at 92%, which is 12% higher than the national Year 1–3 average and 16% higher than the Arizona state average for first year teachers (Mary Lou Fulton Teachers College, Teacher Preparation Research and Evaluation Project, 2015). Retention data was collected and analyzed by the Teacher Preparation Research and Evaluation Project or T-Prep, a department within the Teachers College.

Much of this success is attributed to the support teacher candidates receive by site coordinators as they complete their senior year residency. Teacher preparation programs traditionally have faculty responsible for course instruction, and additional university supervisors responsible for field based experiences. The utilization of the aforementioned site coordinator roles, which work to combine course instruction with supervision, increases the likelihood of teacher candidate satisfaction of the teaching profession. DeAngelis, Wall, and Che (2013) found a direct association between perceived preparation quality and leaving teaching. The satisfaction of the iTeachAZ teacher candidates is measured by an end of semester survey which measures the high quality of communication and support provided by the site coordinator.

As quoted by the assistant dean, "The College has put more responsibility on faculty to support students" (Dr. Nancy Perry, personal communication, April 1, 2016). These numbers demonstrate that teacher candidates strongly agree with the level of coaching and supervisory support received, and signal satisfaction.

The site coordinator plays a significant role in the quality of the teacher preparation program. Site coordinators model, observe, and or engage in dialog with teacher candidates, which Knight (2007) attributes to the goal of meeting differentiated needs of teacher candidates. The combined responsibilities of site coordinators as administrator, coach, and instructor results in teacher candidate satisfaction, which strengthens teacher retention. This is significant because in a survey conducted by the Arizona Schools Administrators Association (ASA) in November 2013, 62% of respondents reported vacant teaching positions within their schools. Therefore, the Arizona State University Mary Lou Fulton Teachers College acknowledged its capacity to address the teachers' shortage through the teacher preparation program. The Teachers College restructured its teacher preparation program with the induction of a new full time faculty position known as the site coordinator. This need was also highlighted by Ingersoll, Merrill & May (2014) in determining that the quality of teacher preparation programs was positively associated with teacher retention. Pre-service teachers who had more teacher training, were less likely to leave the profession. It is important to address the retention of teachers as there is an increase in numbers of teachers who are not qualified working in classrooms. According to the Arizona Department of Education (2014) Highly Qualified Database, 938 districts and charter schools reported that vacant teaching positions were filled by substitute teachers. This was a 29% increase over the previous school year. The findings signal an urgency for teacher preparation programs to strengthen the support provided within clinically rich teacher preparation programs through the site coordinator role.

CONCLUSION

The implications of these findings hold promise for other teacher preparation programs, state education agencies, school districts and most importantly, student learning. Jorrisen (2002) found that longer teacher preparation programs, which combine pedagogical training with field based supervision are more likely to produce candidates who are satisfied and remain in the profession. The facilitation of clinically embedded coursework over the course of a year-long program with attention to pedagogy and professionalism skills taught in district locations by site coordinators is a useful model to producing candidates who stay. Additionally, Freedman and Appleman (2009) point to several factors under the control of teacher preparation programs that the authors hypothesize contribute to teachers staying in the field. They contend that preparation that included both the practical, the academic, and the harmony between the two, and training in assuming the reflective stance were important reasons beginning teachers stayed in the classroom. In their roles, site coordinators in the iTeachAZ program are key players in the clinically embedded coursework that teacher candidates receive and help teacher candidates become high quality and reflective teachers using aforementioned practices. It is suggested that teacher preparation programs encompass high levels of coaching and support offered by one person, similar to that of a site coordinator.

As previously mentioned, longer teacher preparation programs and clinically embedded coursework have a positive relationship to teacher retention rates. To better understand specific site coordinators practices that are contributing to graduates of a teacher preparation program staying in the profession, further research is needed. At the Mary Lou Fulton Teachers College, exit surveys completed by graduates will need to be analyzed to further determine key components of the program and site coordinator practices that are translating to the levels of satisfaction expressed and the graduates' decision to remain in the profession.

Currently, the College is working with the Arizona Department of Education to analyze P–12 student achievement data for graduates of the iTeachAZ program. This data will be useful to understanding the impact that iTeachAZ graduates are having on student achievement and if graduates are showing higher levels of student achievement in comparison to other teacher preparation programs. Additionally, 70% of iTeachAZ graduates are teaching in Title I schools, and according to Year 1–3 data, are being retained. More research is needed to understand the impact of iTeachAZ new teachers on students in Title I schools. Zhang and Zeller (2016) agree that the likelihood of teacher retention partially depends on the type of preparation teachers receive. Although the type of teacher preparation program is an important factor, predicting retention is far more complex and will continue to require further examination of other factors.

REFERENCES

Allen, J. M. (2011). Stakeholders' perspectives of the nature and role of assessment during practicum. *Teaching and Teacher Education, 27*(4), 742–750.

Ambrosetti, A. (2014). Are you ready to be a mentor? Preparing teachers for mentoring pre-service teachers. *Australian Journal for Teacher Education, 39*(6), 30–42.

Arizona Department of Education. (2015). *Educator retention and recruitment report.* Retrieved from https://www.azed.gov/wp-content/uploads/2015/02/err-initial-report-final.pdf

Creswell, J. W., & Miller, D. L. (2010). Determining validity in qualitative inquiry. *Theory into Practice, 39*(3), 124–130.

DeAngelis, K. J., Wall, A. F., & Che, J. (2013). The impact of preservice preparation and early career support on novice teachers' career intentions and decisions. *Journal of Teacher Education, 64*(4), 338–355.

Edwards-Groves, C. J. (2014). Learning theory practices: The role of critical mentoring conversations in teacher education. *Journal of Education and Training Studies, 2*(2), 151–166.

Freedman, S., & Appleman, D. (2009). "In it for the long haul": How teacher education can contribute to teacher retention in high poverty, urban schools. *Journal of Teacher Education, 60*(3), 323–337.

Friend, M. (2007). *Co-teaching connection.* Retrieved from http://www.marilynfriend.com/approaches.htm

Hanna, R., & Pennington, K. (2015). *Despite reports to the contrary, new teachers are staying in their jobs longer.* Retrieved from https://www.americanprogress.org/issues/education/news/2015/01/08/103421/despite-reports-to-the-contrary-new-teachers-are-staying-in-their-jobs-longer/

Hobson, A., Ashby, P., Malderez, A., & Tomlinson, P. (2008). Mentoring beginning teachers: What we know and what we don't. *Teaching and Teacher Education, 25*(1), 207–216.

Ingersoll, R., Merrill, L., & May, H. (2014). What are the effects of teacher education and preparation on beginning teacher attrition? (Research Report #RR-82). Philadelphia: University of Pennsylvania.

Ingersoll, R., Merrill, L., & Stuckey, D. (2014). Seven trends: The transformation of the teaching force, updated April 2014 (CPRE Report #RR-80). Philadelphia, PA: University of Pennsylvania.

Jorissen, K. (2002). Retaining alternate route teachers: The power of professional integration in teacher preparation and induction. *The High School Journal, 86*(1), 45–56.

Knight, J. (2007). *Instructional coaching: A partnership approach to improving instruction.* Thousand Oaks, CA: Corwin Press.

Kocolowski, M. D. (2010). Shared leadership: Is it time for change? *Emerging Leadership Journeys, 3*(1), 22–33.

Kretlow, A. G., & Bartholomew, C. C. (2010). Using coaching to improve the fidelity of evidence-based practices: A review of studies. *Teacher Education and Special Education, 33*(4), 279–299.

Mary Lou Fulton Teachers College. (n.d.). iTeachAZ site coordinator job description [Flyer]. Retrieved from https://education.asu.edu/sites/default/files/jd_iteachazsitecoordinator-1.pdf

Mary Lou Fulton Teachers College, Teacher Preparation Research and Evaluation Project. (2015, March). T-Prep. Unpublished raw data.

Marzano, R. J., & Simms, J. A. (2013). *Coaching classroom instruction.* Bloomington, IN: Marzano Research Laboratory.

McCaffrey, D. F., Koretz, D. M., Lockwood, J. R., & Hamilton, L. S. (2004). *Evaluating value-added models for teacher accountability.* Santa Monica, CA: RAND.

McLaurin, S., Smith, W., & Smillie, A. (2009). Teacher retention: Problems and solutions. Retrieved from http://files.eric.ed.gov/fulltext/ED507446.pdf

Mitchell, E., Cocchiarella, M., Harris, P., & Ludlow, C. (2016). *ASU president's award for innovation application.* Unpublished manuscript, Teachers College, Arizona State University, Tempe, Arizona.

National Institute for Excellence in Teaching. (2013). *Instructionally focused accountability.* Retrieved from http://www.niet.org/tap-system/elements-of-success/instructionally-focused-accountability/

Range, B., Duncan, H., & Hvidston, D. (2013). How faculty supervise and mentor pre-service teachers: Implications for principal supervision of novice teachers. *International Journal of Educational Leadership Preparation, 8*(2), 43–58.

Rodgers, A., & Keil, V. (2007). Restructuring a traditional student teacher supervision model: Fostering enhanced professional development and mentoring within a professional development school context. *Teaching and Teacher Education, 23*(1), 63–80.

Sallis, E. (2002). *Total quality management in education (3rd ed.).* London, England: Routledge.

Shulman, L. S. (1986). Those who understand: Knowledge growth in teaching. *Educational Researcher, 15*(2), 4–14. doi:10.2307/1175860

Stensaker, B., & Vabo, A. (2013). Reinventing shared governance: Implications for organizational culture and institutional leadership. *Higher Education Quarterly, 67*(3), 256–274.

Taylor, A. (2008). Developing understanding about learning to teach in a university—Schools partnership in England. *British Educational Research Journal, 34*(1), 63–90.

U.S. Department of Education, National Center for Education Statistics. (2012). NCES Schools and Staffing Survey (SASS). Retrieved from http://nces. ed.gov/surveys/sass/tables/sass1112_2013314_t1s_001.asp

Zhang, G., & Zeller, N. (2016). A longitudinal investigation of the relationship between teacher preparation and teacher retention. *Teacher of Education Quarterly, 43*(2), 73–92.

SECTION II

OUTCOMES OF NEW PRACTICES

CHAPTER 4

THE ROLE OF PRESERVICE TEACHER COACHING IN CLINICALLY RICH TEACHER EDUCATION

Mary Kay Rodgers, Vicki Vescio, and Jamey Burns,
University of Florida

Lauren Gibbs
University of North Florida

ABSTRACT

This study examined four preservice teachers' learning as they participated in cycles of coaching by their supervisor. The goal of this effort was to analyze the interns' perceptions, the impact on their classroom practices, and the similarities and differences between cycles of coaching and the more traditional process of observation for evaluative purposes historically used in their teacher education program. Data indicate that coaching as supervision provided: individualized, job-embedded support that led to change in interns' daily teaching; elicited collaboration and communication that benefited intern growth; and supported learning of the skills and dispositions necessary

Outcomes of High-Quality Clinical Practice in Teacher Education, pages 63–84
Copyright © 2018 by Information Age Publishing

to intern success as novice teachers. Interns also indicated that coaching fostered a type of continuous learning not experienced with supervision focused on evaluation in their teacher education program. The researchers conclude that using instructional coaching is an essential part of providing clinically rich field experiences for preservice teachers.

Despite decades of reform movements, teacher preparation programs continue to be criticized for a lack of practical preparation for meeting the needs of diverse learners as well as ignoring the voices of teacher candidates (Russell, McPherson, & Martin, 2001). While there is a growing consensus that clinically based experiences hold the key to improved teacher preparation (Darling-Hammond, 2014), these programs remain undervalued and underfunded (Zeichner, 2010). Traditional teacher education programs often display significant gaps (Russell et al., 2001), with instructors addressing evidence-based practices in courses but providing little follow-up support in field-based settings (Scheeler, Bruno, Grubb, & Seavy, 2009). Though efforts to improve teacher education have recently accentuated the importance of well-supervised clinical practice (Darling-Hammond, 2014), in order for novice teachers to successfully implement theory-based practices, the focus of their learning must include well supported clinical practice that emphasizes the individual challenges teachers encounter when teaching in real classrooms (Elmore, 2006).

While professional learning for in-service teachers has become vital in school reform (Darling-Hammond & McGlaughlin, 1995), professional learning for preservice teachers is often overlooked because of the demands of coursework as well as the lack of quality professional facilitation skills possessed by those who work most closely with preservice teachers (Burns & Badiali, 2015; Zeichner, 2010). Because teacher educators have often disagreed as to the value of supervision and the role of the university supervisor, this labor-intensive role of supervisor has often been relegated to those who do not possess the necessary knowledge of teacher education or skill set for providing quality professional development such as new faculty, graduate students, adjunct faculty, and/or retired teachers (Burns, Jacobs, & Yendol-Hoppey, 2016b; NCATE, 2010; Slick, 1998; Zeichner, 2010). In addition, once teacher candidates begin student teaching, supervision models that purport to be about field based learning often assume an evaluative stance that closely monitors these novice educators (Nolan & Hoover, 2010). This can result in a loss of the vision of preservice teachers as colearners, collaborators, and facilitators in the construction of knowledge about teaching (Slick, 1998).

In the professional development literature for practicing teachers, school-based coaching has been heralded as an effective form of teacher learning that promises to improve instruction (Knight, 2009; Neufeld & Roper, 2003). Instructional coaching, which focuses on providing appropriate supports to teachers so they are able to implement scientifi-cally-proven teaching practices in the classroom (Cornett & Knight, 2009; Kowal & Steiner, 2007; Knight, 2007, 2009) depends on three broad cat-egories of coaching skills: pedagogical knowledge, content expertise, and interpersonal and facilitation skills. Instructional coaching has been shown to change the culture of a school, raise proficiency rates in literacy and nu-meracy, and create a successful school-wide phenomenon of change (Cor-nett & Knight, 2009; Killion & Harrison, 2006).

Due to the success of instructional coaching with practicing teachers, this approach has recently surfaced as a viable method of professional learning for preservice teachers (Butler & Cuenca, 2012; Kretlow & Bartholomew, 2010). With clinical supervision often being reduced to observation and evaluation in many teacher education programs (Nolan & Hoover, 2010), a supervision model which includes instructional coaching for preservice teachers would provide professional learning *in* practice and create con-nections with preservice teachers' theoretical foundations. While research on coaching for practicing teachers has shown instructional improvement and achievement gains (Cornett & Knight, 2009; Joyce & Showers, 1996; Knight, 2007), research on coaching with preservice teachers is scarce and needs further exploration.

REVIEW OF LITERATURE

Examining the experiences of preservice teachers in the field requires an understanding of the empirical literature related to effective teacher preparation, traditional supervision models and the role of the university supervisor in the student teaching experience, and instructional coaching for professional learning. The complex nature of the intersections between these stakeholders' lies at the heart of the "close coupling of theoretical and practical preparation" (NCATE, 2010, p. iii) needed for effective pre-service teacher learning and practice.

Effective Teacher Preparation Programs

The American Association of Colleges for Teacher Education (AACTE, 2013) reports, "preparation programs that are focused on the work of the classroom . . . tend to produce first year teachers who are more likely to remain in the profession than those from less clinically based programs" (p. 9). In addition, Darling-Hammond (2008) claims, "the weight of the evidence suggests that teachers who have more complete preparation are better rated and more effective" (p. 1318). The cumulative impact of this literature suggests it is imperative for teacher educators to pay particular attention to providing clinically based field experiences in their teacher preparation programs.

When discussing the gap between preparation and practice, Russell et al. (2001) report that beginning teachers convey an inability to cope with essential elements of the job, including time and classroom management, evaluation, long-range planning, and student relationships. Unfortunately, typical practicum situations result in preservice teachers being left to decipher the pedagogical principles underlying effective classroom practice on their own. As Russell et al. (2001) also state, "Unless these teachers are challenged to question their image, understanding, and role as classroom teachers, they fail to see past the actions of teaching to the pedagogical foundations that let them think like a teacher" (p. 42). Korthagen, Loughran, and Russell (2006) further indicate that innovative programs take preservice teachers' experiences as central in discussions that enable them to study their own practice; create collaborative environments with teacher educators, supervisors, and mentors; and make explicit what successful teachers do and think in the course of planning, implementing, and evaluating their teaching.

Traditional Supervision and the Role of the University Supervisor

The bulk of supervision research focuses on the roles, tasks and responsibilities of the supervisor as well as relationships between the supervisor, preservice teacher, mentor teacher, school, and university. For example, a meta-analysis of the empirical literature from 2001 to 2013 revealed that the most prevalent supervision models enact a "tasks and practices" vision aimed at developing preservice teachers for the betterment of PreK–12 students (Burns, Jacobs, & Yendol-Hoppey, 2016a). The typical "observe and give feedback" supervision model used by many teacher education programs has been argued to ensure competence for teacher practice, but neglect the cultivation of teacher learning for student achievement (Kretlow & Bartholomew, 2010; Nolan & Hoover, 2010).

Many scholars of instructional supervision have debated about the connection between supervision and evaluation (Glanz & Neville, 1997; Nolan & Hoover, 2010), and if these two instructional tasks are serendipitous or mutually exclusive. Nolan and Hoover (2010) identified seven components that distinguish supervision from evaluation (purpose, rationale, scope, relationship, data focus, expertise, and perspective) and argue that these differences are often lost in practice because the supervisor is charged with enacting both these tasks simultaneously. A lack of understanding of the different goals, theories and competencies of supervision and evaluation have resulted in the confusion of the two in practice, which has translated to mixed outcomes for preservice teachers (Basmadjian, 2011; Burns & Badiali, 2015; Burns et al., 2016b).

Burns and Badiali (2015) examined skills and dispositions needed for effective learning from supervision, and noted pedagogical skills such as noticing, ignoring, intervening, pointing, unpacking, and processing as imperative to the process. The researchers concluded these skills are indicative of "a pedagogy of supervision...which illuminates the complexity of supervision as a role that is highly complex, conceptual and interactive" (p. 27). As the function of university supervisor becomes more critical and nuanced in supporting the connection between theory and practice for preservice teachers in field experiences, the dispositions, knowledge, and experiences of supervisors also become critical.

Instructional Coaching as Supervision

School-based coaching has been defined as a "form of inquiry-based learning characterized by collaboration...that involves professional, ongoing classroom modeling, supportive critiques of practice and specific observations, and discussions" (Poglinco, Bach, Hovde, Rosenblum, Saunders, & Supovitz, 2003, p. 1). While there are varying models, theories, and goals of coaching described in the literature, this professional development model has been heralded as effective, and provides promise to improve instruction (Knight, 2007; Neufeld & Roper, 2003) as well as create positive outcomes in combination with other professional learning strategies (Bean, Draper, Hall, Vandermolen, & Zigmond, 2010; Deussen, Coskie, Robinson, & Autio 2007; Walpole, McKenna, Uribe-Zarain, & Lamitina, 2010). Using instructional coaching as an alternative to the more traditional evaluation process of observation and feedback, provides individual inquiry-based support for preservice teachers' clinical practice and learning.

Coaching and Preservice Teacher Learning

There is a small but growing subset of literature on instructional coaching that directly examines coaching as a form of professional learning for preservice teachers. Butler and Cuenca (2012) discuss a model of coaching that incorporates elements of mentoring as part of the student teaching experience and conclude that coaches should approach mentoring with a mindset of assisting with, rather than advocating for, classroom practices. In their review of 13 studies on coaching, Kretlow and Bartholomew (2010) state that preservice clinical preparation has the potential to be one of the most influential factors in increasing teachers' fidelity and implementation of evidence-based practices. These authors suggest that within teacher education programs, preservice teachers need (a) high-quality instructive guidance; (b) multiple opportunities to practice newly learned strategies with real students; and (c) individualized observation, feedback, and modeling through coaching whenever possible. The authors conclude that in student teaching experiences, coaching should be a replacement for the typical "observe and give feedback" (p. 293) format most often used by faculty supervisors and mentor teachers, and that this could make the experience more powerful and valuable.

PROGRAM AND RESEARCH CONTEXT

To better understand the role of instructional coaching in preservice teacher development, this study examined four teacher candidates and three university supervisors who participated in the Elementary Teacher Education (ETE) program at a large southeastern university. In this research, the intern (preservice teacher, teacher candidate) refers to a graduate student enrolled in a yearlong internship experience in a K–5 elementary school. The interns in this particular research context worked with classroom teachers (referred to as mentor teachers) and university supervisors who provided practical learning and support. The university supervisors in this study were all doctoral students who had designed and implemented an instructional coaching model previously with in-service teachers, and had been assigned to oversee a number of interns in their field experience. To adequately understand the context of this research, it is imperative that we provide an overview of the ETE program, as well as describe the coaching model employed in the study.

The Elementary Teacher Education Program

The ETE program is a 5-year program with the goal of preparing teachers with a dual emphasis in elementary education and working with children with mild disabilities. Program themes are connected to cultivating the democratic values of equity and collaboration as well as fostering a commitment in preservice teachers to accept responsibility for the learning of all students (Bondy & Ross, 2012). Starting their junior undergraduate year, students enrolled in the ETE program engage in a field placement every semester, gradually increasing their responsibilities and culminating with a yearlong internship during the fifth/graduate year.

During the yearlong internship, students are assigned to a K–5 classroom for two semesters, which results in a 32-week field experience. ETE interns are integrated into the day-to-day work of their classroom and school with the guidance of a mentor teacher and university supervisor. The intern and mentor work as co-teaching partners, and the university supervisor works as part of this team to facilitate the intern's experience. In conjunction with their field placement, interns take a series of online courses designed to support the learning that occurs at their school site. For example, interns take a course on culturally responsive classroom management, in which they conduct "try its" to implement evidence-based practices from their coursework. The interns are asked to collect data on the impact of these strategies, and reflect upon the strategy's effectiveness in terms of their teaching and student learning.

Pathwise Observation System

In the first semester of their internship, teacher candidates engage in a supervision as evaluation. During this semester interns are assessed by their university supervisor on their classroom teaching ability and lesson planning during four cycles using the Pathwise observation system developed by Danielson (2009). This process requires the intern to submit a lesson plan and have a pre-observation conference with her/his university supervisor. The supervisor then observes the lesson and collects data in the designated instructional domains. After the observation, the supervisor and intern have a conversation to discuss reflections related to noted practices and areas for improvement. Finally, the intern submits a written reflection, and the supervisor writes a summary that is connected to the Pathwise framework, as well as the educator accomplished practices (EAP) with which interns are evaluated after each semester. This process of conducting Pathwise cycles is in line with the more traditional observation and feedback model typically used in traditionally preservice teacher supervision.

Instructional Coaching Model

Developed in 2011, the instructional coaching model used in this study is grounded in Knight's (2007) partnership coaching theory and a comprehensive instructional coaching framework that synthesizes two popular teacher observation systems (Danielson, 2009; Marzano, 2007), a system that evaluates teacher–student interactions (Pianta, Le Paro, & Hamre, 2008), and a culturally responsive observation protocol (Powell & Rightmeyer, 2011). This synthesized framework helps coaches and teachers by emphasizing effective instructional strategies, students' cultural backgrounds, and practices to meet diverse learners needs (Ross, 2011). The framework also provides a common language of instruction to enable teachers and coaches to talk in-depth and develop perspectives and strategies for improved instruction (Ross, 2011). This coaching model and instructional coaching framework were adapted to develop the preservice teacher coaching model investigated in this study.

The coaching model is designed for university supervisors to use coaching skills and strategies to facilitate interns' professional learning. In this study, the coaching model took place during the 2nd semester of the year-long internship and replaced the assessment and evaluation-based Pathwise observation system that the interns experienced during their first semester. The goal of using this preservice teacher coaching model is to facilitate learning and move away from those more traditional forms of supervision that more strongly lend to evaluation and subsequent assessment (Tschannen-Moran & Tschannen-Moran, 2011).

Implementation of the Preservice Teacher Coaching Model

At the end of their first semester, interns, mentors, and supervisors collaboratively created an inquiry-based professional development plan (PDP) for the intern based on previous Pathwise observations as well as mentor and intern reflections. The intern and supervisor then consulted the instructional coaching framework (Ross, 2011) to align individual needs/ goals with specific domain(s) to determine a focus for the intern's initial coaching cycle.

The coaching cycle contained progressive steps beginning with: (a) the determination of a coaching focus from professional development literature, the PDP, and/or an intern's coursework; (b) the pre-observation interview which determined details about the focus and data collection for the observation; (c) the coaching observation; (d) the creation of a data display; and (e) the coaching conversation and data presentation with interns, supervisors, and mentor teachers. Supervisors and interns engaged in two complete coaching cycles where these steps were followed. Coaching differed from the evaluative supervision that the interns experienced during the first semester of their internship. The coaching model allowed interns to determine the focus of their observation. Interns collaborated with their supervisor and mentor to decide on a mutually determined focus as well as the types of data that would inform this focus. The interns also had input into how the supervisor displayed the data collected from the coaching observation. The Pathwise model of supervision that interns experienced

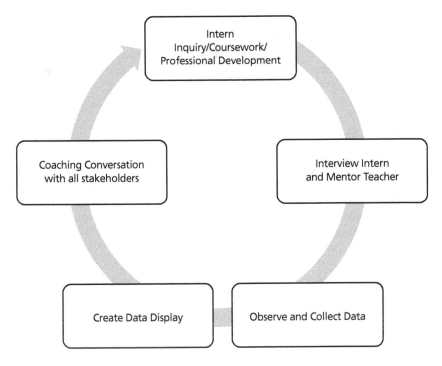

Figure 4.1   Coaching as supervision model.

during the first semester was a directive model of supervision based on assessment and evaluation. The coaching as supervision model of supervision is a facilitative model that is based on intern voice, trust, and targeted, data-driven conversations.

Due to this innovative combination of providing an instructional framework to focus on preservice instructional practice, coaching is a *comprehensive, inquiry-based investigation* that promotes reflection and cycles of constant growth in preservice teacher learning and improvement in their practice. Thus, the coaching model differs from traditional supervision models by creating the connection between preservice teacher learning and practice without fostering an evaluative stance based on proficiency of skills.

METHODOLOGY

With the goal of studying this phenomenon, a team of four researchers examined preservice teacher learning from participating in instructional coaching cycles. The coaching cycle used in this study includes five distinct steps (see Figure 4.1). These steps are: (a) the examination of course work including individual inquiry and professional development to build new knowledge; (b) supervisor interview with the intern and mentor teacher to determine a focus area; (c) predetermined data collection during an observation; (d) creation of a non-judgmental data display; and (e) a data-driven coaching conversation with supervisor, intern, and mentor teacher. The coaching cycle is an ongoing, cyclical process built on Knight's (2007) partnership principles for instructional coaching.

This qualitative study explores the implementation of a coaching model that was based upon a comprehensive instructional framework (Ross, 2011) and the partnership theory of coaching (Knight, 2007) for the supervision of yearlong interns. In this model, the university supervisor acted as the instructional coach facilitating connections between theory and practice, while also providing support for interns and their mentor teachers. The research questions that guided this study were as follows:

1. How do interns experience the process of instructional coaching during a yearlong internship, and what impact does instructional coaching have on their practice, learning, and development?
2. What similarities and differences do the interns see between a traditional supervision model that focuses on evaluation of competencies used in their first semester, and an instructional coaching model used during their second semester of a yearlong internship?

A constructivist epistemological paradigm undergirds this study as the researchers started with the premise that "all knowledge, and therefore all meaningful reality as such, is contingent upon human practices, being constructed in and out of interaction between human beings and their world, and developed and transmitted within an essentially social context" (Crotty, 1998, p. 42). The participants for the research were recruited from the ETE program. Using a purposive strategy of homogeneous sampling (Plano-Clark & Creswell, 2010), interns and supervisors were identified based upon the following criteria: (a) interns had successfully completed the first semester of their internship, and (b) supervisors were trained to facilitate the instructional coaching model used in this study. This sampling strategy provided "information-rich cases" (Glesne, 1999, p. 29) that would support an understanding of our research questions.

Data Collection

Sources of data for this study include artifacts developed during the coaching cycles, reflections written by the interns and supervisors after coaching cycles, intern interviews, and two distinct focus group interviews.

Artifacts included data displays, data collection tools, and field notes from the supervisors. In addition, two semi-structured interviews were conducted with each intern, one before the coaching cycles and the other at the completion of the coaching process. The interviews were designed for interns to elaborate on key aspects of the supervisory process during each semester of their internship. Interns and supervisors also collectively met at the end of the second semester to discuss the benefits and challenges of the coaching process in a 75-minute focus group interview. Finally, supervisors participated in a focus group interview that centered on their coaching experiences as well as discussed their insights into intern development and learning as a result of the coaching process. Interviews lasted from 20–50 minutes, and were audio-recorded and transcribed verbatim.

Data Analysis

Artifacts, participant reflections, and interview transcripts were analyzed using procedures aligned with Hatch's (2002) process of interpretive analysis. To establish inter-coder reliability, the researchers initially analyzed a common data set from intern interviews. Specifically, we each examined one interview asking what evidence existed in the data that was related to our research questions. For example, we each read the data to code evidence that provided support for the impact of coaching on the interns' practices and learning. From this, we each clustered the data into salient themes and then met to discuss our individual analysis. Next, we sought confirming and disconfirming evidence from other data sets (artifacts, coaching field notes) to triangulate findings and substantiate emerging themes (Glesne, 1999). Once we reached consensus on the themes from the data, the four researchers paired up to analyze additional data sets that included artifacts, intern/supervisor reflections, and interview/focus group transcripts. During this process the researchers met several times to further discuss and refine codes and themes that were emerging. These intensive peer-debriefing sessions along with collecting data from a variety of sources helped to bolster the trustworthiness of this study's findings (Glesne, 1999; Hatch, 2002; Plano-Clark & Creswell, 2010).

FINDINGS

The purpose of this study was to examine the experiences of interns and supervisors when implementing an instructional coaching model for supervision during the second semester of a yearlong internship. We sought to investigate the perceived impact of coaching on intern practice as well as make comparisons to traditional models of supervision. Findings related to our research questions are presented from intern perspectives. In addition, we provide a discussion of the perceived challenges with this model within clinical practice experiences.

Intern Experiences With Coaching as Supervision

The results from analyzing intern artifacts and interviews are illustrated using three broad themes: the impact of coaching on everyday practices, the importance of collaboration and collective mentoring, and the power of coaching for providing an ethos of continuous learning. Collectively, these findings support existing research on coaching as effective for helping interns explore and develop their classroom practices through collaboration in a clinically based experience (Butler & Cuenca, 2012; Richardson, Pate, Yost, & Williams, 2015). In addition, our findings align with the work of Kretlow and Bartholomew (2010) who suggest that the work of teacher educators needs to provide interns with opportunities for practice accompanied by conversations that allow the intern to examine data and reflect on practice in a manner that is offered through cycles of coaching.

Theme One: Focusing Coaching on Everyday Practices

This broad theme focuses on the experiences and perceptions of the interns relative to the impact of coaching on their daily practices. Specifically, analysis indicated that engaging in cycles of coaching supported interns' needs to focus on the real work of teaching in a way that directly impacted what they were doing with the children in their classrooms. The emphasis on problems of practice that each intern was experiencing resulted in a type of differentiation in supervision that gave them opportunities to safely explore various teaching strategies. For example, Intern 4 stated, "I really feel like the coaching cycles meet the needs of interns as teachers as opposed to students," showing the need for preservice teachers to be supported as professionals in practice within their classrooms.

All interns indicated they felt coaching was rooted in the work of *real teaching*, which helped meet their individual needs and led to changes in their everyday practices. Throughout interviews the interns continually talked of how coaching allowed them to closely examine their practices in light of day-to-day issues in the classroom. For these novice teachers, having the ability to focus on their individual needs was a profound learning experience. For example, Intern 1 reflected:

> The biggest benefit is being able to focus on something you really need to work on ... getting feedback on one specific thing versus one very broad

thing... because it is something *you* need to work on, it's not every intern had the same question. (emphasis in original)

Intern 3 also expressed this sentiment when she spoke of how engaging in cycles of coaching motivated her to improve her teaching:

> With the coaching cycles it was, "Oh, wow this is something I want to change, this is something that I have noticed in my teaching practice, that I want to work on." No one is telling me what to do...I chose the focus...how I wanted to address that need and improve it.

In fact, all of the interns said that coaching was beneficial because it focused on aspects of their practice that *they* identified as important. For example, Intern 2 talked about recognizing that a challenge in her teaching was time and classroom management.

This ability to focus coaching observations on specific needs led the interns to change their practices. After Intern 4 used a coaching cycle to study her guided reading strategies, she exclaimed, "this is something that I am going to use *forever*...these strategies I learned...I think that's special, I think that's been so helpful." The individual focus on instruction and subsequent change in practice was in direct contrast to the outcomes of cycles of supervision from the first semester for these interns. Intern 3 expressed this difference when she said:

> I might have minorly [sic] been touching on classroom management in a broad sense but I wasn't targeting those specific areas that needed improvement. My teaching practice never really improved and with the coaching cycles I was able to say, "this is one thing that I want to focus on, and I am going to focus on it until I figure out how to improve it.

Another key part of coaching that interns identified as contributing to their development was the data display created by the university supervisor. Interns stated that data from the coaching process provided a *concrete picture of their teaching*, and gave them a view of their instructional practice that was not evident from conversation alone. At some point, each of the interns discussed the importance of the data display for giving them a different perspective on their teaching. Specifically, Intern 2 talked about how the data display opened her eyes to the inconsistency between how she thought a lesson went and how it really went. She said, "After [the lesson] I would say, I thought this went well and this went well and this went well and then she would show me the data display and then it was like, hmmm, maybe not so much." In addition, Intern 1 talked at length about the value of the data display that her supervisor provided:

> You actually get to see some sort of concrete data to know what's happening in your classroom, versus someone telling you. It is so different when you see the data and you are like, I only waited 3 seconds between that question and some kid answering. [My supervisor] could have told me all day everyday that I didn't wait long enough, but if I didn't see those numbers in front of me I might not have thought it was as bad as it is ... there is a concreteness to having some sort of data that is very different.

Collectively, the sentiment of the interns was that the data display produced by their supervisors increased the overall impact of coaching because it provided a window into their teaching and motivated them to improve instantaneously.

Theme Two: Enhancing Collaboration and Collective Mentoring

A second theme that manifested in the data was the importance coaching provided for collaboration and communication between the intern, university supervisor, and mentor teacher. Three of the four interns explicitly mentioned how coaching cycles fostered collaboration and communication in a way that benefited their growth and supported their efforts to learn the skills and dispositions necessary to become successful teachers. For example, Intern 1 noted:

> I felt like with [my supervisor] and then my mentor teachers as well, we were brainstorming and trying to think, How can I take this to make my teaching practice become better? What are some practical ways that I can do that? I felt like I was really supported in that because, one it was focused and two, they know me well enough as a teacher to say, this is what I think you could work on.

Likewise, Intern 4 talked about how her university supervisor was strong at talking with her to "truly think about why it went well" and what she needed to do to continue to grow in her teaching. As a result of this interactive process, Intern 4 stated, "I think that was *really* helpful. ... to sit down and think ... with [my supervisor] and mentor teacher, it really helped me get my thoughts together and see where I need to go from there." Finally, in talking about the importance of collaboration in the coaching cycle Intern 2 explained:

> I thought that overall the coaching cycles offered more communication between the mentor, supervisor, and intern. Together we were able to work and give insightful feedback, and a lot of this happened during the reflection process, talking about what we observed and [my supervisor] was telling us what she observed and going back and forth.

In comparing the traditional observation and feedback supervision model used in the first semester to coaching as supervision, interns thought communication and collaboration was significantly increased. This was evident in a reflection from Intern 2, where she wrote, "With Pathwise, I didn't feel like my mentor teacher was required to be as involved." She added that in contrast during coaching cycles her mentor "played a lot more of an important role." She indicated this was beneficial because her mentor "was able to provide her insight and together we were able to team up and discuss what we thought was going to be best... for our students." Similarly, Intern 1 expressed:

> I felt like with [my supervisor] and then my mentor teachers there as well, we were brainstorming and trying to think, "How can I take this to make my teaching practice become better? What are some practical ways that I can do that?" I felt like I was really supported because it was focused on me, and they know me well enough as a teacher to say, "This is what I think you could work on, you could do this aspect well.

The heightened communication and collaboration during coaching resulted in enhanced experiences for these interns. This, in turn, led them to feel supported in their learning and safe in their efforts to take risks, which impacted their development as well as their everyday classroom practices.

Theme Three: Cultivating an Ethos of Continuous Learning

The cumulative effect of using coaching as supervision went beyond impacting the everyday practices of the interns and providing greater communication and collaboration. Although these two findings are important and are represented in the coaching literature, the interns in our study believed that coaching fostered an ethos of continuous learning that would aid them throughout their careers. When talking about this, Intern 2 simply said, "Through the coaching conversation, and the reflection process, you are able to determine whether you mastered something and what you want to do differently." Intern 1 spoke of coaching as giving her more questions to think about for future improvement, and Intern 3 said,

> [Coaching] is a continuous cycle of development and improving your practice. And so, that's exactly what I felt like ... I was doing these cycles, that each had a different focus but it brought up a new focus I wanted to address.

The reflection and pursuit of growth that coaching fostered for these interns was reinforced by the fact that they each talked about a desire to continue this process throughout the remainder of their internship and beyond. For example, Intern 3 said, "If you're not continuously reflecting on your practice and evaluating yourself as a teacher, you're not doing your job, and that needs to be happening every single day." With this enthusiasm for using coaching cycles as professional development, the interns also recognized the possible tension of continuing support for this type of learning depended on the culture of the schools where they become employed. Despite this uncertainty, interns talked about continuing their own professional development using the strategies and techniques they learned from coaching cycles.

Another important point made by interns was that coaching provided them with the opportunity to *look at their practice holistically, beyond a moment in time*. Coaching allowed interns to shift the focus of observations from a specific lesson to their overall teaching practice, which interns considered invaluable for their learning. Intern 2 underscored this when saying,

> With coaching cycles it's not focused on how well the lesson design is, it's rather, what are some things I can do to change the way that I am connecting with my students, through teaching and their learning? I thought that was kind of an awesome thing for my teaching.

Intern 4 said, "Coaching...made you be more reflective than the Pathwise...because it helped to pinpoint what to reflect upon....whereas in Pathwise it was just how was your teaching, was your behavior management good, was the content taught well?"

While this type of professional development was crucial for learning, these interns admitted that coaching as supervision proved difficult for several reasons. Moving from the general to a more specific examination of their practice was not something these typically successful students were used to. On a few occasions interns expressed how this shift created struggle for them because of an emerging critical analysis that went from a macro to a micro gaze of their instructional practice. Specifically, Intern 1 wrote, "I felt like the coaching cycle actually ends up being a little bit more painful for the intern because you are actually pinpointing something that he or she is really weak on." She went on to discuss how this was different than previous observations of her teaching where supervisors always gave her positive feedback.

All four interns reported that they felt coaching as supervision was a comprehensive, inquiry-based investigation that promoted reflection and cycles of constant growth in their learning and improvement in their practice. One goal of the ETE program is to foster an inquiry stance in its preservice teachers, and the data from this group of interns indicates that coaching helped to instill this type of thinking about their teaching practice. The cumulative impact of cycles of reflection and action along with being able to focus on what each of the interns had identified as important in their practice helped to make these novice teachers feel ready for the next step in their teaching careers. Collectively they expressed that participating in coaching cycles helped them to feel more comfortable and confident going into their first year of teaching. Perhaps this was best summed up by Intern 3 who said, "I feel a lot more prepared for next year when I have my own classroom."

Challenges to Implementing Coaching in Preservice Teacher Supervision

While this study provides promise for the role coaching can potentially play in developing high quality clinical experiences, it also illuminated challenges to consider when moving this work forward. All of the interns voiced challenges they experienced related to time, their mentor teachers, and school and university partnerships and structure. The most resounding challenge for interns was the time associated with completing this process. This specific coaching model required significant time meeting to discuss a focus, identifying professional resources, collecting data, and then discussing the data in the coaching conversation. When asked about challenges of this process, Intern 2 stated, "With the coaching cycle, you do have to devote more time to meet with your supervisor, which . . . could be a complication for some teachers or interns with limited time. That can definitely be a challenge." However, while time was a factor, the participants did not consider this time wasteful or unproductive, and interns reported that actually increasing the number of coaching cycles (more than two) would be beneficial for their practice. With the completion of each coaching cycle, interns were more highly motivated to continue reflecting and improving on their practice.

Another challenge recognized by the interns was the role and responsibility of the mentor teacher in coaching. As is generally supported in the literature, the mentors' training and abilities widely varied. Additionally, the role of the mentor teacher in the coaching process differed for each classroom. Interns articulated that the mentor-intern relationship was significant in how involved or supportive the mentor was during the coaching process. While Interns 1 and 2 had collaborative relationships with their mentor teachers, according to Interns 3 and 4, they did not have the same working relationship with their mentors and thus felt there was not as strong a connection of the teaching triad during coaching cycles. These mentor teachers participated at a minimal level, and the interns felt this created a lack of cohesion that impacted the collaborative nature of the process. For example, Intern 4 discussed how this coaching process helped her implement new strategies despite her mentor teacher's lack of involvement:

> I thought it gave me the opportunity to try different things because I think it almost gave me an excuse to say, "Oh, you know I'm doing this coaching cycle

and I need try this out." It gave me an excuse to try new and different things because without the coaching, my mentor wouldn't have tried any of this.

IMPLICATIONS AND CONCLUSION

While this coaching model provided avenues of growth, development, collaboration, and communication for all stakeholders, there are many implications for future programmatic changes and research to continue moving this work forward. When discussing the ETE yearlong internship, it became evident through this research that both the Pathwise observation system and the coaching model provided specific learning at specific times in interns' development. Pathwise observations were praised for providing specific scaffolded learning regarding lesson planning and organization in a broad, non-contextual platform, while coaching provided effective practical learning for lesson implementation in real classrooms with real students. The challenge brought to light by this research is *when* to implement these models and how to *combine* them into a hybrid supervision system to seamlessly provide powerful, practical learning experiences combining theory and practice for interns. More research is needed to determine how and in what capacity these dueling supervision systems can be used to support clinically based teacher education.

Second, as many coaching scholars have stated (Deussen et al., 2007; Killion 2009; Knight, 2007; Kowal & Steiner, 2007), coaching novice teachers requires tremendous trust and rapport in the coaching relationship, as well as scaffolding of learning and strategies due to lack of intern capacity and knowledge of classroom systems. By having university supervisors take on the role of coach while simultaneously having to evaluate interns during their internship year, a paradox of roles for the university supervisor can arise. While other programs (Richardson et al., 2015) have incorporated the mentor teacher as coach, or utilized the university supervisor in different capacities with regard to intern evaluation, this poses a dilemma for the supervisor-intern relationship. Thus, faculty in teacher education programs need to carefully evaluate the roles and responsibilities of university supervisors and their position within the teaching triad, and consider innovative organizational structures of intern evaluation when implementing this non-traditional model of supervision.

An important finding from this research that needs further investigation is the connection of learning between the mentor teacher and intern, and the possibility of this professional development model to provide deep, inquiry-based learning for *all* stakeholders. It is important to note that while mentor teachers were not focal participants in the study, findings discussing the role of mentor teachers were prevalent, and thus need more investigation in further research. As stated earlier, some interns felt that this coaching model had the capability to impact both intern and mentor teacher practice, thus creating a comprehensive model for classroom professional development. With the supervisor as coach, the teaching triad took on new significance and nuances within these relationships. When interns were being coached, sometimes their mentor teachers were indirectly being coached, and conversely, mentor teachers showed the capability to continue the coaching process on a daily basis when the supervisor was not in the classroom. Future implementation of this model must consider and cultivate these classroom relationships, and determine in what capacity mentor teachers, interns, and supervisors can work together to strengthen instructional learning and change.

Finally, and most critical, this research has provided empirical evidence of the importance of the teacher candidate's voice in their own learning and success in teacher preparation. Darling-Hammond's (2014) blanket description of "extended clinical experiences that are carefully chosen to support the ideas presented in simultaneous, closely interwoven coursework" (p. 549) was examined in this study, and the benefits and challenges of this process were illuminated through the voices of the teacher candidates. While this research provides evidence of intern development from using a coaching model, future research must consider and investigate the integration of coursework within this model, and thus it is imperative to listen to teacher candidates and observe their experiences moving forward with this work.

Teacher candidates deserve individualized learning and support that in turn provides them the knowledge and practices to teach diverse learners in their classroom. This study provides evidence of an innovative approach to teacher education which fosters preservice teacher development through coaching. By attempting to provide the connection of high-quality instructive training, multiple opportunities to practice newly learned strategies with real students, and individualized observation and feedback through coaching, this research helped to raise intern voices in advocacy of their own learning and improvement of practice, while simultaneously supporting their learning needs. It is our hope the continued examination of coaching as an essential form of supervision will move teacher education programs in the direction of more adequately developing clinically rich experiences for preservice teachers.

REFERENCES

American Association of Colleges of Teacher Education. (2013). *The changing teacher preparation profession*. A report from American Association of Colleges for Teacher Education's Professional Education Data System. Retrieved from https://secure.aacte.org/apps/rl/res_get.php?fid=145

Basmadjian, K. G. (2011). Learning to balance assistance with assessment: A scholarship of field instruction. *Teacher Educator, 46*(2), 98–125.

Bean, R., Draper, J., Hall, J., Vandermolen, J., & Zigmond, N. (2010). Coaches and coaching in Reading First schools: A reality check. *The Elementary School Journal, 111*(1), 87–114.

Bondy, E., & Ross, D. D. (Eds.). (2012). *Preparing for inclusive teaching: Meeting the challenges of teacher education reform.* Albany: State University of New York Press.

Burns, B., Jacobs, J., & Yendol-Hoppey, D. (2016a). Preservice teacher supervision within field experiences in a decade of reform: A comprehensive meta-analysis of the empirical literature from 2001–2013. *Teacher Education and Practice, 29*(1), 46–75.

Burns, B., Jacobs, J., & Yendol-Hoppey, D. (2016b). The changing nature of the role of the university supervisor and function of preservice teacher supervision in an era of clinically-rich practice. *Action in Teacher Education, 38*(4), 410–425.

Burns, R. W., & Badiali, B. (2015). When supervision is conflated with evaluation: Teacher candidates' perceptions of their novice supervisor. *Action in Teacher Education, 37*(4), 418–437.

Butler, B. M., & Cuenca, A. (2012). Conceptualizing the roles of mentor teachers during student teaching. *Action in Teacher Education, 34*(4), 296–308.

Cornett, J., & Knight, J. (2009). Research on coaching. In J. Knight (Ed.), *Coaching: Approaches and perspectives* (pp. 192–216). Thousand Oaks, CA: Corwin Press.

Crotty, M. (1998). *The foundations of social research.* Thousand Oaks, CA: SAGE.

Danielson, C. (Ed.). (2009). *Talk about teaching: Leading professional conversations.* Thousand Oaks, CA: SAGE.

Darling-Hammond, L. (2008). Knowledge for teaching: What do we know? In M. Cochran-Smith, S. Feiman-Nemser, D. J. McIntyre, & K. E. Demers (Eds.), *Handbook of research on teacher education: Enduring questions in changing contexts* (3rd ed., pp. 1316–1322). New York, NY: Routledge

Darling-Hammond, L. (2014). Strengthening clinical preparation: The holy grail of teacher education. *Peabody Journal of Education, 89*(4), 547–561.

Darling-Hammond, L., & McLaughlin, M. (1995). Policies that support professional development in an era of reform. *Phi Delta Kappan, 76*(8), 597–604.

Deussen, T., Coskie, T., Robinson, L., & Autio, E. (2007). *"Coach" can mean many things: Five categories of literacy coaches in Reading First* (Issues & Answers Report, REL 2007-No. 005). Washington, DC: U.S. Department of Education. Retrieved from http://ies.ed.gov/ncee/edlabs/regions/northwest/pdf/REL _2007005.pdf

Elmore, R. F. (2006). *School reform from the inside out: Policy, practice, and performance.* Cambridge, MA: Harvard Education Press.

Glanz, J., & Neville, R. F. (1997). *Educational supervision: Perspectives, issues, and controversies.* Norwood, MA: Christopher-Gordon.

Glesne, C. (1999). *Becoming qualitative researchers: An introduction.* (2nd ed.). New York, NY: Longman.

Hatch, A. (2002). *Doing qualitative research in educational settings.* Albany: State University of New York Press.

Joyce, B., & Showers, B. (1996). The evolution of peer coaching. *Educational Leadership, 53*(6), 12–16.

Killion, J. (2009). Coaches' roles, responsibilities, and reach. In Knight, J., (Ed.), *Coaching: Approaches and perspectives* (pp. 7–28). Thousand Oaks, CA: Corwin Press.

Killion, J., & Harrison, C. (2006). *Taking the lead: New roles for teachers and school-based coaches*. Oxford, OH: National Staff Development Council.

Knight, J. (2007). *Instructional coaching: A partnership approach to improving instruction*. Thousand Oaks, CA: Corwin.

Knight, J. (2009). *Coaching: Approaches and perspectives*. Thousand Oaks, CA: Corwin.

Korthagen, F., Loughran, J., & Russell, T. (2006). Developing fundamental principles for teacher education programs and practices. *Teaching and Teacher Education, 22*(8), 1020–1041.

Kowal, J., & Steiner, L. (2007). *Instructional coaching*. Retrieved August 23, 2013 from https://files.eric.ed.gov/fulltext/ED499253.pdf

Kretlow, A. G., & Bartholomew, C. (2010). Using coaching to improve the fidelity of evidence-based practices: A review of studies. *Teacher Education and Special Education, 33*(4), 279–299.

Marzano, R. J. (2007). *The art and science of teaching: A comprehensive framework for effective instruction*. Alexandria, VA: Association of Supervision and Curriculum Development.

National Council for Accreditation of Teacher Education. (2010). *Transforming teacher education through clinical practice: A national strategy to prepare effective teachers*. Report of the Blue Ribbon Panel on Clinical Preparation and Partnerships for Improved Student Learning. Retrived from www.highered.nysed.gov/pdf/NCATECR.pdf

Neufeld, B., & Roper, D. (2003). *Coaching: A strategy for developing instructional capacity, promises and practicalities*. Washington, DC: The Aspen Institute. Retrieved from http://www.annenberginstitute.org/publications/coaching-strategy-developing-instructional-capacity

Nolan, J., & Hoover, L. A. (2010). *Teacher supervision and evaluation: Theory into practice*. Hoboken, NJ: Wiley.

Pianta, R. C., La Paro, K., & Hamre, B. K. (2008). *Classroom assessment scoring system (CLASS) manual, pre-K*. Baltimore, MD: Paul H. Brookes.

Plano-Clark, V. L., & Creswell, J. W. (2010). *Understanding research: A consumer's guide*. Boston, MA: Pearson.

Poglinco, S., Bach, A., Hovde, K., Rosenblum, S., Saunders, M., & Supovitz, J. (2003). *The heart of the matter: The coaching model in America's choice schools*. Philadelphia: University of Pennsylvania. Retrieved from http://www.cpre.org/heart-matter-coaching-model-americas-choice-schools

Powell, R., & Rightmyer, E. C. (2011). *Literacy for all students: An instructional framework for closing the gap*. New York, NY: Routledge.

Richardson, G., Pate, C., Yost, D., & Williams, M. (2015, February). *Cooperating teachers as instructional coaches: Building supportive relationships with preservice teachers*. Paper presented at the annual meeting of the Association of Teacher Educators, Phoenix, AZ.

Ross, D. D. (2011). *Lastinger Instructional Coaching Framework*. Gainesville, FL: Lastinger Center for Learning.

Russell, T., McPherson, S., & Martin, A. (2001). Coherence and collaboration in teacher education reform. *Canadian Journal of Education, 26*(1), 37–55.

Scheeler, M. C., Bruno, K., Grubb, E., & Seavey, T. L. (2009). Generalizing teaching techniques from university to K–12 classrooms: Teaching preservice teachers to use what they learn. *Journal of Behavioral Education, 18*(3), 189–210.

Slick, S. (1998). The university supervisor: A disenfranchised outsider. *Teaching and Teacher Education, 14*(8), 821–834.

Tschannen-Moran, B., & Tschannen-Moran, M. (2011). The coach and the evaluator. *Educational leadership, 69*(2), 10–16.

Walpole, M., McKenna, M., Uribe-Zarain, X., & Lamitina, D. (2010). The relationships between coaching and instruction in primary grades: Evidence from high-poverty schools. *The Elementary School Journal, 111*(1), 115–140.

Zeichner, K. (2010). Rethinking the connections between campus courses and field experiences in college and university-based teacher education. *Journal of Teacher Education, 61*(1–2), 89–99.

CHAPTER 5

CREATING SPACES FOR BECOMING

Interrogating the Voices That Arise in Clinical Practice

Sharon B. Hayes
West Virginia University

Johnna Bolyard
West Virginia University

ABSTRACT

This study investigated how the spaces and dialogues integral to clinical practice contributed to how our prospective teachers created narratives of their teaching, recognized the dilemmas of their practice, interrogated/problematized what they experienced and believed, and how they explored multiple possibilities for future action and the teachers they would become. Findings indicate our prospective teachers were beginning to problematize the status quo and to challenge the sacred stories of their classrooms/school, but often struggled to negotiate the tensions among the historical, social, and political discourses in which they practiced. Our contexts and the ways in which

Outcomes of High-Quality Clinical Practice in Teacher Education, pages 85–104
Copyright © 2018 by Information Age Publishing

we, prospective teachers, practicing teachers, and teacher educators alike, are discursively positioned by our colleagues and institutions can provide barriers to the hybrid spaces and border crossings that would enrich clinical practice. Thus, we suggest re-visioning the traditional seminar courses in teacher education programs as professional learning communities in which all stakeholders might engage in questioning *what is* in order to imagine possibilities for *what might be.*

Although this is not a new proposition, the NCATE Blue Ribbon Panel (2010) suggests that teacher education should be turned "upside down," and that the most effective way to accomplish this transformation would be to re-vision/re-design clinical practice. The panel notes that teaching is a "profession of practice" as learning to teach is intricately embedded in the real world; therefore, prospective teachers must have opportunities to learn how their professional knowledge, often gained through university coursework, might inform the ways in which they work with their students to promote the learning of all. Moreover, as Feiman-Nemser (1983) has argued, learning to teach is a lifelong endeavor and one of the responsibilities of teacher education is "preparing people [teachers] to begin a new phase of learning to teach" (p. 157), to learn how to teach from studying teaching... their own teaching, and the teaching of others (Hammerness, Darling-Hammond, & Bransford, 2005; Hawkins, 1973; Hiebert, Morris, Berk, & Jansen, 2007). Thus, our clinical placements and practices can be designed to create spaces in which prospective teachers, mentor teachers, teacher educators, and other stakeholders can problematize "what is" in order to discover what could be.

However, experience alone does not necessarily lead to learning; reflection of various types/at various times is essential for learning from experience (Loughran, 2002). This reflection is not simply a series of steps to be followed; it is a disposition, a habit of mind that is essential for responsible and ethical practice (Bolton, 2010). It is a way of responding to problems so that our teaching and interactions with students are not reactive, a way of being a teacher that embraces three attitudes: open-mindedness (the desire to consider alternative possibilities), responsibility (careful consideration of the personal, academic, social and political consequences of our actions), and wholeheartedness (embracing an attitude that there is always something to learn; Dewey, 1933). Teachers who are developing as reflective practitioners are willing and able to reflect on the origins, purposes, and consequences of their actions, to question their assumptions and beliefs, and to problematize not only their teaching, but also the institutional and cultural contexts in which they teach (Zeichner & Liston, 2013). Such an active exploration of who we are as teachers, as well as what we do in and outside of our classrooms during our clinical practice, embodies *inquiry-as-stance* (Cochran-Smith & Lytle, 2009), a way of being in the world that encourages questioning, deconstruction, reconstruction, and transformation of teachers' practices and identities, and the traditions, sacred stories (see Clandinin & Connelly, 1996), and policies of the educational status quo, a "critical habit of mind that informs professional work in all its aspects" (Cochran-Smith & Lytle, 2009, p. 121).

We know that if prospective teachers are to be well-prepared for the complexity and diversity they will experience in real world schools, it is not enough to simply be placed in a classroom; the nature of the space created by the people who live and work within and outside of that classroom matters. The spaces we create need to provide rich opportunities to question and construct knowledge, to connect theory and practice, and to engage individually and with others in reflection on practice with the intent of creating classrooms in which all children learn and an educational system that is equitable (Darling-Hammond & Baratz-Snowden, 2007). In other words, clinical placements can and should be learning environments for all who enter, PK–12 students, prospective and practicing teachers, teacher educators, and other stakeholders (Zeichner, 2010). As we considered the space(s) we wished to create with our prospective teachers, as they engaged in their full-time internships, we turned to Zeichner's (2010) suggestions for creating hybrid spaces, or third spaces (see Soja, 1996), as well as Bakhtin's (1981) chronotope, life in the public square, which "emphasizes the agency of individuals within the realities of space and time.... [in which] we have the ability to take charge of our living and learning" (Shields, 2007).

Thus, classrooms can become our public squares as we attend to the words, thoughts, and actions of the other individuals who are a part of classroom life. Because the contexts in which we live and learn are social and political, it is important to create spaces—learning communities that welcome our disparate histories and memberships in multiple discursive communities. Such spaces, which encourage heteroglossia and the dissonance created by encounters with alternative, even conflicting, discourses and perspectives, provide opportunities for teachers to negotiate, question, and transform the meanings of their experiences and explore possibilities for their teacher identities and future practice and advocacy (Cochran-Smith & Lytle, 1999; Eaker, DuFour, & DuFour, 2002; Gee, 2005, 2011; Lieberman & Miller, 2008).

These histories that teachers bring with them, include their long *apprenticeships-of-observation* (Lortie, 1975) as students in schools, their experiences as citizens in our culture, and their exposure to the various images/myths associated with teaching/learning (Britzman, 1986), as well as a myriad of ecological interconnections (Bronfenbrenner, 1979). Thus, the interplay between the histories, voices, and the local and global contexts in which our prospective teachers are/were situated, as well as the ways in which they are able to engage in improvisation at the boundaries/interstices of these social/cultural contexts/constructions (Holland, Lachicotte, Skinner, & Cain, 1998) influence the possibilities for disrupting the commonplace, interrogating multiple perspectives, focusing on sociopolitical issues, and taking action to promote social justice (see Lewison, Flint, & Van Sluys, 2002).

Living and working in these spaces brings any number of discourses (see Gee, 2005, 2011) into dialogue, which engages participants in the "performance[s], negotiation[s], and recognition...that goes into creating, sustaining, and transforming them" (Gee, 2011, p. 38). Engaging in dialogue invites us to be intrigued by the perspectives of others and opens up a space for uncertainty, inquiry, and meaning making. Thus,

> Living dialogically means being open to the Other, to difference, and to the possibility of new understandings...when one moves dialogically towards another, different idea, one does not automatically embrace it, but returns to one's own place, inalterably changed. (Shields, 2007, p. 9)

As we engage in these dialogues, we position ourselves and are positioned in particular ways, which we may adopt, alter, or resist (Harré & van Langenhove, 1999). It is important to note that the spaces in which these dialogues occur may influence our decisions to adopt or resist particular positionings, as well as whether or not we give credence to our own voices. Thus, the creation of a hybrid space, in which binaries are rejected and the voices of teachers are heard, would seem essential for developing rich clinical experiences for our prospective teachers.

Our interest in the spaces we might create for our prospective teachers, in which they developed the knowledge, skills, and dispositions they would need to learn to teach over the course of their professional life spans, led us to explore how our prospective teachers created narratives of their teaching and recognized the dilemmas of their practice, interrogated/problematized what they experienced and believed, and how they explored multiple possibilities for future action and the teachers they would become. We also attended to the influence of the tensions among the disparate contexts/ discourses in which education is enacted/discussed.

METHODOLOGY

Because we wished to study the stories our prospective teachers told/documented of their practice, as well as to tell stories of the spaces we constructed to explore and question those stories, we turned to narrative inquiry, which embraces narrative as both the methodology and the phenomena of study (Pinnegar & Daynes, 2007). We wondered: (a) "How does the nature of the context(s) in which prospective teachers are/were situated as they study teaching influence their reflection and discursive practices?"; and (b) "How do the spaces we construct for studying teaching influence the positions/practices/identities the prospective teachers embrace and/or resist in the PLC and other contexts?"

For both prospective and practicing teachers, narrative provides a way of being and becoming a professional (Rex, 2011). Teachers think in terms of stories of their practice and they use these stories to understand and question their lives with students in classrooms in order to make sense of what did take place and to explore the possibilities for what might/should be. These stories can be used to provoke dialogue with listeners who can engage with the storyteller in critical reflection and learning with and from each other as they interpret, deconstruct, and reconstruct lived experiences. Narratives can also do political work (Riessman, 2008) and encourage social action (Atkinson & Delamont, 2006); particular narratives may embolden us to interrogate the status quo and advocate for transformation. Ultimately, narratives "help guide action and are a socioculturally shared resource that gives substance, artfulness, and texture to people's lives. They form the warp and weft of who we are and what we might or might not do" (Sparkes & Smith, 2008, pp. 295–296). Thus, narrative inquiry informed the design our study and our analysis of the oral and video narratives we asked our prospective teachers to create/capture of their practice.

Our participants were seven prospective teachers (elementary education majors with specializations in SPED, 5–9 math, English or social studies), in their fifth year of our 5-year teacher education program. All participants were Caucasian females, were currently enrolled in their internship/full-time teaching semester, and were engaged in designing and conducting a teacher inquiry. These seven prospective teachers met with two teacher educators in bimonthly PLCs. Prior to this semester, each had completed multiple placements, from 2 to 12 hours per week, in various grade levels in the same school at which they completed their student teaching. The two teacher educators (authors of this paper) had taught all or some of the students during some of their required professional education courses.

We met seven times over the course of the semester. At each meeting, two prospective teachers shared videos of their practice and student work samples for reflection and collegial discussion. Although the focus of our discussions was on the practice of the two interns who presented their videos, our intent was for each prospective teacher to connect what was learned from studying teaching and learning in these videos with their own practice and to actually make changes to their subsequent teaching that benefitted their students.

Prior to the PLC meeting, the prospective teachers who were scheduled to share videos of their practice developed an instructional plan including learning goals, a description of the instructional task, and a plan for the assessment. They implemented and video-taped the lesson and collected student work samples. They reviewed their videos before our meeting, making note of instances they wished to discuss with the group. During the PLC meeting, prospective teachers introduced their videos by providing an overview of their lesson goals, the instructional task, and their assessment criteria. They then shared their videos, stopping at their preselected points to discuss questions/issues with the group. Other group members could request that the prospective teacher stop the video at other points of interest. Student work samples were also shared and discussed.

The PLC meetings ended with a whole group debrief related to issues that arose during the video viewing. The week following the PLC meeting, prospective teachers reflected on the PLC discussions and the implications of what was questioned/learned for their future practice. All PLC conversations were recorded and we collected the interns' videos, student work samples, lesson plans, and the reflections they wrote after each PLC meeting.

We focused our analyses on the narratives two of our prospective teachers constructed of their practice and the dialogic interactions that occurred among the PLC participants, borrowing from several analysis methods, including discourse analysis (Fairclough, 2003; Gee, 2001, 2005, 2011; Johnson, 2011) and narrative analysis (Mishler, 1995; Riessman, 2008) in order to understand the layers of meaning embedded in our discursive interactions. Further, we examined the interactions among the spaces/contexts in which our prospective teachers were or had been situated, including our PLC, their university experiences, field placement experiences, and the cultures of their schools.

FINDINGS

In this chapter, we share analysis of selected excerpts of conversations that occurred with Carrie and Sally during our PLC meetings, highlighting prospective teachers' learning and the ways in which our space and dialogue contributed to the learning. We end the chapter with a summary of our findings.

Carrie

In our first meeting, Carrie (a prospective teacher with specializations in mathematics and special education) shared a lesson for students with special needs that examined the use of arrays to represent multiplication. Her narrative demonstrates her efforts to make meaningful use of curricular resources while responding to students' mathematical thinking. She explained that the focus of the lesson was to support students' connections between an equal groups model of multiplication and an array model. In previous lessons, students had worked with an online tool that organized a designated quantity of ladybugs into equal sized groups, placed on leaves. Students could manipulate the number of groups (by adding or removing leaves) and examine the results. The students could then command the tool to arrange the ladybugs into an array. In this lesson, Carrie planned to build on that work by presenting different arrays to the students and asking them to look at the groupings.

Carrie shared she found it interesting that her students, when looking at a 3×4 array, did not describe 3 groups of 4 or even 4 groups of 3. Rather, they talked about 2 groups of 6. She described this as a dilemma because she had not expected this response; rather, she assumed they would look at the rows and/or columns as equal groups because, in her mind, that was a clear connection between equal groups and arrays. She acknowledged that, at the time, she did not encourage or take up her students' responses; instead, she directed the conversation toward viewing the arrangement as 3 groups of 4. However, upon reflection, she noted, "but it's [seeing 2 groups of 6] not wrong, it's definitely not wrong," and reiterated that seeing equal groups was part of the lesson's goal. She asked the PLC for help in interpreting her students' responses; seeking other perspectives that might help her to make sense of her students' thinking and how she might respond in order to support them in constructing the mathematical understandings she intended.

To begin, the group interrogated how the tool represented the two different representations—equal groups and arrays—since Carrie had expected the students' work with the tool to support their connections between these two representations. She explained that the tool might first demonstrate, for example, 12 ladybugs equally grouped on 3 leaves. By pushing an "array" button, the students could watch as the 12 ladybugs moved from the 3 leaves into 3 equal rows. She noted, "I think I was trying to show that the 3 groups could be the 3 rows. Like the 3 leaves going to 3 rows." However, as the prospective teachers discussed and analyzed the features of the tool, the group began to realize there might be some dissonance between the tool's approach and Carrie's instructional goals, possibly weakening the authoritarian voice of the technological tool. As the PLC members continued to probe for details of how the tool worked, Carrie noted that the tool did not emphasize the connection between the equal groups and the organization of the array. She noted, "So it didn't talk about them [rows and columns] as being anything; it just kind of showed it." As the discussion proceeded, the group questioned whether the tool's organization of the equal groupings and subsequent transition to an array was structured in a way that explicitly connected the number of groups in the first representation with the number of rows in the array. The conversation turned to an exploration of the connection between the way the content was presented by the computer tool (as ladybugs on leaves) and the way Carrie asked her students to examine it (as arrays) during her instruction.

The dialogue continued, as the prospective teachers moved beyond examining the curricular materials, as written, to the role of the teacher in making decisions about how to use the curricular materials to support student learning. Initially, the prospective teachers attributed the difficulties students had connecting the equal groups and with the arrays to their learning disabilities; they assumed the concept was too abstract for this particular population. The teacher educators, however, challenged that perspective and drew attention to the features of the computer tool and how it may or may not have supported students to make these connections regardless of their learning disabilities. Author 1, first discussed the difficulty of the language of rows and columns and noted it should not be assumed that any students would make the connections intended simply by looking at the ladybugs move from groups on leaves to an array. Author 2 reiterated this idea, and offered suggestions for how Carrie could help facilitate these connections, emphasizing the teachers' role in facilitating the students' learning through the tool:

> **Author 2:** And I wonder if they would need that explicit, "Okay, so we have 3 groups of the same number of ladybugs in each; 3 equal groups of ladybugs. Let's take the same number of ladybugs and let's arrange them into 3 rows that are equal." I think you have to be explicit in saying, "I am asking you to organize them differently," and use the language of equal rows.

Author 2 also pointed out that the context used in the tool is somewhat contrived. Ladybugs do not generally group themselves on leaves and then line up in rows. Therefore, the students may not be inclined to consider connections between representations in contexts for which the representations are not authentic. Author 2 suggested that contexts in which arrays would make sense or feel more natural may be a better way to encourage students to analyze this multiplicative structure.

Carrie's experience in a real classroom created a context in which she had to negotiate a desire to listen and respond to her students while working toward a learning goal that did not seem to align with that thinking. She initially recognized and was troubled by the fact that she had not responded, even seemed to dismiss, the students' responses, although mathematically correct, because her students did not produce the responses required/expected by the curricular materials. In her post-reflection questions, Carrie noted that there were opportunities for learning that could have been connected to her students' responses but these were not pursued. She wondered, "Was the lesson too teacher led?" This stance is an influence of her mathematics methods courses, which emphasized eliciting and interpreting students' mathematical thinking and using the results to respond to students and to plan instruction. Our PLC provided Carrie with a space in which to revisit her teaching as she watched, discussed, and reflected on her video with members of the PLC. The narrative of her teaching, captured on video, afforded Carrie the opportunity to revisit and interrogate her teaching from other perspectives, to focus on making sense of her students' thinking and recognize that the tool she had used, as written, may not have supported the learning she intended. By bringing this dilemma to her PLC and discussing it with the group, Carrie developed her understanding of how to use curricular materials as a resource, carefully considering how a particular tool might support students' developing ideas about the specific goal of her lesson. The dialogue that ensued challenged the notion that the curricular materials were the instructional authority. Rather, materials should be questioned and analyzed to determine their usefulness for supporting students' progress toward learning goals. Through the PLC discussion, Carrie was able to reaffirm that her students' thinking was not "wrong;" instead, it was not focused on the connections she hoped they would make because they had not had the opportunity to engage with the concepts in a way that focused their attention on those connections.

The dialogue the prospective teachers engaged in provided a space to deconstruct the responsibilities of teachers and the role(s) of materials and resources. Ultimately they realized that while materials and tools may support students in considering mathematical connections and relationships, they cannot make connections for the students. It is how the tools or resources are implemented by the teacher in response to students' thinking that creates opportunities for learning. Carrie realized she was able to and, in fact, needed to use her professional knowledge in order to implement, adapt, and facilitate the use of available resources in ways that responded to her students' current understandings while supporting their developing knowledge.

It is possible that if Carrie had not had the opportunity to engage in dialogue and reflect with her PLC, she might have remained focused on the fact that she dismissed her students' different, but correct, thinking. Perhaps she would have made an effort to refrain from dismissing such responses in the future and, instead, accept all correct answers. This may have addressed some of the discomfort she felt with her lesson, but it would not have supported her students' progress toward her stated learning goals. She might also have decided not to use the tool the next time she taught this lesson. While these may be reasonable responses for a novice, Carrie would have missed the learning opportunities provided by the dialogue among PLC members. Without this space for identifying and interrogating this real world teaching dilemma, Carrie may have continued to react to the felt difficulties of her teaching, rather than to engage in praxis and become a thoughtful, critical consumer of curricular tools and resources. Further, Carrie discovered how her knowledge of professional content and students was important for designing and facilitating meaningful learning experiences for her students, as she became a teacher who would modify mandated tools and curricula to respond to the learning needs of her students.

Carrie's learning opportunities may have been at the forefront of the PLC discussion but we, as teacher educators, also learned from this dialogue. Our analysis revealed that Carrie was able to reflect upon her instruction and recognize areas of her practice she wanted to change, specifically her failure to pursue her students' ideas. However, she did not examine instruction in more depth. We realized that the space provided by the PLC to discuss the lesson with colleagues, who provided different perspectives, encouraged Carrie to reconsider her responsibility in selecting and using curricular resources. However, we also noted that much of the dialogue that took place was teacher-educator directed. We had to scaffold our prospective teachers to problematize their practice beyond what may have been initially evident. We also noted that our contributions, as we attempted to do this, tended to normalize the conversation; Carrie and the other prospective teachers seemed to understand our contributions not as perspectives to consider, open for interrogation and interpretation, but as definitive answers to the problems of practice being explored.

Sally

Sally (a prospective teacher specializing in English) shared a video of her teaching about a month later. Like Carrie, Sally had been influenced by her mathematics methods courses and valued an instructional approach that was driven by and responsive to students' developing mathematical thinking. She wished to engage her students in mathematics discussions to elicit student thinking and develop a community of learners who collaboratively generated understandings of mathematical concepts. However, her mentor teacher required her to use the teacher's manual and accompanying worksheets for each lesson. Sally wondered how she might integrate some methods/strategies she learned about in methods courses to modify the rather prescriptive nature and authoritarian voice of the school's adopted math series. In the lesson Sally shared with our PLC, she decided that instead of "telling" students about the commutative property, she would demonstrate it for them by asking 3 male students and 2 female students to come to the front of the room—boys on one side and girls on the other. She asked students how many boys, how many girls, and how many total children were in the front of the room, then wrote the corresponding equation on the board

(3 + 2 = 5). Next, she asked the 3 boys and 2 girls to switch positions, pointing this move out to the class, in order to demonstrate the commutative property. She again repeated her questions about the number of male, female, and total students and wrote a corresponding equation on the board (2 + 3 = 5). Next she asked the students if the parts changed. The dialogue below is the interaction Sally had with her students:

> **Sally:** Did our parts change?
> **Students:** Yeah!
> **Sally:** They just switched order.... They didn't change, they just switched places, right? We still have two girls. And we still have three boys. How many altogether?

At this point, Author 2 asked Sally to stop the video to discuss the students' response and Sally's reaction to it.

> **Author 2:** When you said, the parts change and they said, yes, what do you think they were thinking?
> **Sally:** Changing order, like, you know, I kind of led them up to that, I should have said, did the number, did the number of girls change, did the number of boys change? So....
> **Author 2:** Or you could have put it back on them and said, what did change?
> **Sally:** Yeah. (softly) What did change?

Author 2 and Sally continued to discuss ways to phrase questions that might elicit students' thinking about what did and did not change in the scenario. Sally noted, "I should of, instead of just telling them, I should have had, seen what they thought about it."

It was evident that this demonstration of the commutative property was led by Sally and did not provide opportunities for students to construct their own understandings, although none of the group members chose to problematize this. Rather, the teacher educator stepped in to ask questions in an attempt to draw Sally's attention to the fact that her approach and questions did not serve to elicit her students' thinking about the concept. While these activities (including the number sentences Sally wrote on the whiteboard) did provide a visual representation of the commutative property, no one questioned the ways in which teacher and students were positioned during this task or what students learned. Although Sally wished to escape the transmission model of teaching, she found it difficult to engage in the alternative ways of teaching she had learned in her mathematics methods course which were more student-led, possibly because she did not experience these models as a K–12 student or see them modeled in her clinical placement. She recognized aspects of her practice that she wished to develop, such as using discussion to elicit students' thinking and support their learning, but had difficulty identifying how she might modify her practice in order to align it with her beliefs about teaching and learning. The teacher educator provided questions Sally might pose in future lessons, which, similar to Carrie's case, served to normalize the conversation, rather than opening it for an exploration of other possibilities. This lack of response on the part of the other prospective teachers may have been further reinforced by the ways in which they positioned themselves and the teacher educators.

Later in the lesson, Sally posted an anchor chart on which she had written some of the language students were encountering in their math problems and the "definitions" associated with that language. She told her students she made the chart to help them learn and remember the "important words." While her video played, Sally said, "When I thought about it, I should have made [the anchor chart] with them, but I figured this would save time. But I should have just gone ahead and made it with them." Sally had learned about the use of anchor charts in her coursework and obviously understood that they are most useful when the students have a voice in constructing them. However, Sally felt constrained by the time limits imposed by her institutional context and had been unable to identify possibilities for working the system and living her beliefs. Author 2 returned to the anchor chart a little later in the conversation and encouraged Sally to problematize the language she used on the chart. Sally shared that she felt if she had made the chart with her students, she could have asked them to recall words they had been taught related to specific operations. She provided the example of the phrase "in all" as an indicator of addition. Author 2, questioned her about this and pointed out that a "key word" approach such as this was not always accurate. She gave the following example:

> **Author 2:** So, I think I heard you say, "in all" means addition? So let me ask you this, what if the problem was . . . I had three pencils. My mom gave me some more. Now I have five pencils in all . . .
> **Sally:** (Long pause) Yeah.

Author 2 then pointed out that a more effective focus would be on examining the action in the problem. She noted that Sally had discussed with students the terms "parts" and "total" as they analyzed the problems and suggested focusing on this aspect as a way to support students in generalizing their understanding of problems that can be modeled with addition or subtraction. By examining what is missing—the part or the total—students can reason about which operation would make the most sense. Sally took up this idea and connected it to work students had been doing on other addition-related tasks: "Yeah, they've been using that part, part whole...And so they see if the...thing says eight is the whole...and they see in that one part is four, they just go one, two, three, four and then fill in five, six, seven, eight."

Author 2 identified an aspect of Sally's practice that needed to be problematized and provided scaffolding during the ensuing dialogue that supported Sally in not only recognizing, but understanding what needed to be changed. In fact, Sally was able to connect other strategies she had taught her students that helped her to make sense of what Author 2 suggested—that the ways in which language is used in mathematics needs to be carefully analyzed. Although Sally positioned Author 2 as the expert, she was not a passive participant during this exchange. She connected what she had been doing with her students (part, part, whole) with what she heard Author 2 say, actively constructing new understandings of what it means to teach mathematics and for her students to do mathematics. It is possible that this space and dialogue provided Sally with an opportunity to understand the language of mathematics in more nuanced and sophisticated ways.

Sally was also learning to question the status quo and work within the system to meet the needs of her students and align at least some of her teaching with her beliefs about "good" teaching. Sally's mentor teacher had made it very clear that while she could engage her students in mathematics discussions, this could only happen two days a week and Sally needed to be sure the students completed all the worksheets required by the mandated curriculum. Author 2 returned to Sally's opening exercise in which she engaged her students in demonstrating the commutative property. Author 2 began a dialogue with Sally that explored possibilities for engaging her students in further discussion to promote deeper understandings of the property under study.

> **Author 2:** Does the series [the math series used by the school] eventually ask questions like, "Why do we get the same sums?"
>
> **Sally:** There's an interactive page for every lesson. She [her mentor teacher] doesn't use that page, but I'll use ideas or the question from that page every time...just personally I always ask them [her students] "why?" And so, I've been doing that. I mean, I don't know if most teachers would...do that. I think they just kind of follow the worksheets.
>
> **Author 1:** So are the interactive pages more aligned with the kinds of things you want to do?
>
> **Sally:** Mm hmm.
>
> **Author 2:** It seems like, asking a questions like that, why is it still five?...there would be something to talk about.
>
> **Sally:** Yeah.

In this exchange, Sally demonstrated she was working to use the required curricular materials in ways that more closely aligned with her teaching identity. She used the resources within the materials that engaged her students in a discussion of their thinking. However, rather than pursuing this line of thought, this conversation was abruptly ended, when several of the prospective teachers shared their ideas for how to teach students to make use of a variety strategies that did not directly connect to exploring the commutative property. This divergence from the topic under consideration had happened numerous times in previous conversations. Although the teacher educators attempted to return to issues that had been raised earlier in the dialogue, our prospective teachers did not necessarily take up the talk and explore their felt difficulties in more depth. They were often able to analyze the immediate effects of their instruction, but were not always cognizant of the complex relationships among their context, pedagogy, content, and students and understanding how those interactions could inform the stories they choose to live in their classrooms, as well as the roles they might choose to play in the broader social, cultural, and political contexts that surround schooling.

Summary of Findings

Our analysis revealed that the space we created for studying teaching (our PLC), provided opportunities for our prospective teachers to negotiate the contexts in which they practiced in order to realize the teacher identities they had begun to develop during our teacher education program, while working within systems that often felt opposed to some aspects of those identities. Specifically, our prospective teachers were developing teacher identities that valued using students' thinking to guide instruction; thus, the instructional philosophies they espoused emphasized eliciting, interpreting, and responding to student thinking to facilitate learning. However, their attempts to enact these approaches in their clinical placements were influenced by their contexts (e.g., use of prescribed curricular materials, sacred stories of their schools, contrasting philosophies of their mentor teachers, constraints of time and the pressure of high stakes testing). Through our PLC conversations, we noticed how our prospective teachers were learning to negotiate the challenges of adhering to and continuing to develop their teaching identities within these contexts. Furthermore, they began to value the intricate relationships between theory and practice, as they learned how to develop their own theories of practice and to problematize and even resist, when necessary, the authoritarian voices of mandated curricular resources, standardized testing, and the sacred stories of their contexts. We, as teacher educators learned as well, developing deeper understandings of what is necessary to effectively support prospective teachers' continued learning from clinically rich experiences.

DISCUSSION

Since teacher education cannot impart a body of knowledge that comprises everything teachers will ever need to know, it must lay a foundation for life-long learning. This study explored how the nature of clinical practice and the spaces created for dialogue and reflection on that practice, which may be in or outside of the classroom walls, might result in teachers who are able to learn to teach from studying their teaching and who develop *inquiry as stance,* which would enable them to interrogate current conditions in order to create alternative possibilities for meeting the needs of their students. Our analysis revealed some of the tensions that exist between and among the spaces in which we practice and engage in reflection, as well as how the expectations of our institutions and the ways in which we are positioned by those institutions and each other impose barriers that must be overcome in order to create the hybrid spaces in which the work of learning to teach and problematizing the sacred stories of traditional schooling might occur.

We believe that professional learning communities can become spaces that encourage reflective action (Dewey, 1933), in which what is learned during clinical practice is considered "in light of the reasons that support it and the further consequences to which it leads" (Zeichner & Liston, 2013, p. 9), enriching the nature of the clinical placement itself. We found that as our prospective teachers became more comfortable in the space created by our PLC, they began to question their interpretations of what students were doing, to entertain alternative approaches to instruction, and to challenge some of the ways in which we do school. However, while our prospective teachers were willing to problematize their teaching and the ways we do school and to identify "answers" for their problems of practice, they were somewhat reticent to engage with each other in collegial conversations that would "provide a forum for reflection and honest feedback, for challenge and disagreement, and for accepting responsibility without assigning blame" (Lieberman & Miller, 2008, p. 18). Questions posed by teacher educators, which were intended to prompt prospective teachers to more closely examine and problematize their practice, did result in a movement from descriptive exchanges to exploration of alternative courses of actions. However, in many cases, if the teacher educator suggested a course of action or alternative interpretation, the prospective teacher positioned the teacher educator as the expert or content coach, who provided "the answer," thereby ending the conversation. In other words, the teacher educator was positioned as the more knowledgeable other, while the prospective teachers positioned themselves as novice teachers and rather passive learners, who accumulated/accepted the authoritative words of the experts. Our prospective teachers resisted our attempts to position them as having agency to identify connections between theory/professional knowledge and the real world and to engage in the construction of new knowledge, as well as the deconstruction/interrogation of what is useful and dangerous in particular practices and ways of seeing the world.

This result has important implications for the identities and practices of teacher educators and the ways in which we work with our prospective teachers to create spaces that enhance their clinical practice. While the expertise and knowledge of teacher educators is essential for supporting prospective teachers as they engage in collegial conversations that deeply analyze the problems of practice, teacher educators must also be mindful of being positioned by the prospective teachers as the only source of knowledge/understanding. We (teacher educators) must become more comfortable with silence and not rush to "save" our prospective teachers as they engage in productive struggles. In this study, our prospective teachers appeared to value the knowledge-for-practice, provided by the teacher educators, over the knowledge they constructed in practice. We want to create spaces in which our prospective teachers view themselves as intellectuals (Giroux, 1998) and are positioned as "knowing subjects" (Freire, 2000), who are always engaged in constructing, deconstructing, and reconstructing knowledge independently and collaboratively. Thus, we, as teacher educators, must emphasize the importance of the many ways in which knowledge is constructed. We must explicitly position ourselves as learners, who, alongside our prospective teachers, are actively interrogating instructional practices and contexts in order to develop new knowledge that is local and global.

Given their many years in American schools, our prospective teachers seem to be influenced by the belief that there is an answer to the problems of teaching: one way for students to demonstrate knowledge, one "best" instructional approach to meet all students' needs, a best model for demonstrating a concept, and/or one task that will be understood by all students. Indeed, our prospective teachers have experienced this culture as K–12 students, and they continue to experience it as prospective teachers working in professional development school settings. In the public school context, prospective teachers are exposed to the struggles and pressures teachers face in this era of accountability. Moreover, institutions of higher education are often more focused on a teacher educator's published research, rather than her commitment to crossing the borders between public schools and the university. In these ways, our institutional contexts (K–12 schools and institutions of higher education) have imposed barriers to creating the hybrid spaces that might contribute to rich clinical practice. The PLC we created with our prospective teachers took place on our own time and without the important contributions of practicing teachers. Therefore, we need to reconsider the structures of public schools and universities that do not provide time for or welcome these spaces, as well as to problematize the ways in which we, teacher educators, practicing and prospective teachers traditionally position each other.

We propose that the seminar courses in which clinical placement hours are typically housed in teacher education programs might be problematized and re-visioned as professional learning communities in which all stakeholders invested in the process of *becoming* teachers, of learning to teach (e.g., prospective teachers, mentor teacher, teacher educators) engage in collegial dialogues that trouble our beliefs, curricula, practices, and traditions in order to create more equitable classrooms and schools. Such hybrid spaces might provide a place for all of us to negotiate and challenge these institutional, cultural, and political tensions, balancing the issues related to accountability with an understanding of how students learn and how we might teach to meet the needs of diverse learners. The problematization of current professional practice and policy that might occur in these transformed seminars could serve to position us as inquirers, knowledge workers, and agents of "educational and social" change (Cochran-Smith & Lytle, 2009).

As we end this chapter, we return to our beginning and the suggestions made by many scholars that

> learning from teaching ought to be regarded as the primary task of teacher education across the professional life span. By 'learning from teaching' we mean that inquiry ought to be regarded as an integral part of the activity of teaching and ... classrooms and schools ought to be treated as research sites. (Cochran-Smith & Lytle, 1993, pp. 63–64)

Ultimately, we are all students of teaching—prospective teachers, practicing teachers, and teacher educators alike—and we must all learn from studying our teaching and uncovering deeper understandings of our own practice(s) and their implications for students and schools. We must become more aware of, and challenge, the taken-for-granted aspects of practice and hidden assumptions that are shaping our practices so that we might work collaboratively and independently to create more equitable classrooms/schools. All of us must become comfortable with making our practices public, with living in the public square. We must make ourselves vulnerable and open our beliefs and identities to questioning and critique. Ultimately, we must become more open-minded, willing to listen to and accept many sources of understanding, in order to understand the ideologies and consequences of our own and others' perspectives. The creation of third spaces, which encourage border crossing between public schools and universities, might provide a place for the critical dialogues that are necessary to interrogate our practices, as well as the educational status quo, so our "learning in and from practice is educative and enduring" (Zeichner, 2010, p. 91) and ensures we are able to work with others to enhance the learning and life chances of all students.

REFERENCES

Atkinson, P., & Delamont, S. (2006). Rescuing narrative from qualitative research. *Narrative Inquiry, 16*(1), 164–172.

Bahktin, M. M. (1981). *The dialogic imagination.* (Caryl Emerson & Michael Holquist, Trans.) (pp. 3–40). Austin: University of Texas Press.

Bolton, G. (2010). *Reflective practice: Writing & professional development* (3rd ed.). Los Angeles, CA: SAGE.

Britzman, D. P. (1986). Cultural myths in the making of a teacher: Biography and social structure in teacher education. *Harvard Educational Review, 65*(4), 442–456.

Bronfenbrenner, U. (1979). *The ecology of human development: Experiments by nature and design.* Cambridge, MA: Harvard University Press.

Clandinin, D. J., & Connelly, M. F. (1996). Teachers' professional knowledge landscapes: Teacher stories, stories of teacher, school stories, stories of school. *Educational Researcher, 25*(3), 24–30.

Cochran-Smith, M., & Lytle, S. L. (1993). *Inside/outside: Teacher research and knowledge.* New York, NY: Teachers College Press.

Cochran-Smith, M., & Lytle, S. L. (1999). Relationships of knowledge and practice: Teacher learning in communities. *Review of Educational Research, 24*(1), 249–305.

Cochran-Smith, M., & Lytle, S. L. (2009). *Inquiry as stance: Practitioner research for the next generation.* New York, NY: Teachers College Press.

Darling-Hammond, L., & Baratz-Snowden, J. (2007). A good teacher in every classroom: Preparing the highly qualified teachers our children deserve. *Phi Delta Kappan, 85*(2), 111–132.

Dewey, J. (1933). *How we think.* Chicago, IL: Henry Regnery.

Eaker, R., DuFour, R., & DuFour, R. (2002). *Getting started: Reculturing schools to become professional learning communities.* Bloomington, IN: Solution Tree.

Fairclough, N. (2003). *Analyzing discourse: Textual analysis for social research.* New York, NY: Routledge.

Feiman-Nemser, S. (1983). Learning to teach. In L. S. Shulman & G. Sykes, (Eds.), *Handbook of teaching and policy* (pp. 150–170). New York, NY: Longman.

Freire, P. (2000). *Pedagogy of the oppressed.* New York, NY: Continuum.

Gee, J. P. (2001). Identity as an analytic lens for research in education. *Review of Research in Education, 25*(1), 99–125.

Gee, J. P. (2005). *An introduction to discourse analysis: Theory and method* (2nd ed.). New York, NY: Routledge.

Gee, J. P. (2011). *An introduction to discourse analysis: Theory and method* (3rd ed.). New York, NY: Routledge.

Giroux, H. (1998). *Teachers as intellectuals: Toward a critical pedagogy of learning.* Westport, CT: Bergin & Garvey.

Hammerness, K., Darling-Hammond, L., & Bransford, J. (2005). How teachers learn and develop. In L. Darling-Hammond & J. Bransford (Eds.), *Preparing teachers for a changing world: What teachers should learn and be able to do* (pp. 358–389). San Francisco, CA: Jossey-Bass.

Harré, R., & van Langenhove, L. (1999). Introducing positioning theory. In R. Harré & L. van Langenhove (Eds.), *Positioning theory* (pp. 14–31). Oxford, England: Blackwell.

Hawkins, D. (1973). What it means to teach. *Teachers College Record, 75*(1), 7–16.

Hiebert, J., Morris, A. K., Berk, D., & Jansen, A. (2007). Preparing teachers to learn from teaching. *Journal of Teacher Education, 58*(1), 47–61.

Holland, D., Lachicotte, W., Skinner, D., & Cain, C. (1998). *Identity and agency in cultural worlds.* Cambridge, MA: Harvard University Press.

Johnson, A. S. (2011). Understanding (moral) viewpoints through layered interpretations of teachers' stories. In L. A. Rex & M. M. Juzwik (Eds.), *Narrative discourse analysis for teacher educators: Managing cultural differences in classrooms* (pp. 55–75). New York, NY: Hampton Press.

Lewison, M., Flint, A. S., & Van Sluys, K. (2002). Taking on critical literacy: The journey of newcomers and novices. *Language Arts, 79*(9), 382–392.

Lieberman, A., & Miller, L., (Eds.). (2008). *Teachers in professional communities: Improving teaching and learning.* New York, NY: Teachers College Press.

Lortie, D. C. (1975). *Schoolteacher: A sociological study.* Chicago, IL: University of Chicago Press.

Loughran, J. J. (2002). Effective reflective practice: In search of meaning in learning about teaching. *Journal of Teacher Education, 53*(1), 33–43.

Mishler, E. G. (1995). Models of narrative analysis: A typology. *Journal of Narrative and Life History, 5*(2), 87–123.

National Council for the Accreditation of Teacher Education. (2010). Transforming teacher education through clinical practice: A national strategy to prepare effective teachers. Retrieved from http://www.highered.nysed.gov/pdf/NCATECR.pdf

Pinnegar, S., & Daynes, J. G. (2007). Locating narrative inquiry historically: Thematics in the turn to narrative. In D. J. Clandinin (Ed.), *Handbook of narrative inquiry: Mapping a methodology* (pp. 3–34). Thousand Oaks, CA: SAGE.

Rex, L. A. (2011). Narrative discourse analysis for teacher educators: Considering participation, difference, and ethics. In L. A. Rex & M. M. Juzwik (Eds.), *Discourse analysis for teacher educators: Managing cultural differences in classrooms* (pp. 1–29). New York, NY: Hampton Press.

Riessman, C. K. (2008). *Narrative methods for the human sciences.* Thousand Oaks, CA: SAGE.

Shields, C. M. (2007). *Bakhtin.* New York, NY: Peter Lang.

Soja, E. W. (1996). *Thirdspace: Journeys to Los Angeles and other real-and-imagined places.* Cambridge, MA: Blackwell.

Sparkes, A. C., & Smith, B. (2008). Narrative constructionist inquiry. In J. A. Holstein & J. F. Gubrium (Eds.), *Handbook of constructionist research* (pp. 295–314). New York, NY: Guilford Press.

Zeichner, K. (2010). Rethinking the connections between campus courses and field experiences in college- and university-based teacher education. *Journal of Teacher Education, 60*(1–2), 89–99.

Zeichner, K. M., & Liston, D. P. (2013). *Reflective teaching: An introduction* (2nd ed.). New York, NY: Routledge.

CHAPTER 6

CURRICULUM-BASED VAM

An Alternative to Traditional VAM in Clinically Rich Teacher Education

Michael P. Brady and Katie M. Miller
Florida Atlantic University

ABSTRACT

Rich teacher preparation is the key to improving teacher candidate performance as well as bridging the research to practice gap in university and school partnerships. However, teacher and teacher preparation accountability models, including the value-added model (VAM) for measuring teacher effectiveness, have unintended consequences that affect the teacher preparation efforts and K–12 students. This chapter describes the current educational evaluation climate, discusses consequences of the VAM effort, and offers solutions by introducing a curriculum-based, action research alternative VAM approach for clinically rich teacher education. Recent studies highlighting the results of one teacher preparation program's (TPP) efforts to incorporate an alternative VAM are discussed, and future directions for research are proposed.

Most professionals involved in the preparation of teacher design programs that highlight the importance of clinical applications. In contrast, many

Outcomes of High-Quality Clinical Practice in Teacher Education, pages 105–126
Copyright © 2018 by Information Age Publishing

critics of public education argue that teacher preparation programs (TPPs) do not provide rich clinical experiences for developing teachers, and as a result teachers enter the profession ill equipped to deliver effective instruction to children (Hess, 2001). As a result, any number of groups and individuals have advocated teacher preparation "reforms" that increase regulation of TPPs, increase scrutiny and oversight of TPPs, and even replace traditional models of teacher preparation with private, vendor-driven models. Attacks on public education that were previously aimed toward teachers have shifted to those who prepare these teachers—including university-based preparation programs.

Couched in language that promotes "accountability" and "educational reform," vast changes in the regulation of public education occur with the political climate changes that accompany each election cycle (Lincove, Osborne, Dillon, & Mills, 2014). In a *Nation at Risk* (1983), critics demanded reforms involving: (a) content and curriculum, (b) expectations for high school graduates, (c) time spent learning, and (d) method used in teaching—all of which targeted improvements in teacher preparation (Jorgensen & Hoffman, 2003). This report was the impetus for a new preoccupation with standardized testing as a way to promote accountability.

Accountability measures incorporating K–12 student standardized assessments were fully implemented in 2001 with the implementation of *No Child Left Behind* (NCLB), the reauthorization of the *Elementary and Secondary Education Act* (ESEA). NCLB firmly established a new era of accountability, and authorized explicit changes to teacher preparation. These changes included providing an explicit link between teacher preparation and K–12 standardized student assessment results.

A decade later, President Obama and his Secretary of Education began to grant NCLB waivers to states as it became clear that neither the national goals for students (performing at 100% proficiency in grade level math and reading) nor teachers (achieving a status of "highly qualified") would be achieved (Goldhaber, 2008). These waivers required states to identify high achieving schools based, in part, on students' standardized test scores; states then would use these scores as part of their teacher and principal evaluation systems (Ayers & Owen, 2012). The use of K–12 student assessment results took on an even greater role with President Obama's *Race to the Top* (RTTT) initiative in which states linked teacher effectiveness to these assessment results. As the stakes for student assessments increased, RTTT defined "highly effective" teachers as those whose students achieved high rates of growth on state assessments. Thus, the era of "value-added" models (VAMs) of student achievement was codified, with major consequences for teachers, districts, and states in terms of funding and evaluation (Lincove et al., 2014), and these consequences continued with the passage and development of regulations for the *Every Student Succeeds Act* in 2015.

As these regulatory changes demonstrate, critics of public education tie their messages and change efforts to political ideologies that often have contradictory prescriptions. Often these critics have little expertise in delivering or reforming public education, but call for accountability measures to control curriculum delivered to children, increase subject matter requirements for future teachers, and regulate credentials of the professionals who prepare these future teachers. The efforts to control public education are linked less to genuine accountability efforts, but reflect a public uncertainty toward educational practice. For example, Bushaw and Lopez (2012) report that recent surveys of Americans' satisfaction with public education call for more and less regulation, more and less local control over school practices, and more and less attention to resources for schools. These contradictory positions reflect Americans' opinions that (a) too much or too little funding targets low achieving students, (b) English language learning students and students with disabilities require too much or receive too little teacher attention, while (c) schools provide too much money for programs for gifted and talented students who receive too few educational opportunities. The result is a public all too willing to accept "reform" efforts untested with actual children and teachers.

An unfortunate irony of this accountability logic is that using statewide standardized assessments as the primary measure of K–12 student learning assumes that a student–teacher relationship can be tracked from year to year, and across a series of teachers and subject areas—and that this dynamic can isolate the effects of each individual teacher. To make sense of this accountability model, it would be necessary to isolate the impact of a single teacher in a group of K–12 students. For example, during a 3-year period when students move from fifth to seventh grade, they are likely to have *at least* three different teachers. Each teacher would have contributed differently to the K–12 students' learning. For schools that use a block schedule or other "shared teacher" arrangement, students could face numerous teachers during that period. In classes with co-teachers, the impact of isolating individual teacher effects is even more complex. And for K–12 students who receive supplemental or pullout instruction (e.g., students with disabilities, English language learners, students who receive remedial instruction) have numerous other educators contribute to their learning (e.g., speech-language pathologists, reading coaches, occupational therapists, ELL language specialists). Finally, consider schools with strong partnerships with TPPs from local colleges and universities. K–12 students in these schools are taught by any number of teacher candidates completing field experiences, practica, or student teaching. The result is that K–12 students are frequently instructed from a pool of a dozen or more teachers, for vastly different lengths of time. Any of these teachers and teacher candidates are likely to make different contributions to student learning in this school. As

TABLE 6.1 Unintended Consequences of High-Stakes Assessment VAM		
Impact on Students	**Impact on Teachers**	**Impact on District and College Partnerships**
Performance on standardized assessments identifies students as ineffective learners in spite of content mastery on authentic curriculum tasks Reduced curriculum and instruction not directly tied to test preparation	Identified as ineffective teachers due to K–12 students' performance on standardized assessments Implications of ineffectiveness on teacher evaluations on salary, future teaching positions, and professional identity	Difficulty recruiting district cooperating teachers to supervise and mentor practicum and student teaching interns Teacher reluctance to invest professionally in activities that do not explicitly involve preparation for assessments

Berliner (2005) and McCaffrey, Sass, Lockwood, and Mihaly (2009) point out, using standardized assessments to isolate the effects of these individual teachers is an absurd exercise, fraught with unmet and unintended consequences. Table 6.1 summarizes several unintended effects of using K–12 students' standardized assessment results as the primary measure of VAM.

VAM AND TEACHER PREPARATION PROGRAMS

As these change efforts are applied to teacher preparation programs (TPPs), the mandates from state departments of education, federal and state legislators, and accreditation agencies have become increasingly prescriptive. Ironically, many of these mandates require that TPPs implement practices that have little grounding in empirical evidence; in some cases, an evidence base is completely absent. For example, with no empirical support that linking teacher evaluations to K–12 student assessments would actually improve K–12 student learning, *NCLB* and *RTTT* mandated that states (and ultimately TPPs) implement teacher evaluation models that make this link. Often criticized as unreliable for children, these assessments are now used as an indicator of school, teacher, and even TPP effectiveness. Because K–12 students were taught in schools, by teachers who, in turn, were graduates from TPPs, these student assessment data become a measure of effectiveness for efforts *four times removed* from their original intent. That is, data with a history of validity and reliability challenges for first-order decision-making (children) are now applied for fourth-order effects, with purposes for which the data were never intended, and with no demonstration as an evidence-based practice. Figure 6.1 presents a schematic of the broadening impact of student assessment data. Although teacher educators have long advocated that TPPs should examine their impact on K–12 student performance (Greenwood & Maheady, 1997; Shores, 1979), the logic of this

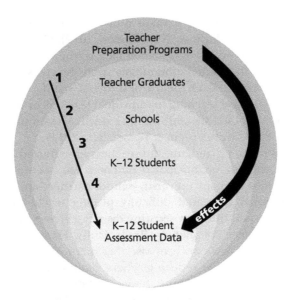

Figure 6.1 First, second, third, and fourth order effects of K–12 student assessment data.

accountability assumes that TPPs are a controlling factor in the day-to-day teaching behavior of teacher graduates.

While teacher educators agree that the whole point of teaching is to promote student learning, numerous educational empirical reports identify many factors influence teachers' performance long after leaving the TPP that prepared them for their initial employment (Amrein-Beardsley, 2008; Berliner, 2005; Cochran-Smith, Piazza, & Power, 2013). To begin with, dozens of school and classroom factors over which teachers have no control contribute to student learning (e.g., class size, school resources, and administrative policies). Even broad state policies affect school district policies which, in turn, affect individual schools, teachers, and children. The administration in each school affects a school's learning climate. School philosophies vary, just as teacher philosophies of education vary. The administrative chain from each individual school, district, and state can vary greatly, creating uneven learning climates—and these schools make teacher-to-teacher comparisons impossible. In the real world, students are taught by multiple teachers, and isolating the impact of a single teacher is nearly impossible on a broad-based standardized measure. Student variables also affect achievement (e.g., student attendance, socioeconomic status, lack of prior knowledge) regardless of classroom or teacher placement.

In addition to school and student variables, the personal lives of teachers (marriage, family, economics, and health issues) obviously affect their instruction on any given day, perhaps more so than the impact of their preparation programs (Berliner, 2014; Floden, 2012). Floden also observed that as teachers respond to labor market factors, they are forced to accept teaching positions that differ substantially from the roles for which their TPPs prepared them. To date, the use of students' standardized assessment data to identify effective teaching in individual teachers or in TPPs has not lived up to even minimal standards as an evidence-based practice (AERA, 2015; Berliner, 2014; Morganstein & Wasserstein, 2014).

Finally, as more K–12 students and teachers are affected by these VAM consequences, another unanticipated outcome has been a deterioration in the effectiveness of many university–school partnerships. For example, TPPs have reported increased difficulty placing teacher candidates in schools, and increased difficulty securing district teachers to mentor teacher candidates and new completers (Brady, Duffy, Hazelkorn, & Bucholz, 2014; Johnson, 2015). As concerns rise that mentoring student teachers or recent completers could reduce teachers' attention to preparing K–12 students for high-stakes assessments, fewer teachers are willing to risk their own evaluations by participating in these activities. These changes in evaluation practices have had a major impact on clinical practice and preparation partnerships.

LINKING INSTRUCTIONAL DELIVERY TO STUDENT LEARNING

Many teacher educators are searching for valid measures that link teachers' instructional delivery to verifiable indicators of K–12 student learning. For teacher preparation programs to promote clinically rich practices *and* rational accountability models, it is necessary to explore measures to evaluate teacher candidates other than K–12 student standardized assessments (AERA, 2015). In their examination of VAMs, Brady, Heiser, McCormick, and Forgan (2016) proposed four minimum standards for VAM assessments. First, the logic behind VAM is to identify the contributions of individual teachers on K–12 student learning. To accomplish this, measures of student learning should be linked to the actual curriculum content provided by the teachers or teacher candidates under review. Student testing results on instruction that was not delivered by the teachers under review do not portray these teachers' instructional effectiveness. Second, K–12 student learning measures should be based on multiple, authentic student work samples. These measures should target K–12 student *task performance* rather than student's ability to perform on standardized assessments. Third, the measures ought to directly reflect the array of curricular content delivered to students, rather than the content areas that make up high-stakes state assessments. Currently, VAM measures are based on K–12 student scores on standardized assessments in reading, language arts, and mathematics. These measures have little relevance for large numbers of students (and their teachers) who are not participating on grade-level curriculum, and who participate in alternative curricula. This includes many students with disabilities, students in vocational and career education classes, and many English language learners. Finally, any use of VAM measures ought to generate useful feedback that would improve instructional programs for K–12 students and their teachers, teacher candidates, and TPPs. If the VAM effort is to become an evidence-based practice, then the effort must generate information that enables professionals to improve practice. A summary of standards and expectations for VAM is found in Table 6.2. If high-stakes standardized test scores are not sensitive enough to show the contributions of individual teachers on K–12 student learning and are not valid and reliable for VAM (AERA, 2015; Brady, Heiser, et al., 2016; Darling-Hammond, 2015), then educators are left with a central question: Are there valid and reliable models that can directly measure the effects of a preservice teacher's instruction on student learning?

A few alternatives do exist. Teacher portfolios incorporating observations and self-reports have attracted the attention of some policy makers (Elliott, Roach, & Kurz, 2014), and portfolios such as edTPA, have been advocated as a possible evaluation system for teacher candidates (Pecheone, Shear, Whittaker, & Darling-Hammond, 2013). Unfortunately, these alternatives are costly, and require resource and time supports. Another alternative to standardized student assessments is the use of classroom observations of a teacher's instructional behavior (Goldring et al., 2015; Jones & Brownell, 2014). However, the results of teacher observations may yield different results based upon the nature of the instrument, focus of the teacher, and background of the observer (Goldring et al., 2015; Swank, Taylor, Brady, & Freiberg, 1989).

TABLE 6.2 Minimum Standards for VAM Measures to Reflect an Evidence-Based Practice
1. K–12 student learning gains should be explicitly linked and limited to the *actual teachers and teacher candidates* who taught them.
2. K–12 student learning gains should be based on measures of student *performance on multiple, authentic work samples* rather than their performance on standardized assessments.
3. VAM measures should be based on K–12 student learning gains on *curriculum content* actually delivered to them by teachers and teacher candidates.
4. VAM measures should inform teachers, teacher candidates, and TPPs of their effectiveness in teaching, and provide feedback that acknowledges or improves future instruction and professional development.

Perhaps the most direct VAM is a curriculum-based measure that incorporates students' progress on their learning objectives as a measure of their learning. Although teachers cannot always control factors that influence a student, they can change their own instructional methods and assessment procedures. A curriculum-based assessment using action research is consistent with clinically based teacher preparation, and most action research models incorporate direct measures of student learning.

A CURRICULUM-BASED ASSESSMENT
USING ACTION RESEARCH

Action research incorporates teacher-directed inquiry into classroom practice, linking improved teaching to student learning (Cochran-Smith & Lytle, 1993). Hensen (1996) described action research as a process which (a) helps teachers develop new knowledge directly related to their classrooms, (b) promotes reflective teaching and thinking, (c) increases knowledge of pedagogy, (d) puts teachers in charge for their teaching, (e) reinforces the link between teacher practice and student performance, (f) increases an openness towards learning and incorporating new strategies, and (g) gives teachers accountability of effective practices. This model of action research helps to bridge the gap between research and practice, a process that is also implicit in establishing a VAM for evaluating teachers and teacher candidates.

Action research in teacher preparation programs typically incorporates an expectation that teacher candidates design a lesson in which they intend to make an impact on student learning. As instructional activities are delivered, student performance data are collected and analyzed, outcomes are communicated, and refinements to the instruction are made (Stringer, 2008). A key component of action research in clinically rich teacher preparation is professional learning tied to an instructional methods course in which teacher candidates are prepared to implement different teaching strategies and methods with their K–12 students. In addition, professional learning via action research can be integrated across courses in a program that embeds effective teaching practices into the pedagogy. This occurs at a critical time for developing teachers as they have an instructional coach (i.e., methods instructor; internship supervisors), providing immediate feedback and analysis for improvement.

Action research expects the teacher candidates to deliver instruction aligned to specific curriculum standards. Candidates task analyze the curriculum content, create a specific learning objective, and then design specific lessons that will help students master the objective. Pre- and post-test data linked to the learning objective are collected. Learning growth is determined by changes in K–12 student performance on pre-to-post learning measures. Slow growth, or no growth, results in candidates making changes to their instruction. Student change that indicates adequate growth or mastery results in candidates making decisions about next steps. In short, candidates do what they are taught to do by the TPPs: They deliver instruction based on student assessment results!

An additional part of a curriculum-based VAM for a TPP is the professional development that accompanies candidates' progression through their programs. In clinically rich programs teacher candidates participate in instructional methods course while they participate in their clinical experiences. TPPs provide coaching from a field supervisor, so that candidates obtain frequent and regular feedback as they learn to teach. This coaching and feedback contributes significantly to their instruction, and to K–12 student performance. A curriculum-based VAM defines a teacher candidate as effective, in part, by the candidate's ability to promote student learning—the very essence of VAM as an accountability model. As important, TPPs make changes to improve individual candidate's performance, as well as entire program changes, based on the impact of their candidates on student learning. That is, a curriculum-based VAM establishes a direct path between candidates and K–12 students.

FLORIDA ATLANTIC UNIVERSITY: A CURRICULUM-BASED MEASURE FOR TEACHER PREPARATION

To respond to the policy directive that TPPs should be able to demonstrate that their teacher candidates make an impact on K–12 student learning, we began a series of three exploratory investigations with our own teacher preparation efforts at Florida Atlantic University (FAU). Two principles drove our explorations. First, we accepted the premise that effective TPPs should be measured, in part, by improvements in their candidates' impact on K–12 student performance (Shores, 1979). Second, we proposed that any link between teacher candidates and K–12 student learning must be an explicit and direct link. That is, teacher candidates' contributions to K–12 student learning should not be implied or inferred from learning measures and activities in which the candidates had no direct role. This means that any link between teacher candidates and K–12 students must include a curriculum link—that assessing candidates' contributions must be based on candidates' instructional efforts. Though this assumption seems fairly logical, it is not part of the assumption of most current VAM efforts, where K–12 student standardized assessment results are linked to candidates who make little or no instructional contributions to the students. As described previously, our initial efforts to explore a rational and usable VAM reflected a curriculum logic rather than a logic based on standardized assessment results. Table 6.3 summarizes the purpose and findings of the FAU exploratory investigations.

TABLE 6.3 Summary of Findings in the FAU VAM Explorations

Study	Participants	Purpose	Findings	Summary of Statistics
First Exploration Study[a]	Undergraduate and Graduate Teacher Candidates (TCs)	Examine the impact of TC delivery of a Learning Sequence (LS) on two learning gain measures in K–12 students across three TC cohorts	K–12 students showed statistically significant pre/post learning gains on the LS delivered by their TC Majority of K–12 students met their learning objectives delivered by their TC	Pre/post differences on LS delivered by their TC (56% increase; $p < 0.001$; ES = 2.22) 83% of K–12 students met their learning objectives
Second Exploration Study[b]	Undergraduate TCs	Identify variables that might predict the relationship between TC instruction and K–12 student learning gains (part time practicum vs. full time student teaching placements; academic vs. functional lessons; TC GPAs)	K–12 students of TCs in part-time and full-time placements met their learning objectives There was no significant *difference* in K–12 student learning gains when comparing TCs in part-time vs. full-time placements There was no significant difference in K–12 student learning gains for academic vs. functional lessons When TC GPAs were ranked from high to low, K–12 students of TCs in the top 1/3 showed largest learning gains	Statistically significant number of students met learning objectives in part-time placements (58.7%; $p < 0.001$; ES = 1.10) and full-time placements (68.9%; $p < 0.001$; ES = 1.80) There was an increase in students meeting objectives as TCs moved from part-time to full-time placements but increases were not statistically significant ($p > 0.214$; ES = 0.358) No statistically significant differences for K–12 students in academic vs. functional lessons on pre/post differences ($p = 0.267$; ES = 0.525) or on meeting their objectives ($p = 0.386$; ES = 0.43) K–12 students from TCs in top 1/3 group showed statistically significant greater differences on meeting the learning objectives ($t = 3.9$; $p < 0.01$) and for pre/post differences on the LS ($t = 2.42$; $p < 0.05$)

(continued)

TABLE 6.3 Summary of Findings in the FAU VAM Explorations (continued)

Study	Participants	Purpose	Findings	Summary of Statistics
Third Exploration Study[c]	University Supervisors; Undergraduate TCs	Examine whether a select set of TC teaching indicators on the observation instrument (NOS) predicted K–12 learning gains	Selected indicators on observation instrument did not predict K–12 learning gains	No significant predictive value for pre/post differences or meeting learning objectives ($p > 0.05$) for selected observation indicators
		Determine whether any specific TC behaviors predict K–12 learning gains	The cluster of observation indicators representing classroom management predicted whether K–12 students met their specific learning objectives	Cluster of all classroom management indicators (combined) did not predict pre/post changes on the LS ($p > 0.05$), but was a significant predictor for K–12 students meeting their learning objectives ($p < 0.01$; ES = 0.479)

[a] Brady, Heiser et al., 2016
[b] Brady, Miller et al., 2016
[c] McCormick et al., 2017

First Exploratory Study

In our first exploratory study (Brady, Heiser, et al., 2016), we examined teacher candidates who were enrolled in both undergraduate and graduate special education teacher preparation programs. Across three cohorts, consisting of 37 candidates, we examined K–12 students' learning by measuring their gain scores, reported as percentages or rates of change in student learning. We identified two measures of student learning:

- pre/post changes in K–12 student learning on lessons taught by our teacher candidates, and
- the percentage of K–12 students who met their learning objectives on lessons delivered by the teacher candidates.

In this first exploration, the first student teacher cohort had a substantial impact on K–12 students, with more than 91% of their K–12 students meeting the designated objective of the lessons delivered by these student teachers. Further, the students increased their pre-to-post learning gains by an average of more than 35 percentage points. In a second cohort of undergraduate candidates in a preparatory practicum (pre-student teaching) experience, the average pre-to-post gain scores increased by more than 39 percentage points. In a third cohort with graduate interns, candidates showed similar results: Nearly 96% of the candidates' K–12 students met the learning objectives of the curriculum targeted for instruction, with a mean gain of nearly 40 percentage points in students' scores. All measures of K–12 student learning showed statistically significant increases, with strong effect sizes, in spite of the small sample sizes.

This first exploration of a curriculum-based VAM was telling, if not surprising. When assessing whether our teacher candidates promoted learning gains in the K–12 students whom they taught, we found that these teacher candidates demonstrated substantial learning in students they were learning to teach. As important, candidates were effective regardless of whether they were enrolled in undergraduate or graduate teacher preparation programs, and whether they were in their initial practicum experiences or in their full-time student teaching experiences.

Second Exploratory Study

Following our initial investigation, we explored further this curriculum-based VAM with another cycle of teacher candidates—this time limited to undergraduate students during their practicum and student teaching experiences. In our second study (Brady, Miller, McCormick, & Heiser, 2016), we sought to replicate our first VAM findings, and extend those results by exploring variables that we previously did not consider. Specifically, we investigated a number of variables that might *predict* whether teacher candidates' instruction might be related to student learning gains. In one analysis, we investigated whether certain types of lessons delivered by the candidates (i.e., academic vs functional daily living skills) might predict whether K–12 students would show learning gains. We also investigated whether teacher candidates might improve their effectiveness with K–12 students as the candidates progressed from their part-time practicum to full-time student teaching. Finally, we investigated whether there might be any differences in K–12 students' learning gains based on teacher candidates' GPAs during their teacher preparation coursework.

In this second exploration, 30 undergraduate teacher candidates produced statistically significant ($p < 0.001$) pre- to post-test changes in their K–12 students' learning during their part-time Fall practicum ($M = 36.94$, 95% confidence interval [CI] = [26.89, 46.99], $SD = 23.79$). These learning gains showed a strong effect size ($d = 1.10$). During the teacher candidates' Spring full-time student teaching, the K–12 students also showed statistically significant ($p < .001$) pre- to post-test changes ($M = 45.76$, 95% CI [34.99, 56.54], $SD = 25.50$), with an effect size of $d = 1.80$. A statistically significant ($p < .001$) number of these K–12 students met their learning objectives ($M = 3.23$, 95% CI [2.59, 3.87], $SD = 1.58$). The effect size during practicum ($d = 0.814$), and the effect size during student teaching ($d = 0.716$) indicate that the number of K–12 students meeting the learning objectives can be attributed to their participation in the teacher candidates' learning sequences. When the candidates progressed *from* practicum *to* student teaching, there was an increase in K–12 student learning gains ($M = 8.83$, 95% CI [5.45, 23.12], $SD = 33.83$), although these gains were not statistically significant ($p > 0.214$; $d = 0.358$) with a minimal effect size. The analysis also showed that K–12 students who participated in lessons of an academic nature showed more improvement than those who participated in functional lessons, although these differences were not statistically significant.

In the final analysis of this second exploration, we investigated K–12 student learning gains of teacher candidates who were grouped by their GPAs. For candidates in the Top GPA group, over 76% ($SD = 30.57$) of their K–12 students met their learning objectives. For candidates in the Middle and Bottom GPA groups, nearly 59% ($SD = 25.93$) and 69% ($SD = 41.19$) of their K–12 students met their learning objectives. This resulted in a statistically significant difference between the Top and Middle GPA groups ($t = 3.9$, $df = 14$, $p < .01$). Results *did not* reveal statistically significant differences between the Top and Bottom GPA groups ($t = 1.25$, $df = 14$, $p > .05$), or the Middle and Bottom groups ($t = -1.93$, $df = 14$, $p > .05$).

Thus, the results of our second exploration of a curriculum-based VAM reinforced our belief that a different type of VAM was not only possible, but that certain teacher and other contextual variables might be helpful in predicting VAM outcomes in K–12 students. Because teacher candidates differed substantially in the hours and intensity of their teaching during practicum and student teaching, and that candidates in both experiences were able to help K–12 students make learning gains, we gained additional confidence that a curriculum-based VAM was indeed an effective metric for assessing the value-added logic. Also important in a VAM that relies on candidates actual instructional delivery, our candidates appeared equally effective whether they delivered instruction to students that was limited to pure academics (e.g., narrative writing or solving math word problems), or when delivering lessons that were more practical or functional in nature (e.g., community living or social interaction skills).

Third Exploratory Study

Having established the viability of a rational, curriculum-based VAM in two studies that explicitly linked K–12 student learning to the lessons taught by teacher candidates from a TPP, we next sought to explore specific teacher candidate behaviors that might allow us to *predict* K–12 student learning gains (McCormick, Brady, Morris, Heiser, & Miller, 2017). To accomplish this, we assembled a team of six faculty and university supervisors who had experience supervising teacher candidates during their preservice clinical experiences. First, we asked this team to identify observation indicators from the observation instrument used by the TPP that they believed would be most likely to predict candidates' teaching effectiveness. These indicators reflect teaching behaviors that have long been identified as effective in increasing student engagement and learning, and have withstood the test of time (Brophy & Good, 1986; Creemers & Reezigt, 1996; Grossman & McDonald, 2008). From the 75 observation indicators representing eight teaching domains on this instrument, the clinical supervision team identified 36 individual items that they believed would best predict candidates' clinical effectiveness in practicum and student teaching. From this list, the number of observation indicators was narrowed by selecting items nominated by at least four members (a majority) of the clinical supervision team. This process resulted in 6 observable candidate behaviors that were selected for the first round of data analysis (see Table 6.4).

In the first round of data analysis, we investigated whether teacher candidates with the highest ratings on the selected observation indicators (i.e., the independent variable) would predict the K–12 student learning gains (i.e., the dependent variable). To our surprise, none of the observation

TABLE 6.4   Observation Instrument Indicators Nominated By Faculty and Supervisors

Domain	Observation Item
General Teaching Skills	Uses model-lead-test procedure as appropriate
Activities Prior to Instruction	Lesson plans are effective for planning instruction
Questioning & Feedback	Provides appropriate feedback to student response
Guided Practice	Gives students clear instructions
Evaluation of Student Progress	Sets criteria, collects data, and monitors progress toward mastery of individual student objectives
Management of Student Behavior	Utilizes behavior management systems effectively and consistently

indicators nominated as the best indicators of teaching effectiveness by the clinical supervision team were related to the K–12 student learning gains. A regression model predicting pre-post change from the 6 individual NOS items indicated the changes were not significant [$F(6,16) = 2.092$, $p > .05$ where R^2 was .431, and the adjusted R^2 was .230]. For the percentage of K–12 students meeting learning objectives, results were also nonsignificant [$F(6,16) = 1.337$, $p > .05$, where R^2 was .333 and the adjusted R^2 was .081]. That is, none of the six selected observation indicators significantly improved our ability to predict K–12 students' learning gains. Reflecting on this we asked, "Are all of our observation indicators equally effective (or ineffective) in predicting student learning gains?"

Given these findings, a second round of data analysis was conducted. In this analysis, we used the complete observation instrument to investigate teacher candidates' impact on K–12 student learning gains. This analysis revealed that candidates' ratings within Domain 8 (*Management of Student Behavior*) significantly predicted whether K–12 students met their specific learning objectives on lessons delivered by the teacher candidates [$F(8,14) = 3.645$, $p = 0.017$, $R^2 = .676$]. Specifically, candidates' ratings in the Management of Student Behavior domain made a significant contribution only when all eight items were observed together, and these results yielded a large effect size [overall fit of $r = .822$, f^2 ($R^2/(1 - R^2)$) resulting in an effect size of 2.086]. Deletion of any items decreased ability to predict K–12 student learning.

To some extent, the results of this third VAM investigation were surprising. The observation indicators that we initially predicted would have a positive impact on K–12 student learning did not predict learning gains any better than any other observable teaching behavior on the instrument. On the other hand, the cluster of classroom management behaviors on the instrument did predict K–12 learning gains; specifically candidates' ratings on this domain predicted whether K–12 students met their learning objectives on lessons delivered by these candidates. However, these results should not be too surprising as the link between effective classroom management and organization skills and K–12 student learning has long been identified as a hallmark of successful teaching (Colvin & Sugai, 1988; Madsen, Becker, & Thomas, 1968; Rosenberg & Jackman, 2003). Interestingly, these results have not been integrated into any of the other VAMs to date. Results of this third exploration for a rational VAM reinforces a truism often neglected in current VAM discussions: Teacher candidates' classroom management effectiveness predicts K–12 student learning.

FUTURE DIRECTION FOR RESEARCH AND PRACTICE

During the first three investigations, the FAU research team established the viability of a curriculum-based VAM as a metric sensitive enough to isolate the impact of individual teacher candidates, regardless of the students and content they taught. In addition, the team identified an initial set of variables that predict candidates' effectiveness in promoting student learning. Yet, these findings are based on program evaluation efforts and must be considered exploratory. Future studies are needed to identify other variables that predict K–12 student learning.

Our initial explorations of *K–12 student characteristics* only scratched the surface of predictors of student learning, but several student characteristics are obvious targets for research. Variables such as students' ages could have a major impact on learning given issues involving readiness to learn and other developmental factors. Along with age, the grade levels of students are logical areas for study. Student characteristics such as language proficiency and, in particular, reading levels could become robust predictors of student learning. Other student characteristics including presence or absence of a disability, and the nature of the disability, are logical topics for investigation. Family background has long been identified as a mediator of learning, as have students' attendance rates and delinquency rates.

In our research, we did explore certain *teacher variables.* However, our investigations of teacher variables were limited to candidates' GPAs and a single observation instrument to identify particular teacher behaviors that we speculated might be indicators of effectiveness (McCormick et al., 2017). We did not explore whether candidates' ratings from their university supervisors and cooperating classroom teachers were predictive of their impact on student learning. We also did not investigate whether grades in individual classes (e.g., an instructional methods or assessment class) might influence their VAM ratings.

Several other teacher variables have been suggested as indicators of effectiveness that could be helpful in predicting specific VAM relations. For example, lessons learned by teachers during their first years of teaching could provide valuable information to TPPs and school administrators that, in turn, could affect lessons delivered to K–12 students. Also, teacher perceptions and expectations for students have long been correlated with student achievement, although no direct VAM link has yet been made. Also, teacher involvement in curriculum development, and instruction in metacognitive strategies has been established as indicators of effective instruction, although neither have been directly linked to student growth as a VAM predictor. Teachers' implementation of frequent evaluations of their students' learning is known to promote student engagement, but like the other teacher variables, evaluation frequency has not been established as a VAM predictor. Finally, professional attributes such as judgment, tact, reliability, dependability, collegiality, and ethical behavior are seldom included in most classroom observation assessments, yet have the potential to predict teacher effectiveness in a VAM context. Professional attributes directly affect a teacher's ability to work across school environments. The ability to capture and measure professional attributes remains a challenge although these attributes often have an impact on student learning. For example, if a teacher does not collaborate with other professionals in the school, this absence of collaboration could hinder student success if valuable information is not shared. These and other teacher candidate variables should be studied to establish whether they might be useful as predictors of student learning.

At least three *curriculum variables* could have predictive value in future VAM studies. First, the pace of a teacher's lesson has often been cited as a correlate of effective teaching. Second, the nature of the instructional delivery system (such as whether the format involves whole class vs small group instruction) has also been a frequent target of research. Third, a great deal of information is available about teacher questioning; while some research has suggested that certain types of questions (higher vs lower order) are more likely to correlate with improved student outcomes, the most reliable finding has been that simply posing *more* questions to students is the best predictor of engagement and learning (Hamilton & Brady, 1991). It is highly likely that other curriculum variables have similar predictive capacity for a VAM context.

Finally, a host of school and contextual variables have been correlated to school and teaching effectiveness, but whether these variables rise to the level as VAM predictors is unknown. For example, school size, class size, school culture, and student/teacher ratios have drawn the attention of many school effectiveness researchers. Other researchers have shown links between how instruction is organized by teachers and whether students make instructional gains. The use of homework, a relatively narrow focus, contrasts with an amorphous contextual variable such as the leadership style of principals and other school leaders. Both have been identified as effectiveness indicators, although neither have been studied as VAM predictors. Finally school safety is frequently linked to student learning. School safety correlates at a micro level (e.g., specific classroom management strategies), as well as at a macro level (e.g., perceptions of the safety and orderliness of the school climate). To understand VAM better, these and other research and practice explorations are needed to discover variables that are most likely to predict K–12 student learning.

CONCLUSION

In an age of educational reform, teacher accountability, and high-stakes testing, TPPs need to demonstrate that their candidates are effective with all learners in our diverse classrooms. Rich teacher preparation in which university research and evaluation is connected to classroom practice is essential. State and federal legislators have mandated VAM as a way to measure the impact of TPPs on K–12 students. The reaction of teacher educators to the VAM mandate has ranged from critical to skeptical, with a hint of cautious willingness to explore possible, rational opportunities. At best, teacher educators have complied with state agency and accreditation agency mandates, unwilling to risk the reputations of their college and university programs to the punitive consequences of not putting their programs under the VAM microscope (Darling-Hammond, 2015; Floden, 2012; Lincove et al., 2014). At worst, some professionals have traded their skepticism for cynicism, reflective of educators who have endured a long line of mandates from critics do not believe that public resources are well spent on university-based teacher preparation (AERA, 2015; Berliner 2005, 2013; Cochran-Smith et al., 2013).

The curriculum-based action research model summarized in this chapter represents a nuanced reaction to the VAM phenomenon. We believe that it is not unreasonable to expect TPPs to demonstrate that as candidates progress through their preparation programs, they should indeed be able to show that their efforts have a positive impact on student learning. This position is not an effort to curry favor with accreditation reviewers. Rather, the proposition that TPPs should expect their candidates to produce learning gains reflects beliefs of teacher educators for over 35 years who embraced the logic and found empirically demonstrated methods of doing so (Shores, 1979).

Many teacher educators have spent the last two decades committed to the idea that public education should be based on practices that have a solid evidence base. There should be no surprise that VAMs that are *not* rooted in evidence-based practice have generated serious controversy. Relying on high-stakes student assessments as the metric for determining learning gains is not an evidence-based practice. Given the numerous validity and reliability challenges (AERA, 2015; Amrein-Beardsley, 2008; Ballou & Springer, 2015; Buzick & Laitusis, 2010; Hill, Kapitula, & Umland, 2011; Holdheide, Goe, Croft, & Reschly, 2010; Jones, Buzick, & Turkan 2013; McCaffrey et al., 2009; Morganstein & Wasserstein, 2014; Papay, 2011; Steinbrecher, Selig, Cosbey, & Thorstensen, 2014), this metric does not rise to even an "acceptable practice" for establishing a VAM metric.

If teacher educators are to take seriously the logic of VAM as relevant to preparing teacher candidates and as a measure of program effectiveness, what metric does make sense for this purpose? As presented in this chapter, we believe a curriculum-based VAM based on action research principles is an obvious metric for evaluating the impact of teacher candidates on K–12 student learning. A VAM metric based on teacher candidates' actual instruction is both intuitively and empirically sound, and meets the minimum standards proposed by Brady, Heiser, et al. (2016) as an evidence-based metric for VAM. A curriculum-based VAM links K–12 student learning gains to the teachers and teacher candidates who actually taught the students. Second, student learning gains are based on measures of student performance on subject area content that was actually taught, with actual work samples representing that content. We believe the VAM demonstrations in the FAU explorations summarized in this chapter establishes an evidence base for a curriculum-based VAM.

REFERENCES

American Educational Research Association. (2015). AERA statement on use of value-added models (VAM) for the evaluation of educators and educator preparation programs. *Educational Researcher, 44*(8), 448–452.

Amrein-Beardsley, A. (2008). Methodological concerns about the education value-added assessment system. *Educational Researcher, 37*(2), 65–75. doi:10.3102/0013189X08316420

Ayers, J., & Owen, A. (2012). No Child Left Behind waivers: Promising ideas from second round applications. *Center for American Progress.* Retrieved from https://www.americanprogress.org/wp-content/uploads/issues/2012/07/pdf/nochildwaivers.pdf

Ballou, D., & Springer, M. G. (2015). Using student test scores to measure teacher performance: Some problems in the design and implementation of evaluation systems. *Educational Researcher, 44*(2), 77–86.

Berliner, D. C. (2005). The near impossibility of testing for teacher quality. *Journal of Teacher Education, 56*(3), 205–213. doi:10.1177/0022487105275904

Berliner, D. C. (2013). Problems with value-added evaluations of teachers? Let me count the ways! *The Teacher Educator, 48*(4), 235–243. doi:10.1080/08878730.2013.827496

Berliner, D. C. (2014). Exogenous variables and value-added assessments: A fatal flaw. *Teachers College Record, 116*(1), 1–31.

Brady, M. P., Duffy, M. L., Hazelkorn, M., & Bucholz, J. (2014). Policy and systems change: Planning for unintended consequences. *The Clearing House: A Journal of Educational Strategies, Issues, and Ideas, 87*(3), 102–109.

Brady, M. P., Heiser, L. A., McCormick, J. K., & Forgan, J. (2016). Value-added models for teacher preparation programs: Validity and reliability threats, and a manageable alternative. *Educational Forum, 80*(3), 339–352. doi:10.1080/001 31725.2016.1173150

Brady, M. P., Miller, K., McCormick, J., & Heiser, L. A. (2016). A rational and manageable value added model for teacher preparation programs. *Educational Policy.* https://doi.org/10.1177/0895904816673741

Brophy, J., & Good, T. L. (1986). Teacher behavior and student achievement. In M. C. Wittrock (Ed.), *Handbook of research on teaching* (3rd ed., pp. 328–375). New York, NY: Macmillan.

Bushaw, W. J., & Lopez, S. J. (2012). Public education in the United States: A nation divided. The 44th annual Phi Delta Kappa/Gallup Poll of the public's attitudes toward the public schools. *Phi Delta Kappan, 94*(1), 9–25.

Buzick, H. M., & Laitusis, C. C. (2010). Using growth for accountability: Measurement challenges for students with disabilities and recommendations for research. *Educational Researcher, 39*(7), 537–544.

Cochran-Smith, M., & Lytle, S. L. (1993). *Inside/outside: Teacher research and knowledge.* New York, NY: Teachers College Press.

Cochran-Smith, M., Piazza, P., & Power, C. (2013). The politics of accountability: Assessing teacher education in the United States. *Educational Forum, 77*(1), 6–27. doi:10.1080 /00131725.2013.739015

Colvin, G. T., & Sugai, G. M. (1988). Proactive strategies for managing social behavior problems: An instructional approach. *Education and Treatment of Children, 11,* 341–348.

Creemers, B. P. M., & Reezigt, G. J. (1996). School-level conditions affecting the effectiveness of instruction. *School Effectiveness and School Improvement, 7*(3), 197–228.

Darling-Hammond, L. (2015). Can value added add value to teacher evaluation? *Educational Researcher, 44*(2), 132–137.

Elliott, S. N., Roach, A. T., & Kurz, A. (2014). Evaluating and advancing the effective teaching of special educators with a dynamic instructional practices portfolio. *Assessment for Effective Intervention, 39*(2), 83–98.

Floden, R. (2012). Teacher value added as a measure of program quality: Interpret with caution. *Journal of Teacher Education, 63*(5), 356–360. doi:10.1177/0022487112454175

Goldhaber, D. (2008). Teachers matter, but effective teacher policies are elusive. In H. Ladd & E. B. Fiske (Eds.), *Handbook of research in education finance and policy* (pp. 146–165). New York, NY: Routledge.

Goldring, E., Grissom, J. A., Rubin, M., Neumerski, C. M., Cannata, M., Drake, T., & Schuermann, P. (2015). Make room value added: Principals' human capital decisions and the emergence of teacher observation data. *Educational Researcher, 44*(2), 96–104.

Greenwood, C. R., & Maheady, L. (1997). Measurable change in student performance: Forgotten standard in teacher preparation? *Teacher Education and Special Education, 20,* 265–275.

Grossman, P., & McDonald, M. (2008). Back to the future: Directions for research in teaching and teacher education. *American Educational Research Journal, 45*(1), 184–205.

Hamilton, R., & Brady, M. P. (1991). Individual and classwide patterns of teachers' questioning in mainstreamed social studies and science classes. *Teaching and Teacher Education, 7*(3), 253–262.

Hensen, K. T. (1996). Teachers as researchers. In J. Sikula (Ed.), *Handbook of research on teacher education* (4th ed., pp. 53–66). New York, NY: Macmillan.

Hess, F. M. (2001). *Tear down this wall: The case for a radical overhaul of teacher certification.* Washington, DC: Progressive Policy Institute.

Hill, H. C., Kapitula, L., & Umland, K. A. (2011). Validity argument approach to evaluating teacher value-added scores. *American Educational Research Journal, 48*(3), 794–831.

Holdheide, L., Goe, L., Croft, A., & Reschly, D. (2010). *Challenges in evaluating special education teachers and English language learner specialists.* Washington, DC: National Comprehensive Center for Teacher Quality. Retrieved from http://www.gtlcenter.org/sites/default/files/docs/July2010Brief.pdf

Johnson, S. M. (2015). Will VAMs reinforce the walls of the egg-crate school? *Educational Researcher, 44*(2), 117–126.

Jones, N. D., & Brownell, M. T. (2014). Examining the use of classroom observations in the evaluation of special education teachers. *Assessment for Effective Intervention, 39*(2), 112–124.

Jones, N. D., Buzick, H. M., & Turkan, S. (2013). Including students with disabilities and English learners in measures of educator effectiveness. *Educational Researcher, 42*(4), 234–241.

Jorgensen, M. A., & Hoffmann, J. (2003). *History of the No Child Left Behind Act.* Upper Saddle River, NJ: Pearson Education.

Lincove, J. A., Osborne, C., Dillon, A., & Mills, N. (2014). The politics and statistics of value-added modeling for accountability of teacher preparation programs. *Journal of Teacher Education, 65*(1), 24–38.

Madsen, C. H., Becker, W. C., & Thomas, D. R. (1968). Rules, praise, and ignoring: Elements of elementary classroom control. *Journal of Applied Behavior Analysis, 1,* 139–150.

McCaffrey, D. F., Sass, T. R., Lockwood, J. R., & Mihaly, K. (2009). The intertemporal variability of teacher effect estimates. *Education Finance and Policy, 4*(4), 572–606.

McCormick, J., Brady, M. B., Morris, J. D., Heiser, L. A., & Miller, K. M. (2017). *Further examination of a rational Value-Added Model for teacher preparation programs: Do classrooms predict K–12 student learning?* Manuscript submitted for publication.

Morganstein, D., & Wasserstein, R. (2014). ASA statement on value-added models. *Statistics and Public Policy, 1*(1), 108–110. doi:10.1080/2330443X.2014.956906

Papay, J. P. (2011). Different tests, different answers: The stability of teacher value-added estimates across outcome measures. *American Education Research Journal, 48*(1), 163–193.

Pecheone, R. L., Shear, B., Whittaker, A., Darling-Hammond, L. (2013). *2013 edTPA Field Test: Summary Report.* Stanford, CA: Stanford Center for Assessment, Learning and Equity.

Rosenberg, M. S., & Jackman, L. A. (2003). Development, implementation, and sustainability of comprehensive school-wide behavior management systems. *Intervention in School and Clinic, 39*(1), 10–21.

Shores, R. E. (1979). Evaluation and research. *Teacher Education and Special Education, 2*(3), 68–71. doi:10.1177/088840647900200326

Steinbrecher, T. D., Selig, J. P., Cosbey, J., & Thorstensen, B. I. (2014). Evaluating special educator effectiveness: Addressing issues inherent to Value-Added Modeling. *Exceptional Children, 80*(3), 323–336.

Stringer, E. T. (2008). *Action research in education* (2nd ed.). Upper Saddle River, NJ: Pearson.

Swank, P. R., Taylor, R. D., Brady, M. P., & Freiberg, J. (1989). Sensitivity of classroom observation systems: Measuring teacher effectiveness. *Journal of Experimental Education, 57*(2), 171–186.

SECTION III

OUTCOMES OF NEW COURSEWORK–FIELDWORK
INTEGRATION

CHAPTER 7

"WE NEED TO BE PREPARED!"

Teacher Candidates' Third Learning Space With University ELLs

Yukari Takimoto Amos
Central Washington University

ABSTRACT

The qualitative research study investigated the impact of regular interactions with English language learners (ELLs) who were enrolled in a university's ESL program on two teacher candidates with "third spaces" as a theoretical framework. In third spaces, boundaries of teachers and students get blurred, and new ways of thinking about ELL teaching emerge. The study found that third spaces provided the participants with opportunities to make their own assumptions problematic, inquired into the relationships between academic and practical knowledge, and discovered new findings on their own. The findings indicate that feedback teacher candidates receive from university instructors plays an important role for clinically rich experiences to be successful and effective.

Outcomes of High-Quality Clinical Practice in Teacher Education, pages 129–147
Copyright © 2018 by Information Age Publishing

129

Despite the projection that English language learners (ELLs) will comprise 40% of public school students by 2030 (U.S. Department of Education & National Institute of Child Health and Human Development, 2003) and that this population represents the fastest growing segment of the school age population (García, Jensen, & Scribner, 2009), the population of teachers will likely remain predominantly White and native speakers of English. In 2011, for example, White native speakers consisted of 84% of full-time teachers (Feistritzer, 2011). These teachers, according to Matias (2016), "have little to no experience nor previous relationships with people of color" (p. 85), while the majority of ELLs are students of color. On top of the racial/ethnic gap between teachers and ELLs, the majority of these teachers are monolingual English speakers (Feistritzer, 2011).

The problem above is further exacerbated because most of these teachers are largely untrained to work with ELLs (Reeves, 2006). According to National Center for Education Statistics (2002), only 12.5% of U.S. teachers have received eight or more hours of recent training to teach ELLs. Echevarria, Short, and Powers (2006) lament that mainstream teachers have a deep understanding of their subject matter, but may not "have a commensurate level of understanding of second-language acquisition, ESL methods, or sheltered teaching methods" (p. 196). It is most likely that ELLs learn content in mainstream classes with little accommodation from untrained teachers (Dellicarpini, 2009). Since ELLs are held to the same accountability standards as native English speakers (Short & Boyson, 2012), these White monolingual teachers need to develop "sufficient breadth and depth of knowledge and range of skills" (Samson & Collins, 2012, p. 4) to meet the unique academic needs of ELLs.

To produce teacher candidates who possess such knowledge, skills, and dispositions, teacher candidates are required to take a class, EDBL 401: Principles and Practices for Educating English Language Learners. The class covers the history of ELL education, basic second language acquisition theories, and sheltering techniques to help ELLs develop their academic language proficiency. Many teacher candidates, however, have had zero to very little experience of interacting with ELLs before this class. While teaching the class, I observed their lack of exposure to the ELL population has been undermining their understanding of ELLs' academic needs and has been hindering them from acquiring the knowledge, skills, and dispositions necessary for ELL teaching.

Lucas and Grinberg (2008) assert that extended contact with nonnative speakers of English has a positive impact on teachers' attitudes towards ELLs. In order to increase this contact, my class partners with a university ESL program that offers ESL classes to nonnative international students who wish to improve their English language skills. In this collaboration, teacher candidates are required to regularly interact with university ELLs in and outside the class and officially teach mini-lessons to them as well. While this clinical experience with university ELLs has been well-received by the teacher candidates what was unknown is the actual impact on their development of the knowledge, skills, and dispositions appropriate for ELL teaching. Therefore, this research investigated the impact of the clinical experience with university ELLs on teacher candidates. The chapter attempts to answer the following questions: (a) "How do teacher candidates apply what they learn in the EDBL 401 class when they interact with university ELLs?"; and (b) "What new learnings emerge through these interactions?"

ELL TEACHING IN CLINICALLY RICH TEACHER EDUCATION

For decades, the importance of incorporating and improving clinical experiences in teacher education has been called for (Darling-Hammond, 2006, 2010; Grossman, Hammerness, & McDonald, 2009; Zeichner, 2010). This growing consensus suggests that much of what teachers need to learn must be learned in and from practice rather than in preparing for practice (Hammerness, Darling-Hammond, & Bransford, 2005). Benefits of these experiences are many. Clinical experiences require teacher candidates to connect and apply what they learn from university based classes to what they experience with real students in the field (NCATE, 2010). The experiences basically offer teacher candidates "a context for understanding the link between theory and practice" (Coffey, 2010, p. 335). From direct experiences, according to Hollins and Guzman (2005), teacher candidates could bolster their capacity to understand, relate to, and work with students.

For largely White monolingual teacher candidates, the exposure not only to the sociocultural characteristics of the ELL population but also the preparation to enact effective instructional practices for ELL learning becomes critical for their development of appropriate knowledge, skills, and dispositions for the ELL population. Lucas, Villegas, and Freedson-Gonzalez (2008) urge teacher education programs to require teacher candidates to spend time in schools and classrooms where they will have contact with ELLs during field-based courses because the direct contact will provide teacher candidates with opportunities to "apply what they are learning about linguistically responsive teaching" (p. 370) in traditional courses.

More importantly, Lucas et al. (2008) argue that direct contact with ELLs allows teacher candidates to see ELLs as individuals instead of abstract beings and away from prevalent media stereotypes of immigrants. Most importantly, such experiences provide teacher candidates with much needed opportunities to practice. For example, McGraner and Saenz (2009) found that teacher preparation programs that included field experiences with diverse student populations, not only deepened teacher candidates' understanding of the ELL population, but also prepared them to create more effective instructional practices for ELLs.

Contact and exposure alone, however, do not guarantee a positive impact. They may work to reinforce, rather than to break down, any negative stereotypes that teacher candidates may bring to the contact (Ballantyne, Sanderman, & Levy, 2008; Lucas, 2005). In order to avoid this pitfall, McGraner and Saenz (2009) recommend that structured observation and reflection be implemented during clinical experiences. Studies revealed that teacher candidates' practices with ELLs were greatly enhanced when collaborated with and given feedback from the mentor teachers and university supervisors (Athanases & de Oliveira, 2010; Sakash & Rodriguez-Brown, 2010). In addition, through reflections, teacher candidates can see their own growth, learn from mistakes, obtain valuable feedback from instructors, and look critically at their experiences. The advantages of these structured observations and reflections were detailed in Abbate-Vaughn's (2008) study where teacher candidates who did a year-long urban field experiences with ELLs used process writing to reflect on their attitudes towards working with ELLs. At the end of the practicum year, most teacher candidates had shifted their focus away from a deficit perception to more clearly seeing ELLs' assets and embracing their own responsibility in reaching out across cultures.

In summary, teacher candidates must be exposed to a variety of issues and techniques from the beginning of their educational program followed by coordinated clinical experiences. Ideally, teacher candidates should be given opportunities to spend time in an academic environment with ELLs to see how they apply what they learn in traditional classes.

THEORETICAL FRAMEWORK: THIRD SPACES

Given the increasing number of ELLs in mainstream classes, Lucas et al. (2008) suggest that a separate course on ELLs be added to the teacher education curriculum and that teacher candidates spend time in schools and classrooms where they will have contact with ELLs in field-based courses. Although this suggestion sounds reasonable, Zeichner (2010) argues that disconnect between university-based and field-based classes has been one of the central problems that has plagued traditional university-based preservice teacher education for many years. In the historically dominant "application of theory" model, teacher candidates are supposed to learn theories at the university and then go to schools to practice or apply what they learned on campus (Korthagen & Kessels, 1999). Although most university-based teacher education programs now include multiple field experiences, disconnect between what students are taught in campus courses and their chances for learning to enact these practices in field-based classes is often very great (Bullough et al., 1999; Zeichner, 2007).

To intentionally connect between academic knowledge in university-based courses and practitioner knowledge in field-based courses, Bhabha's (1990) concept of third spaces is useful. Third spaces involve a rejection of binaries such as practitioner and academic knowledge, and theory and practice, and involve the integration of what are often seen as competing discourses. Eventually an either/or perspective is transformed into a both/also point of view. In Bhabha's (1994) mind, third spaces attempt to put together "traces of certain meanings or discourse" giving "rise to something different, a new area of negotiation of meaning and representation" (p. 211). In third spaces, boundaries of teachers and students get blurred, and new ways of thinking emerge.

Third spaces have more to do with the emergence of new ways of thinking about teaching and learning rather than with the changes of class locations and class instructional modes. Cochran-Smith and Lytle (1999) argue that inquiring into the relationship between academic and practical knowledge is the key to interrupting the hierarchy often found between these two types of knowledge. When teacher candidates "make problematic their own knowledge and practice" (Cuenca, Schmeichel, Butler, Dinkelman, & Nicholas Jr., 2011, p. 1069), third spaces emerge and provide new ways of thinking, thus new learning. This allows the boundary between teaching and learning, or academics and practitioners, to become blurred and teacher candidates are able to see things from different perspectives. Zeichner (2010) summarizes that creating third spaces in teacher education involves an equal and more dialectical relationship between academic and practitioner knowledge in support of teacher candidates' learning. With third spaces as a theoretical framework, this chapter explores how interactions with university ELLs provide teacher candidates with third spaces and how new learning emerges in such spaces.

SETTING AND METHOD

Rationales for Collaborating With University ELLs

Ideally, the contact with ELLs should be conducted at a K–12 setting because teacher candidates are going to be certified at this level. However, I was presented with two realities. First, our traditional teacher education program that produces approximately 500 teacher candidates each year strictly divides coursework and clinical work. Second, the community where our university is located is a small and predominantly White community with only a few ELL populations in the school district. Therefore, I found it impossible to find schools that can take in the large number of teacher candidates for the class assignment. In order to overcome this dilemma, I began requiring teacher candidates to interact with university ELLs as conversation partners on a regular basis and complete academic assignments together.

Compared to K–12 students, older learners, like university ELLs, tend to be practical, purposeful, and self-directed (Florez & Burt, 2001), thus more motivated to learn a foreign language. Older learner's prior education and their ability to read and write in their native language can also have both facilitating and complicating effects on their second language learning (Harper & de Jong, 2004). Despite these age-related differences, university ELLs are similar to K–12 ELLs because they go through linguistically similar processes in acquiring English. Because of this, I believe that teacher candidates can apply the theoretical concepts and sheltering techniques they learn in the methods class which are all meant for teaching K–12 ELLs to the interactions with university ELLs.

Participants

Two teacher candidates who were both White and monolingual English speakers and who were enrolled in the methods course participated in the study. Laura was an undergraduate in her early 20s who majored in elementary education and minored in literacy. She confessed that she had hardly ever conversed with ELLs before the class. Mariko, a university ELL from Japan, became Laura's conversation partner. They regularly met in person on campus throughout the quarter, and completed the academic assignments together. Laura also taught a mini-lesson three times to university ELLs in the methods class.

Nick was a mathematics teaching major in his late 60s, and took the online version of the method class. He was already accustomed to nonnative English in two ways. At his previous work, he worked with many Southeast Asian immigrant workers who spoke only broken English. Further, at his religious group meeting, he regularly talked to many women from Japan. Nick was assigned to Toshi, a university ELL from Japan, and interacted with him via Skype to complete the weekly assignments together. All the names in the study are pseudonyms.

Procedure

After interacting with their partner ELLs, both participants wrote a one-to-two pages long reflection paper each time they met. I read their reflection papers first, and then discussed, either in person or via Skype, what they had written for further reflections and clarifications. During the discussions, I took field notes. The comments made by the participants during the class were written immediately after the class. Finally, a formal interview with each candidate was conducted at the end of the term. The interviews were tape-recorded and transcribed.

Multiple data was triangulated—the reflection papers, the discussion field-notes, the comments, and the interviews—to enhance trustworthiness of the study (Glesne, 2006). By using multiple data sources, I was able to "relate them so as to counter-react the threats to validity identified in each" (Berg, 1995, p. 5). All the data sources were open coded using line-by-line analysis which involved "close examination of data, phrase by phrase and sometimes word by word" (Strauss & Cobin, 1998, p. 119) to develop categories. I coded the participants' reflection papers, comments, and interviews for words and phrases that stood out related to the study's research questions. The discussion field-notes were analyzed at this time. Then, I conducted "axial coding" (Strauss & Cobin, 1998, p. 124) in which categories were related to subcategories through statements denoting how they were related to each other. I compared each participant's categories and sorted into common groupings. These common groupings were subsequently compared and contrasted against each other to create larger categories.

THIRD LEARNING SPACES WITH UNIVERSITY ELLs

Laura's Case

Throughout the quarter, Laura interacted with Mariko outside the class and completed various assignments together. Before meeting with Mariko in person, Laura watched a video introduction Mariko sent and observed: "Her ability to speak English is very good. I definitely think that I will be able to communicate with her. If there is a miscommunication, I will find other ways of understanding her and helping her understand me." Laura was optimistic about understanding Mariko and making herself understood as well. Her optimism indicates that Laura, at least at the beginning, did not perceive teaching ELLs as challenging.

Shortly afterwards, however, her optimism changed into dismay. On the first day when Laura met Mariko, they were to complete an information gap activity. An information gap activity is an activity commonly used in ESL teaching where Student A and Student B fill in the gap by asking each other questions. When they finish, they are supposed to have exactly the same information. Having evaluated Mariko's language skills as high via the video, Laura expected that Mariko would speak English a lot and that the activity would be completed easily. To Laura's surprise, Mariko rarely spoke and kept trying to copy what Laura wrote on her sheet instead of engaging in the conversation. Furthermore, Laura had a hard time understanding Mariko's English and making herself understood by Mariko as well. Laura admitted that she felt uncomfortable at times talking to Mariko because of her tendency to be silent. Laura finally realized that talking to an ELL was more difficult than she had anticipated.

Although being dismayed and shocked, Laura incorporated a technique she had learned from the class. Laura observed that Mariko did not ask about any words that she did not understand. Several times, Laura asked Mariko if there were any words that she did not understand or any parts that were confusing, Mariko said, "No." However, Mariko's "No" clearly translated to Laura as "Yes" because Mariko looked very confused. Laura recalled that in class, she had learned that asking ELLs such questions as "Do you understand?" or "Does anyone have a question?" was not effective because no ELLs would answer such questions affirmatively, thus, teachers should ask specific questions instead. Realizing that Mariko could be hesitant to admit that there were words she did not understand, Laura switched to a question type and began to ask more specific questions, such as, "Do you know what 'synopsis' means?" To these questions, Mariko started to respond by either "Yes" or "No." Laura saw a value of asking specific questions rather than general questions. After the first encounter, Laura pondered why Mariko did not speak much:

> I can tell that Mariko was reluctant to make mistakes while speaking. She didn't speak unless she was asked questions. She also spoke very quietly in case of mistakes. She could comprehend a lot. She wrote down everything I said perfectly. Besides, some of the vocabulary words were difficult, like the names of the theaters and people. Maybe she may have never heard of those names before.

In this reflection, Laura reached a conclusion that Mariko could have been afraid of making mistakes and unfamiliar with the proper nouns. Her reflection here was analytical, trying to understand Mariko's situation and identify how to accommodate.

Laura's attempt to connect the class content to her interactions continued. After learning that there are two different types of language skills—BICS (basic interpersonal communication skills), social language, and CALP (cognitive academic language proficiency), academic language, and that CALP is more difficult to achieve than BICS (Cummins, 1980), Laura analyzed Mariko's oral proficiency as below:

> I think Mariko has more CALP skills than BICS, which was surprising to me. When I tried to talk to her before and after the assignments, I asked her casually, like, "What's she going to do for a holiday?" I could tell she was not com-

prehending what I was saying. Maybe, she's not used to colloquial English. The other day, I asked her if she had any finals. She kind of stared at me for a minute, and smiled. So, I had to ask her again. But, she would understand when we were doing the assignment.

In the reflection above, Laura speculated that some ELLs, particularly those who hadn't had much interaction with native speakers and had learned English mainly at school in their home country like Mariko, could have a higher level of CALP than BICS. Her speculation suggests Laura's attempt to apply and contextualize the concepts in a specific situation.

Furthermore, Laura realized that ELLs' background knowledge made a difference in comprehension after learning about the importance of checking students' background knowledge in class. When she first taught a minilesson about Pilgrims to another ELL named Kota, he had a relatively easy time filling out the worksheet because he had the sufficient background knowledge about the topic. Kota not only asked questions about the specific sentences in the worksheet but also asked questions about the topic itself. Because of this success, Laura began to create required worksheets/handouts with Kota in mind. She explained:

> When I was making a worksheet after I taught the first lesson, I was thinking of Kota, and how it will benefit him. It's always a good idea to have field experiences with the combination of what we are learning about in class. So that we can actually use it while interacting with the students.

Laura's comment indicates that she saw a clear connection between her methods coursework and her teaching interactions.

However, when she taught a lesson on Native American homes to an ELL named Mika, Laura had a difficulty. Mika had a difficult time comprehending the content simply because she only had a vague idea about Native Americans in general and was not all familiar with the fact that Native Americans were diverse groups of people who are comprised of many different tribes with vastly different cultural traditions, customs, and languages. Comparing Kota and Mika reminded Laura that ELLs were more engaged in the lesson when they had sufficient background knowledge, such as in Kota's case. His background knowledge assisted Kota comprehend the topic, and it was easy for Laura to ask specific questions about the topic as well. Kota's case supports studies that found a positive relationship between students' background knowledge and learning (Fisher, Frey, & Lapp, 2012; Wolfe & Goldman, 2005). In other words, through interacting with Kota and Mika, Laura solidified what she learned in class—that appropriate background knowledge makes a difference in students' learning.

Laura further learned a new perspective about background knowledge. Laura and Mariko needed to complete a worksheet on Thanksgiving together. As a person who grew up in the United States, Laura thought that she knew all about Thanksgiving. However, when Mariko asked a simple question—"How is Thanksgiving related to Pilgrims?"—Laura could not answer it because it was something that Americans tacitly understood. This is when Laura realized that those who did not grow up in the United States may ask questions for which Americans take for granted. Laura said, "We kind of learned together."

Throughout the quarter, Laura focused on giving comprehensible input by speaking slowly and giving as many visuals as possible as she learned in class. The worksheets/handouts she created always had colorful photos and pictures and her speech was deliberate. Kota evaluated her teaching, "It was easy to understand her speech. Because of lots of photos, it was easy to understand the topic." Therefore, witnessing Mika's struggles in her second teaching experience came as a shock to Laura. However, Laura spontaneously made a couple of accommodations while teaching Mika.

First, Mika had trouble comprehending the directions Laura gave when trying to fill out the matrix given to her. Using plus and minus signs on the matrix was confusing to Mika. In class, Laura had learned the importance of giving clear directions and showing examples before ELLs begin their task. Recalling this, Laura quickly directed Mika to follow along with her and they filled out plus and minus signs in the first row together. This accommodation was successful: From the second row, Mika filled out each box all by herself.

Second, Laura noticed that Mika comprehended better when she followed along in the passage while someone else was reading it aloud, rather than her reading aloud. Laura observed:

> Mika was nervous because I asked her to read the first paragraph aloud. She didn't comprehend what she had read. She was just worried about pronouncing the words. She had to go back to the paragraph and find the answer when it was time to fill out the matrix. So, from the second passage, I read it. Mika understood what she was supposed to do. She would underline the parts she would have to remember while I was reading.

Reading a passage aloud pressures ELLs to perform, and while doing so, ELLs' comprehension suffers. However, listening to the passage read aloud while following it in the eyes allows ELLs to concentrate on meanings. While observing Mika's difficulty, Laura quickly figured out where this difficulty was coming from and quickly changed the way she taught. Reflecting on the whole experience Laura summarized:

> Teaching content areas to ELLs is challenging and will be always challenging because each ELL comes from a different country and speaks a different language. We have to accommodate for them differently. So, we'll always be learning about how to help them.

Her comment that ELL teaching will be always challenging makes a sharp contrast with her optimism at the beginning of the quarter. This contrast, however, evidences what she learned. Laura clearly saw a connection between the methods class and the interactions she had with the university ELLs. She was able to put strategies she learned in the class into practice when interacting with the university ELLs, and reconfirmed how important it was for ELLs to use their background knowledge upon learning new materials. Most importantly, Laura learned the value of paying closer attention to the ELLs' performances and spontaneously accommodating based on their unique needs.

Nick's Case

Having been accustomed to hearing nonnative English at work and his religious group meetings, Nick was confident about his ability to complete assignments together with Toshi. When he first talked to Toshi via Skype, however, he found his confidence fading away. Nick sighed, "There was a noticeable language gap. I needed to ask for a repeated comment several times. I got a little frustrated." Although being used to talking to nonnative speakers in a casual setting, it seems that Nick found it difficult to complete the academic assignment with Toshi. The first encounter with Toshi, thus, seems to have solidified Nick's understanding that casual language (BICS) and academic language (CALP) are indeed different, which he learned in class.

For the first month, Nick was preoccupied with the correction of Toshi's pronunciations of "R" and "L." According to him, Toshi's "Robertson" sounded like "Lovetson." Even after being informed that most Japanese people cannot discriminate the English R and L sounds, Nick was determined to make Toshi pronounce correctly. Although constantly stating, "Toshi's quite fluent," Nick apparently perceived Toshi's pronunciation problematic and bothersome to continue conversations. During the first month, there was no sign of reflection on the part of Nick. Instead of thinking what he himself could do, Nick emphasized what Toshi could not do with such comments like "He can't explain ... " and "He has a problem with ... " Moreover, Nick found it difficult to incorporate what he had learned in class. For example, he stated, "We learned in class that we shouldn't ask such a question like 'Do you understand?' But I found it hard not to do so."

Realizing Nick's lack of self-reflection, I began telling him to think more about how to accommodate for Toshi instead of making Toshi accommodate for him. During this time, Nick was literally at a loss and made such comments like, "I've never had to do this before," and "I've never had to think deeply about this before." Obviously, accommodations for ELLs were something Nick had never done before upon interacting with nonnative speakers.

It was after the second month started that Nick's focus gradually shifted from what Toshi could not do to what Nick himself should do/have done to make the interactions go more smoothly. In Week 6, Nick and Toshi needed to complete a Q and A questionnaire survey about love and marriage orally and write down each other's answers. By this time, Nick had already realized that Toshi understood the questions, but never attempted to use complete sentences upon answering, let alone expanding his answers. Toshi continuously answered only in one-two words. After this particular interaction, Nick stated as below:

> It's hard for him. I can see now, ELLs might understand our language, but they can't put the words into sentences. I need to find out how to ask better questions, you know. I'm not good at it yet. I've got to figure out now instead of saying just, "Can you explain more?" I need to expand the ways I question. Just like one of your lesson, "Don't get in the trap of do you understand?" question. I've got to figure out how to work with him.

In the comment above, Nick critically analyzed why ELLs could not spontaneously speak. In this analysis, he frequently started an utterance with "I need to..." This discourse style not only contrasts with his previous emphasis on what Toshi could not do but also displays his attempt to change the ways he had been interacting to facilitate Toshi's spontaneous speech. Evidently Nick began to self-reflect and attempt to accommodate for Toshi.

One of Nick's accommodation plans for Toshi was to use Toshi's strengths to make the conversations go more smoothly. Ever since they started to interact, Nick had noticed the below:

> If he has something to read, he can read it. Everything he did well so far, Toshi actually had written down what he wanted to say and memorized them all. If he writes down the answers, he can actually say them. But he can't just speak spontaneously.

Based on this observation, Nick started to encourage Toshi to write down what he wanted to say before he spoke. This strategy obviously took time to complete an activity. However, Nick did not seem to mind and announced, "No choice. I've become more patient. You can't just say, 'I don't understand.' You have to be compassionate. You have to be patient."

Another strategy Nick came up with was vocabulary related. In Week 8, Nick and Toshi needed to complete an alien invasion activity in which Toshi verbally described the alien, while Nick drew as he was told. The alien was known only to Toshi. The alien figure was made up of geometrical figures, such as squares, rectangles, triangles, and so on. It turned out that Nick had to ask Toshi one question after another rather than Toshi describing the alien. Nick reenacted this activity as below:

I asked him if he could describe it. He said, "Yes." Then there was a pause. So, I asked him to describe the hat. He said, "Big square." "Does it have eyes?" "Yes, big circles." He should have described it to me instead of me asking him questions. But it didn't happen. I'm not surprised with anything anymore (laugh)! If he does this activity in Japanese, he will be able to do it, but he can't translate into English. He couldn't transfer the geometry terms into English. He didn't even use descriptive words like adjectives. If I had a chance to meet with him and coach him before this, I would definitely have gone over the geometry terms.

Although learning the importance of vocabulary and several vocabulary-related strategies in class, it was not until he did the alien invasion activity with Toshi that Nick had a deep understanding of how important it is for ELLs to be taught vocabulary words. Nick added, "We've been given a plenty of good tools in class, like picture dictionary, cloze, visual representations, information gap, etc. Very useful tools. I need to start using them." This comment indicates Nick's attempt to connect the class content to the interactions with Toshi. The comment above also suggests that Nick began to see Toshi as capable rather than deficient, which made a contrast with his attitude towards Toshi at the beginning of the quarter.

At the end of the quarter, Nick summarized his experience:

I have to be sure that I am totally prepared what they're (ELLs) supposed to say. If they don't seem right, try to repeat, and hope they will come back and repeat more completely. If this is gonna be successful, you have to be prepared. I adjusted myself to Toshi's R and L problem. I don't think he got better. I just got used to it. Interestingly, they don't bother me anymore.

Clearly, Nick's final self-reflection suggests that he learned that it was him who needed to be better prepared than Toshi being not prepared. In the attempt to connect the theories and strategies he learned in the class with the interactions with Toshi, Nick began shifting his attention to modify these strategies based on Toshi's unique needs rather than using them as they were in the textbook. In this process, Nick was constantly involved in analyzing and thinking not only about how to help Toshi but also what was lacking in him.

DISCUSSION, IMPLICATION, AND FUTURE RESEARCH

In order to assess the impacts the interactions with the university ELLs had on the participants, it is essential that we analyze how the participants came up with new ways of thinking about ELL teaching. Apparently, third spaces provided the participants with opportunities to make their own assumptions and feelings problematic, inquire the relationships between academic and practical knowledge, and discover new findings on their own.

Upon interacting, both participants were presented with the opposing realities to the assumptions they had held before interacting. Laura's optimism about ELL teaching was immediately shattered when she interacted with Mariko for the first time. Nick's confidence, based on his previous experiences with nonnative speakers of English, was transformed into frustration when he first talked to Toshi. It seems that these realities forced the participants to problematize their own assumptions about ELLs and then generate alternative approaches to continue interactions.

The pressure to generate alternative approaches seems to have given the participants the strong impetus to connect the class content they were simultaneously learning to the interactions. Therefore, there was a merit to incorporate clinical experiences directly into the class. Laura's connections were evidenced when she tested that asking specific questions helped the interaction with Mariko, when she realized that differing background knowledge made a difference in comprehension, and when she used modeling to facilitate Mika completing the worksheet. Nick also saw clear connections between the class content and the interactions when he realized that vocabulary was essential in ELL's utterances and that reading and speaking were totally different skills for Toshi. In addition, both participants witnessed how the theoretical concepts, such as BICS (social language) and CALP (academic language), worked with real ELLs. As several studies emphasized (Hollins & Guzman, 2005; Lucas, Villegas, & Freedson-Gonzalez, 2008; NCATE, 2010), direct contact with university ELLs enabled Laura and Nick to establish a clear connection between theories and practice. In addition, the experience forced both participants to analyze and create more effective practices with ELLs (McGraner & Saenz, 2009).

As the inquiries about the relationships between academic and practical knowledge became more and more analytical with sharpened observation skills among the participants, the distinct role separation between the participants as teachers and their ELL partners as learners seems to have blurred. Since practical knowledge was gained through the interactions with the ELL partners, the participants apparently became learners as well. In other words, as Bhabha's (1990) concept of third spaces reminds us, the participants' knowledge merged with their ELLs' knowledge in new, less hierarchical ways and new ways of thinking about teaching emerged. For example, when Laura reflected about her lack of knowledge on Thanksgiving, it was her ELL partner, Mariko, who pinpointed her ignorance. When Nick used the sentence pattern "I need to . . . " upon thinking about better ways to interact, it was his ELL partner, Toshi, who prompted this type of sentence. Although indirect and silent, their ELL partners seem to have assumed the role as teachers for the participants. It was around this stage that Nick's view of ELLs seems to have shifted from deficient to capable. In other words, these hybrid spaces encouraged a more egalitarian status for both participants and the university ELLs they worked with (Gorodetsky & Barak, 2008).

In the end, both participants produced new thoughts about ELL teaching in their own ways. Laura's biggest new finding was the fact that ELLs are diverse and that each ELL has different academic needs. To Nick, adjusting to ELL instead of making them adjust to him was the biggest intake he learned through the interactions with Toshi. These new discoveries must have given the participants a sense of ownership of the knowledge they themselves generated, rather than merely borrowing the knowledge they learned in class. Apparently, this sense of ownership gave the participants a new impetus to challenge themselves further to better their ELL teaching.

The findings of the study also highlight the importance of feedback teacher candidates receive from university professors/supervisors. For the first month, Nick was unable to immerse himself in third spaces and blamed Toshi for failed interactions and for his lack of proficiency in English. During this time, Nick seems to have perceived Toshi as deficient and emphasized his weaknesses rather than strengths as was evidenced in his insistence on correcting Toshi's pronunciation and his repeated use of the sentence type, "Toshi cannot..." It was after receiving repeated feedback from me that Nick began to direct his attention from Toshi to himself. Grossman et al. (2009) argue that feedback can help novices distinguish features of a complex practice that may be difficult to fully appreciate until one tries to enact the practice. Since the interaction with Toshi took place in the context of coursework, there was a place for coaching of instructional practice to influence Nick's teaching. Through the feedback given to him, Nick seems to have become a "reflective practitioner" (Schön, 1983) who gave up his power as a teacher and was humble enough to learn from the ELL he interacted with. Without the feedback, Nick may not have been able to benefit himself from a third space learning.

Implications

The National Council for Accreditation of Teacher Education (NCATE, 2010) strongly recommends a restructuring of teacher education around clinical practice. However, Martin, Snow, and Torrez (2011) warn that focusing attention simply on creating structures to provide clinical practices is not sufficient. Rather, locating quality clinical contexts is essential and examining whether or not such contexts provide teacher candidates with transformative learning is critical. As the current study implies, the interactions with the university ELLs assisted Laura and Nick with application of the knowledge and skills. However, these skills seem to be at a beginning novice level.

Whether or not their skills and dispositions become ingrained in their teaching practices depends on how teacher educators construct, support, and sustain the emergence of third spaces within the existing structures of teacher education programs. In order to accomplish this, each program should carefully structure quality clinical experiences for teacher candidates. This allows clinical experiences to become embedded in a teacher education programs' existing structure and become a norm. One challenge facing teacher educators is how to find more creative ways to incorporate clinical experiences in a variety of settings. For example, depending on the nature of the course, a clinical experience could be done with international students at a university like this study, creating opportunities for representations of teachers' practices to be brought into courses (Gallas, 2004; Hanson, 2008), or strategically utilizing the expertise that exists in the broader community to educate teacher candidates about how to become successful teachers in their communities (Boyle-Baise & McIntyre, 2008; Sleeter, 2008). The goal should be for every teacher educator to assume a responsibility as a hybrid teacher educator as well so that their teaching content will always be paired with clinical experiences. In other words, the goal is to provide candidates with opportunities to learn in third spaces.

Future Research

The best way to evaluate the effectiveness of the innovative collaborations with university ELLs is to compare and contrast results with teacher candidates in a traditional class that has no clinical experiences. Such a comparison will clearly show differences with regard to teacher candidates' willingness to accommodate based on each ELL's unique academic needs. In addition, research that is longitudinal and continuously monitors outcomes of clinically rich programs are needed. For example, investigating what kinds of clinical learning environments will facilitate Laura and Nick's newly acquired knowledge, skills, and dispositions to grow further is an important step to understand the quality and the quantity of clinical experiences all teacher candidates should have. Clinical experiences need to be planned, implemented, and assessed continuously while examining a variety of outcomes for teacher candidates and ELL students.

REFERENCES

Abbate-Vaughn, J. (2008). Highly qualified teachers for our schools: Developing knowledge, skills, and dispositions to teach culturally and linguistically diverse students. In M. E. Brisk (Ed.), *Language, culture, and community in teacher education* (pp. 175–202). New York, NY: Erlbaum.

Athanases, S. Z., & de Oliveira, L. C. (2010). Toward program-wide coherence in preparing teachers to teach and advocate for English language learners. In T. Lucas (Ed.), *Teacher preparation for linguistically diverse classrooms: A resource for teacher educators* (pp. 195–215). New York, NY: Routledge.

Ballantyne, K. G., Sanderman, A. R., & Levy, J. (2008). *Educating English language learners: Building teacher capacity.* Washington, DC: National Clearinghouse for English Language Acquisition. Retrieved from http://files.eric.ed.gov/fulltext/ED521360.pdf

Berg, B. L. (1995). *Qualitative research methods for the social sciences* (2nd ed.). Boston, MA: Allyn and Bacon.

Bhabha, H. K. (1990). The third space. In J. Rutherford (Ed.), *Identity, community, culture and difference* (pp. 207–221). London, England: Lawrence and Wishart.

Bhabha, H. K. (1994). *The location of culture.* London, England: Routledge.

Boyle-Baise, M., & McIntyre, D. M. (2008). What kind of experience? Preparing teachers in PDS or community settings. In M. Cochran-Smith, S. Feiman-Nemser, & D. J. McIntyre (Eds.), *Handbook of research on teacher education* (3rd ed., pp. 307–330). New York, NY: Routledge.

Bullough, R., Birrell, J., Young, J., Clark, D., Erickson, L., & Earle, R. (1999). Paradise unrealized: Teacher education and the costs and benefits of school university partnerships. *Journal of Teacher Education, 50*(5), 381–390.

Cochran-Smith, M., & Lytle, S. (1999). Relationships of knowledge and practice: Teacher learning in communities. *Review of Research in Education, 24,* 249–306.

Coffey, H. (2010). "They taught me": The benefits of early community-based field experiences in teacher education. *Teaching and Teacher Education, 26*(2), 335–342.

Cuenca, A., Schmeichel, M., Butler, B. M., Dinkelman, T., & Nicholas Jr., J. R. (2011). Creating a "third space" in student teaching: Implications for the university supervisor's status as outsiders. *Teaching and Teacher Education, 27*(7), 1068–1077.

Cummins, J. (1980). The cross-lingual dimensions of language proficiency: Implications for bilingual education and the optimal age issue. *TESOL Quarterly, 14*(2), 175–187.

Darling-Hammond, L. (2006). Constructing 21st-Century teacher education. *Journal of Teacher Education, 57*(3), 1–15.

Darling-Hammond, L. (2010). Teacher education and the American future. *Journal of Teacher Education, 61*(1–2), 35–47.

Dellicarpini, M. (2009). Dialogues across disciplines: Preparing English-as-a-second-language teachers for interdisciplinary collaboration. *Current Issues in Education, 11*(2). Retrieved from https://cie.asu.edu/ojs/index.php/cieatasu/article/download/1573/618/

Echevarria, J., Short, D., & Powers, K. (2006). School reform and standards-based education: A model for English language learners. *The Journal of Educational Research, 99*(4), 195–210.

Feistritzer, C. E. (2011). *Profile of teachers in the U.S. 2011.* Washington, DC: National Center for Education Information.

Fisher, D., Frey, N., & Lapp, D. (2012). Building and activating students' background knowledge: It's what they already know that counts. *Middle School Journal, 43*(3), 22–31.

Florez, M.-A., C., & Burt, M. (2001). *Beginning to work with adult English language learners: Some considerations.* Retrieved from the CAELA website: http://www.cal.org/caela/esl_resources/digests/beginQA.html

Gallas, K. (2004). Look, Karen, I'm running like a jello: Imagination as a question, a topic, a tool for a literacy research and learning. In C. Ballanger (Ed.), *Regarding children's words: Teacher research on language and literacy* (pp. 119–148). New York, NY: Teachers College Press.

García, E. E., Jensen, B. T., & Scribner, K. P. (2009). The demographic imperative: Educating English language learners. *Educational Leadership, 66*(7), 9–13.

Glesne, C. (2006). *Becoming qualitative researchers: An introduction* (3rd ed.). Boston, MA: Pearson.

Gorodetsky, M., & Barak, J. (2008). The educational-cultural edge: A participative learning environment for co-emergence of personal and institutional growth. *Teaching and Teacher Education, 24*(7), 1907–1918.

Grossman, P., Hammerness, K., & McDonald, M. (2009). Redefining teaching, reimagining teacher education. *Teachers and Teaching: Theory and Practice, 15*(2), 273–289.

Hammerness, K., Darling-Hammond, L., & Bransford, J. (2005). How teachers learn and develop. In L. Darling-Hammond & J. Bransford (Eds.), *Preparing teachers for a changing world* (pp. 358–389). San Francisco, CA: Jossey-Bass.

Hanson, D. (2008). Crossing the bridges of culture, color, and language. In C. Caro-Bruce, R. Flessner, M. Klehr, & K. Zeichner (Eds.), *Creating equitable classrooms through action research* (pp. 254–276). Thousand Oaks, CA: Corwin.

Harper, C., & de Jong, E. (2004). Misconceptions about teaching English-language learners. *Journal of Adolescent and Adult Literacy, 48*(2), 152–162.

Hollins, E., & Guzman, M. T. (2005). Research on preparing teachers for diverse populations. In M. Cochran-Smith & K. Zeichner (Eds.), *Studying teacher education* (pp. 477–548). New York, NY: Routledge.

Korthagen, F., & Kessels, J. (1999). Linking theory and practice: Changing the pedagogy of teacher education. *Educational Researcher, 28*(3), 4–17.

Lucas, T. (2005). Fostering a commitment to social justice through service learning: Hopes, plans, and realities in a teacher education course. In N. M. Michelli & D. L. Keiser (Eds.), *Education for democracy and social justice* (pp. 167–188). New York, NY: Routledge.

Lucas, T., & Grinberg, J. (2008). Responding to the linguistic reality of mainstream classrooms: Preparing all teachers to teach English language learners. In M. Cochran-Smith, S. Feiman-Nemser, & J. McIntyre (Eds.), Handbook of research on teacher education: Enduring issues in changing contexts (3rd ed., pp. 606–636). Mahwah, NJ: Erlbaum.

Lucas, T., Villegas, A., & Freedson-Gonzalez, M. (2008). Linguistically responsive teacher education: Preparing the classroom teachers to teach English language learners. *Journal of Teacher Education, 59*(4), 361–373.

Martin, S. D., Snow, J., & Torrez, C. A. F. (2011). Navigating the terrain of third space: Tensions with/in relationships in school–university partnerships. *Journal of Teacher Education, 62*(3), 299–311.

Matias, C. E. (2016). *Feeling White: Whiteness, emotionality, and education.* Rotterdam, Netherlands: Sense.

McGraner, K., & Saenz, L. (2009). *Preparing teachers of English language learners.* Washington, DC: National Comprehensive Center for Teacher Quality.

National Center for Education Statistics. (2002). *School and staffing survey 1999–2000: Overview of the data for public, private, public charter and Bureau of Indian Affairs elementary and secondary schools.* Washington, DC: U.S. Department of Education.

National Council for Accreditation of Teacher Education. (2010). *Transforming teacher education through clinical practice: A national strategy to prepare effective teachers.* Washington, DC: Author.

Reeves, J. (2006). Secondary teacher attitudes toward including English-language learners in mainstream classes. *The Journal of Educational Research, 99*(3), 131–143.

Sakash, K., & Rodriguez-Brown, F. (2010). Fostering collaboration between mainstream and bilingual teachers and teacher candidates. In T. Lucas (Ed.), *Teacher preparation for linguistically diverse classrooms: A resource for teacher educators* (pp. 143–159). New York, NY: Routledge.

Samson, J. F., & Collins, B. A. (2012). *Preparing all teachers to meet the needs of English language learners: Applying research to policy and practice for teacher effectiveness.* Washington, DC: Center for American Progress.

Schön, D. (1983). *The reflective practitioner: How professionals think in action.* San Francisco, CA: Jossey-Bass.

Short, D. J., & Boyson, E. A. (2012). *Helping newcomer students succeed in secondary schools and beyond.* Washington, DC: Center for Applied Linguistics.

Sleeter, C. (2008). Preparing white teachers for diverse students. In M. Cochran-Smith, S. Feiman-Nemser, & D. J. McIntyre (Eds.), *Handbook of research on teacher education,* (3rd ed., pp. 559–582). New York, NY: Routledge.

Strauss, A., & Corbin, J. (1998). *Basics of qualitative research: Techniques and procedures for developing grounded theory* (2nd ed.). Thousand Oaks, CA: SAGE.

U.S. Department of Education, & National Institute of Child Health and Human Development. (2003, October). National symposium on learning disabilities in English language learners. Symposium summary. Washington, DC: Authors.

Wolfe, M. B. W., & Goldman, S. R. (2005). Relations between adolescents' text processing and reasoning. *Cognition and Instruction, 23*(4), 467–502.

Zeichner, K. (2007). Professional development schools in a culture of evidence and accountability. *School–University Partnerships, 1*(1), 9–17.

Zeichner, K. (2010). Rethinking the connections between campus courses and field experiences in college- and university-based teacher education. *Journal of Teacher Education, 61*(1–2), 89–99.

CHAPTER 8

FOSTERING A CIVIC ETHOS

Teacher Candidates as Effective Citizens in an Urban PDS, Special Education Context

Deborah S. Reed
University of North Florida

Darcey J. Gray
*Duval County Public Schools
and University of North Florida*

ABSTRACT

Service learning is an instructional approach derived from the philosophical position of experiential learning. Pedagogically, service learning connects academic content to community experiences and uses critical reflection as a means to promote learning. Service learning has been shown to improve teacher candidate dispositions toward diverse populations, making it a valuable tool for educating teacher candidates. An overview of the University of North Florida professional development school model of preparing teachers in a clinically rich, authentic setting and its impact on one local Jacksonville middle school is discussed. This chapter further looks at the impact of service

Outcomes of High-Quality Clinical Practice in Teacher Education, pages 149–169
Copyright © 2018 by Information Age Publishing

learning in a middle school, special education context on teacher candidates as civically engaged learners.

The focus of this chapter will offer a glimpse into a secondary urban professional development school (UPDS) that uses a model of placing clinical practice as its central focus, and where coursework is designed to support the development of both theory and application within authentic and diverse classrooms and contexts. The National Council for Accreditation of Teacher Education's (NCATE) Blue Ribbon Panel report (2010) drove home the notion that strategic partnerships are imperative for quality clinical preparation in teacher education (CAEP, 2013; NAPDS, 2008). The intentional collaboration between P–12 schools and college preparation programs offers a clinically rich setting for all stakeholders (Burns, Yendol-Hoppey, & Jacobs, 2015). It was our hope to build on these views to ground ourselves in a strong program of learning using clinical practice and inquiry in one of our UPDSs (Dana & Yendol-Hoppey, 2014; Darling-Hammond, 2012; NCATE, 2010).

Teacher candidates, university-based teacher educators, boundary-spanning teacher educators, and other school-based educators have interacted in a "third space" for the past 5 years to foster the ongoing relationship and development of the collective partnership (Gutierrez, 2008; Ikpeze, Broikou, Hildenbrand, & Gladstone-Brown, 2012). The notion of a third space is simply explained as an impartial and neutral workspace where all constituents gather to engage in clinically based practices. It is the space that is created when teacher candidates, mentor teachers and faculty collaborate on problems of practice (Sawyer, Neel, & Coulter, 2016). As the partnership grew and developed its own unique focus, a genuine collaborative environment and commitment to enhancing the school-university culture emerged. We all understood that to realize a shared vision of the UPDS, role parity had to occur. Role parity suggests that everyone's role in the UPDS is deemed as equally important, regardless of position title within their respective organizations. Contributions from all stakeholders are considered valuable and important to the enrichment of clinical practice (NAPDS, 2008). Preparation of teacher candidates and a reciprocal commitment to educating P–12 learners arose from collaborative efforts and mutual acceptance of expertise from all stakeholders.

A brief history of the UPDS partnership at the University of North Florida (UNF) will be discussed, followed by a more detailed look at one of four schools in the urban partnership, Lake Shore Middle School (LSMS). A description of the journey from the beginning stages of development and initial wonderings, to the current stage of progress and ongoing complexities, will offer one example of commitment to improving clinical practice through an extension of learning, inquiry and understanding.

HISTORY OF THE UNIVERSITY OF NORTH FLORIDA
PROFESSIONAL DEVELOPMENT SCHOOL MODEL

The UNF, located in Jacksonville, FL, has a student body of approximately 16,000 students, and has established itself as a community-centered institution. UNF is dedicated to preparing students who will make meaningful and noteworthy community contributions. Learning experiences are intentionally designed by community minded faculty to foster student growth in academic, personal, and civic development. It is expected that community stakeholders will mutually benefit from experiences on and off campus. The Jacksonville community is the 12th most populous city in the United States. Additionally, Duval County Public Schools (DCPS) is the 20th largest school district in the country and the sixth largest in the state of Florida. DCPS currently has 198 schools in total including 149 traditional schools, six dedicated Exceptional Student Education schools, 35 charter schools, seven alternative education centers, and one virtual school. Forty four percent of DCPS students are African American, 36% White or Caucasian, 10% Latino/Hispanic, 5% multiracial, 4% Asian, and less than 1% Native American/Alaskan Native. The graduation rate for the district is 78.8% (using the federal formula) with a dropout rate of 5.3%. There are currently 1,237 part-time staff and 11,876 full-time staff, of which 8,284 of those are teachers. UNF's education programs have emerged as a strong presence in the local community with the development of the college's notable UPDS partnership program in 1997. Our UPDS model was developed using a framework of the nine required essentials of a PDS (NAPDS, 2008). We are committed to all nine of these fundamentals and continually refer to the framework as a guiding tool for ongoing partnership growth (see Table 8.1). The National Association for Professional Development Schools (NAPDS) advocates for PDSs to ensure a "school-university culture committed to the preparation of future educators that embraces their active engagement in the school community" (NAPDS, 2008).

The emphasis of the UPDS partnership between UNF and Jacksonville's DCPS is to prepare future educators in clinical settings, collaborate with school practitioners using an inquiry stance to understand struggling learners, and improve outcomes for P–12 students and the broader community. Our focus on urban school initiatives addresses the critical need of learning how to teach in our most challenging urban settings with a diverse group of students. Today, the partnership is jointly funded and institutionalized by both DCPS and UNF with three elementary schools and one middle school. Plans to enhance our existing UPDS model with additional school partnerships and incorporating components of teacher residency models are under development.

TABLE 8.1   Nine Essentials of a PDS
1. A comprehensive mission that is broader in its outreach and scope than the mission of any partner and that furthers the education profession and its responsibility to advance equity within schools and, by potential extension, the broader community;
2. A school–university culture committed to the preparation of future educators that embraces their active engagement in the school community;
3. Ongoing and reciprocal professional development for all participants guided by need;
4. A shared commitment to innovative and reflective practice by all participants;
5. Engagement in and public sharing of the results of deliberate investigations of practice by respective participants;
6. An articulation agreement developed by the respective participants delineating the roles and responsibilities of all involved;
7. A structure that allows all participants a forum for ongoing governance, reflection, and collaboration;
8. Work by college/university faculty and P–12 faculty in formal roles across institutional settings; and
9. Dedicated and shared resources and formal rewards and recognition structures.

A professor in residence (PIR) and a resident clinical faculty member (RCF) are assigned to each of the UPDS schools. The PIR is a faculty position that receives one course release for engaging in research and service at the UPDS site. RCFs are master level teachers with responsibilities that include supervision of interns and providing support and professional development to first year teachers in PDSs. The school district and the university jointly fund the RCF position. One of the highlights of the model are the undergraduate courses that are taught on site, providing teacher candidates opportunities to learn in an authentic environment early on in the teacher preparation program. The PIR and RCF work closely with school educators to design effective clinical practice experiences, continually develop school-wide evidence-based practices, and provide professional development as needed. Other community connections resulting from the partnership include service on school advisory councils, leadership teams, and/or UPDS steering committees.

The undergraduate program in Exceptional Student Education at UNF currently requires teacher candidates to participate in two levels of field experiences leading up to a semester long final internship. One semester of an unpaid urban teaching experience is required in one of the local district schools. Further, UNF field courses are designed to allow teacher candidates opportunities to experience hands-on lessons that bridge the theory to practice gap as they apply ideas from coursework into practice. For example, teacher candidates observe, create lessons aligned with current curriculum, and implement strategies related to content and classroom management under the guidance of an experienced mentor. The courses prepare teacher candidates to work with diverse populations they may encounter within any school setting. They also are placed with teacher mentors who have their Clinical Educator Training (CET). This certification allows mentors to supervise professionals-in-training by providing feedback on performance, preparation and implementation of professional development plans, and learning how to reflect on practice. The final internship experience at UNF is organized around the state of Florida's framework of accomplished practices (2017). Teacher candidates must meet these as part of their graduation requirements and demonstrate understanding, knowledge, skills, and dispositions needed for making teaching decisions.

Lakeshore Middle School

One local Title 1 urban middle school (Grades 6–8) was eager to participate with UNF and applied to become a professional development school, citing the need for assistance with their large number of students with moderate and severe disabilities, low performing math students and a high number of students identifying as English language learners. Currently, there are 1,180 students at LSMS with approximately 70% minority status and 60% of the students receiving subsidized lunches.

LSMS has a large population of students with autism and other disabilities as approximately 19% of the students at LSMS have been identified as having disabilities. During the 2016–2017 school year, 150 students with disabilities had IEP's and were educated in an inclusion setting, with the majority of students working on the Florida State standards. Another 79 students with IEPs received their free and appropriate public education (FAPE) in a self-contained classroom. The majority of those students are working on Access Points or alternative standards. There are a few students in the self-contained setting who work on the regular standards, and likewise, there are some, albeit few, who work on Access Points in the inclusion setting. There are also a large number of English language learners, with 92 students identified as having "limited English proficiency."

Recent state testing indicates that a large part of the LSMS student body is low performing in major academic content areas. Though the UPDS at LSMS targets the entire student population, it is the students with special needs that were the *initial* focus of the UPDS efforts. University-based faculty, school-based educators, and school administration identified three areas of greatest need: (a) special education services and practices, (b) low performance of students on regular standards in math, and (c) a high TESOL population.

University students are engaged in a continuum of clinical experiences within the LSMS community. The range of clinical experiences varies, from structured observations as part of course requirements, undergraduate classes held on site, field experiences, and a culminating semester of internship.

The PIR and RCF are boundary-spanning educators that work closely with the administration, and school-based educators to design, develop and deliver course content and experiences that will meet the needs of teacher candidates, in-service teachers, and middle school students in Grades 6–8. The following section will offer an example of one methods course developed and taught in the UPDS context, and present initial findings from an analysis of reflections written during the course of the semester.

EEX 4474 Teaching Students With Moderate and Severe Disabilities

The LSMS UPDS officially began in August of 2011, with a focus on special education. This initial semester was used by the PIR to make observations in self-contained classrooms, due to the large number of students receiving their education in this setting and to gain a better understanding of the school culture. Anecdotal information related to instructional methodology, inclusive teaching practices, and general philosophies of teaching students with moderate and severe disabilities were collected from school-based educators and used as a baseline to determine how to proceed with partnership development.

Observation and teacher interviews led to a joint decision that a UNF Special Education course would be offered on site at the middle school and taught by the PIR. This course was intentionally redesigned; moving from a traditional, lecture style of teaching on the university campus with minimal observation hours, to having class on the LSMS campus and incorporating service-learning expectations. Service learning has innumerable benefits when integrated into teacher preparation programs (Anderson & Erickson, 2003; Eyler & Giles, 1999; Jenkins & Sheehey, 2009). To engage the students in a broader appreciation of teaching students with disabilities in a clinically rich setting, and help them gain a sense of personal values and civic responsibility (Bringle & Hatcher, 2009), service learning was added as a requirement for all students. The course was specifically designed to improve clinical practice by moving undergraduate students beyond learning content knowledge, to engaging them in learning opportunities within an authentic classroom setting with the goal of applying this knowledge in practice.

Teaching students with moderate and severe disabilities is a required course for the Exceptional Education teacher preparation program at UNF. Fundamentally, the purpose of the course is to educate teacher candidates on issues facing the population of individuals with moderate to severe disabilities and learn how to use evidence based, high-leverage teaching practices.

It also encourages teacher candidates to be change agents within their community. All told, service learning offered an opportunity for our teacher candidates in the UPDS at LSMS to become actively involved in learning and using evidence based teaching practices in an authentic classroom. Learning on site also gave them an opportunity to become actively involved in the inclusive education movement for students with moderate and severe disabilities by providing a means for social awareness of inclusion and social responsibility for creating change.

Furthermore, learning how to navigate the challenges of teaching students with disabilities is difficult, and even more so if the only experiences related to practice are contrived and based solely upon content from traditional coursework. "Third space" conversations with stakeholders became the focus of the course and asked undergraduate students just beginning their teacher preparation journey to examine their own that occurred in real life, meaningful UPDS settings. These experiences take place early in their teacher preparation program to engage them in clinically rich practices prior to final internship.

A series of activities were co-developed with school-based educators and the RCF to meet the needs of both undergraduate students and the middle school students identified as having disabilities. For instance, classes are structured so that the first half of a weekly class session is held in the middle school media center. Theories of practice and teaching strategies are presented in both lecture and small group activity style. This allows time during the latter part of class for students to immerse themselves in their assigned classrooms for students with moderate and severe disabilities. The PIR and RCF member work closely with teachers and the school-based disability site coach to ensure teacher candidates are placed into classrooms that will allow them to apply theoretically-based content, as well as experience working in self-contained settings alongside teachers and students. Mentor teachers are expected to include in their lesson plans how teacher candidates will be immersed into the classroom.

Teacher candidates are provided with weekly structured activities. For example, if they are learning a new teaching strategy, they are first asked to observe the teacher using the strategy and take notes related to how the teacher incorporated it into the lesson, how the students in the classroom responded, and any questions they might have related to delivery and effectiveness. This information is brought back to the larger group for discussion and to clear up any misconceptions. Teacher candidates are given opportunities in subsequent weeks to practice the evidence-based strategies by first co-teaching with the classroom teacher and ultimately using the strategies independently, with support from the classroom teacher.

Teacher candidates write about their experiences using structured reflection prompts. Guided reflection is used as a way to tie course content into their service learning experience. Reflection is a powerful tool that is often a recommended component of service learning. Carrington (2011) suggests that reflection can take students from being unaware of social inequalities to being aware and inspired to take action. Gibson, Hauf, Long, and Sampson (2011) suggest that reflection on service learning experiences, in addition to the experience itself, may extend academic learning and allow for personal and societal learning to occur. Therefore, moving the undergraduate course on site and restructuring the format allowed teacher candidates to recognize major educational issues impacting the instruction of individuals with moderate to severe disabilities, discuss possible solutions, and in some cases take action, demonstrating their commitment to bettering the community and student education as effective citizens.

UPDS OUTCOMES

While there are many success stories that have come out of the LSMS UPDS, we would like to highlight here a small piece of how our work represents clinically rich teacher education. The National Task Force on Civic Learning and Democratic Engagement (2012) called upon the higher education community to embrace civic learning and democratic engagement as a priority, and to foster civic ethos across campus culture. Our teacher candidates have time and again demonstrated their passion and strengths in working with students with disabilities, but it was not until we saw the richness in their reflections that we truly realized what a special partnership we had with LSMS. We wanted to understand how teacher candidates were making sense of their experiences at LSMS. We were also interested in researching their perceptions as civically engaged learners, in a UPDS.

Methods

UNF teacher candidates completed reflection papers on their special education clinical practice experiences as part of an undergraduate course, *Teaching Students With Moderate and Severe Disabilities*. This is a required course for special education majors that is taught every fall semester. This study examined 3 years of reflection papers to uncover themes that emerged from teacher candidates' experiences. For this reason, a qualitative approach was used to construct meaning from their experiences (Sherman & Webb, 1988).

Research Design

This study emerged from our own wonderings about teacher candidate classroom-based experiences and the dilemmas they encountered while working with students with moderate and severe disabilities. We were interested in understanding how the service learning experiences of the special education methods course impacted teacher candidates. They were assigned to work in a self-contained classroom with students with disabilities over the course of the semester. To encourage discourse on civic engagement and to prepare future teachers for lives as citizens, teacher candidates were asked to describe fundamental democratic values and beliefs they infused into, or felt strongly about, as they participated in their clinical experiences working with students with disabilities at LSMS. They were also asked to describe any issues or struggles related to their classroom experiences with students with moderate and severe disabilities and how they addressed them or would address them in the future.

Three semesters of existing reflection papers were studied and analyzed for themes. Fifty reflections were examined in all (22, 13, and 15 reflections in each respective semester). Teacher candidates explored real-world issues and potential solutions regarding the education of students with moderate and severe disabilities and searched for meaning and understanding of their service learning experience as civically engaged learners. Written reflections were used for teacher candidates to articulate learning that emerged during the service learning experiences.

The reflections studied helped illuminate the experiential component of the semester-long class where students connected coursework with service to the community. During the course, teacher candidates were exposed to the history and theoretical underpinnings of educating students with disabilities. For example, students with moderate and severe disabilities are a unique population of students and often had been excluded from inclusive educational practices. Prior to the mid-1970s students with severe disabilities were not even included in special education programs in public schools (Browder & Spooner, 2011). On the other hand, compelling evidence suggests that students with moderate and severe disabilities are capable of experiencing significant portions of their school day in age-appropriate inclusive contexts and accessing the same general curriculum as their non-disabled peers (Carter & Kennedy, 2006; Jackson, Ryndak, & Wehmeyer, 2010; Ryndak & Alper, 2003). Further, teaching any child is complex, and teaching children with disabilities, in a variety of settings, using a multitude of strategies, makes it even more challenging.

Analysis of the reflections in this study was beneficial as it captured what teacher candidates learned, through articulations from their own written work (Ash, Clayton, & Atkinson, 2005). Reflections emphasized open-mindedness, the worth of students with disabilities, and overall a concern for the well-being of others. This was valuable for looking at course and program effectiveness when preparing teacher candidates both academically and as potential leaders and citizens in their community.

RESULTS

Teacher candidates reflected on their clinically based experiences in self-contained classrooms for students with disabilities. Thematic analysis was used as a method for identifying and analyzing patterns and themes across three semesters of reflection papers (Braun & Clarke, 2006). Schaffer, White, and Brown's (2016) purported five stages of cognitive dissonance was used as the theoretical framework to guide thematic analysis and report findings: (a) creating a felt need, (b) shifting from apprehension to appreciation, (c) moving beyond the deficit approach, (d) closing the gaps, and (e) teaching for social justice. The first three stages challenge internal assumptions and perceptions while stages four and five are externalized. Teacher candidates might begin to act on their wonderings and identified challenges in the last two stages (Schaffer et al., 2016). Reflections on service learning experiences at LSMS indicated that many teacher candidates experienced dissonance and moved through the stages in various, nonlinear ways (Schaffer et al., 2016). Several teacher candidates extended the impact of cognitive dissonance to the larger context of society beyond internalizing the dissonance. They questioned injustices in teaching practices and policies that had been institutionalized, even though they seemed to have a negative impact on students with disabilities.

Creating a Felt Need

Teacher candidates worked alongside students with disabilities in self-contained classrooms. They were asked to think about these classroom-based experiences and further examine any wonderings they had related to the education of students with moderate and severe disabilities. Not only were middle school students receiving their education in an urban school with a high representation of minority children, many students with disabilities were receiving their free and appropriate public education in separate classrooms from the their peers. Teacher candidates were curious about the large number of students in this more restrictive setting and wanted to further their understanding of this issue. The following excerpts highlight a common concern:

> Excerpt #1: I was somewhat alarmed by the way students in my classroom were viewed by the teacher and other professionals. Most importantly, none of the students I worked with had any academic or social opportunities to be with peers without disabilities. How is this preparing them for life after school? How is this preparing a student to enter the workforce? How is this supporting social interaction?

Excerpt #2: Equality is one of the most important values that educators must keep in mind when working with students with disabilities. All students deserve to be given an equal education and to be treated fairly in the educational system. I really wondered why the opposite was happening and why students with disabilities were secluded from the rest of the student body?

Excerpt #3: I am concerned with the number of schools in our district that have numerous general education classrooms, with a few ESE classrooms isolated in makeshift spaces or portables away from the main student body. I have to stop and wonder; is this really an equal education?

The reflection assignment helped teacher candidates to problematize the idea (Dana & Yendol-Hoppey, 2014) and realities of inclusion. Thirty-two teacher candidates, or 64% of the reflection papers included wonderings about the lack of inclusive practices for students with disabilities. The notion of equality was often equated with the concept of inclusion. Once teacher candidates were aware of these felt needs, many moved to the next stage of dissonance for resolution.

Shifting From Apprehension to Appreciation

Many of the teacher candidates were apprehensive about working in classrooms with students with moderate and severe disabilities, especially in the beginning of the semester. Apprehension eased as the semester went on and gave way to appreciation. Teacher candidates felt strongly in their written reflections about the lack of opportunities to be educated with peers without disabilities. Analysis of the existing reflection documents revealed that teacher candidate prior content knowledge related to teaching students with disabilities and teaching in urban schools appeared to conflict with their actual experiences in urban clinical practice sites. Teacher candidates wrestled with this dissonance. As analysis became more refined, the notion of equality emerged.

Service learning experiences in the classrooms not only provided teacher candidates with opportunities to learn about strategies and effective teaching practices, it also gave them an opportunity to see first hand the continued educational practice of segregating students with disabilities away from their peers without disabilities. The following excerpts from the documents reflect this notion:

Excerpt #1: The Declaration of Independence declared, "All men are created equal." People with disabilities, however, have not always been treated as equals. Once believed to be demonic and part of witchcraft, persons born with a disability were put to death or shut away from society to live in deplorable conditions. Society has changed a lot since those times but individuals with disabilities still struggle for equality. Life can be difficult when you don't have the ways and means to communicate your thoughts and feelings. When educating students with disabilities they cannot feel as equals if they are not able to participate and learn with peers without disabilities. Speaking to all students as social equals promotes a feeling of acceptance, fosters respect, and may even improve academic success.

Excerpt #2: I was very moved by the students stories in my classroom and felt deteriorated as they expressed emotions of what a day in their life is like. Most of the middle school students I worked with do not interact with peers outside of their classrooms, and typically spend their day rotating between teachers where they are given worksheet on top of worksheet from the district curriculum. My students do attend gym as an elective but typically sit out because the choices of activities offered were very limited. I understand that money, resources, and community involvement all play a large factor in creating a better environment for students, but there are simple ways of providing equality for students as well. Inclusion is one way. In my opinion, inclusive education benefits all members involved: students with and without disabilities, families, and instructors. I believe that inclusion is the key to gain access to equality.

Excerpt #3: Individuals have the right to social equality...I believe within schools there should be no clear divide among students other than their grade levels. Current legislation calls for inclusive classrooms however individual schools have a seemingly skewed opinion of what an inclusion classroom is. This past semester at LSMS I witnessed the school taking new steps towards inclusion however there is a noticeable divide and inequality across the campus...ESE classrooms are isolated in portables distant from the main campus and other students, which only decreases opportunities to engage with peers. In my opinion, this does not promote equality.

The democratic value of equality was identified in many of the reflection documents as critical to the education of students with disabilities. Teacher candidates expressed the importance of shared values in their descriptions of students with disabilities having equal access and opportunities in all aspects of their life, including education. Thirty-five teacher candidates, or 70% of the documents analyzed, identified the democratic value of equality as highly important, and a notion that should always be considered in the education of students with disabilities. Teacher candidates expressed empathy with some instances of inequalities in their service learning experiences. Most expressed concern with the lack of inclusive opportunities, both academically and socially, for students with disabilities in the self-contained settings. As the semester progressed, teacher candidates continued to challenge their internal assumptions based on the service learning experiences at the UPDS, and began to show movement beyond the deficit approach to educating students with disabilities.

Moving Beyond the Deficit Approach

Multiple perspectives by teacher candidates were appreciated in this stage. While many initially focused on the deficits of students with disabilities who are educated in urban schools, they did recognize students' assets and seemed to value setting high expectations for all students. Diversity was a theme woven throughout several stages, however it was most commonly mentioned from an asset based perspective. Teacher candidates referred to diversity through an understanding that all students with disabilities are unique and their individual differences should be valued. When diversity was explored in the reflection documents, it was often framed around the categories of disability, race, national origin, and socioeconomic status:

Excerpt #1: LSMS is culturally diverse. It provides educational services to a multitude of English language learners, students of all exceptionalities, racial diversity, as well as socioeconomic diversity. The majority of my experiences at LSMS have been with African American males who have disabilities. This has helped create awareness within myself, of the varying cultural differences I experienced in an academic setting. In order to foster an environment of acceptance of individual differences, I was determined to create an understanding of the diverse background of my students. Such an understanding helped decrease cultural boundaries and facilitate the development of a more personal relationship between my students and I.

Excerpt #2: I quickly noticed that LSMS has students from a variety of cultural backgrounds. Within the classrooms, you are sure to find multiple languages being used as well as differentiated learning tasks for students of diverse backgrounds. For example, in one of the classrooms I experienced a teacher using various communication devices such as text-to-talk communication boards for students with disabilities who are in the pre-language stages or non-verbal, the PECS system which incorporates a large use of pictures and matching/pointing/cueing, as well as the English language assignments translated into the student's home language. I was very interested to see how students respond in the classroom when they are comfortable with the communication style they're using. I recall a particular day when I followed a student from one class to another where he visited two separate teachers. In the first class, the teacher considered the students to be non-verbal. But, the second teacher developed strategies and ways around the communication barrier. It was so moving to see this student excel in the classroom when he was able to use the communication technique he was comfortable with. As our communities grow, I feel that it is extremely important that we are aware of the diversity that surrounds us. As future educators, we must develop learning strategies that are beneficial to each and every student.

Diversity was identified as a fundamental democratic value critical to the teacher candidate experiences in many of the reflections. Twenty-nine teacher candidates, or 58% of the reflection papers included narrative about diversity and its importance to understanding a democratic society and educational system. Teacher candidates began to see the importance of teaching students with disabilities based on their individual and diverse needs, rather than focusing on a group of students stigmatized by a label. Teacher candidates expressed the importance of valuing difference and began moving from internalizing their cognitions to externalizing them.

Closing the Gaps

Teacher candidates began to explore the use of evidence based teaching strategies in the classrooms. They shifted their thoughts from thinking about problems and issues to implementing effective practices that would address the identified areas of need. Commitment to action flourished as the PDS grew and relationships developed. Teacher candidates, along with school based educators and administration, worked collaboratively to advocate for and create improved educational experiences for students with disabilities.

Several projects grew from service learning experiences in the UPDS. Some of the collaborative projects included securing funding for the development and creation of a sensory room for students with autism, securing funding and donations for the ongoing development and upkeep of functioning outdoor garden beds, holding book drives for age-appropriate books for students in self-contained classroom settings, and organizing an inclusive career fashion show for students with and without disabilities. The creation of a new peer support elective and grant-funded tablet project stemmed from initial wonderings of teacher candidates through their service learning experiences.

Peer Support Elective

Students with disabilities continue to lag behind their peers academically, and although current legislation exists to prevent inequity, access to and participation in inclusive contexts remains limited for some students with disabilities. Teacher candidates continually identified the importance of equality in their reflections. They talked at length in class and wrote in their reflections about the lack of inclusive opportunities for students with disabilities, framing questions around the areas of placement in self-contained settings and social inclusion. To address this, teacher candidates, along with the PIR and school partners researched peer support strategies (Carter & Kennedy, 2006) and the benefits of formal peer support programs, which led to the development of a peer support elective course for middle school students. Middle school students who take this elective provide academic and social support to students with disabilities who receive their education in self-contained settings. What started off as a pilot program with four students has since grown to an elective with approximately 20–25 students taking the peer supports as an elective class each year. A teacher candidate reflects on the benefits below:

> Programs like peer support is another practice I observed that contributes to the principle of common good. I am grateful to have been a part of developing the peer support system, where students are taught how to effectively work with a diverse population of individuals toward a common goal, which models society as a whole and prepares students for a more integrated adult life with the capacity for collaborative work and interactions.

Tablet Project

Several students with autism at LSMS had difficulty with communication and social skills. Noting the lack of technology for these and other students, teacher candidates wondered early on in the partnership about using tablets as a strategy to increase opportunities for communication and learning. They wondered if the use of tablets would give students with disabilities a "voice," and provide them with the support they needed to engage with others. Teacher candidates and the PIR acted on this wondering, by writing a grant for 14 Nexus 7 tablets. The grant was funded by a local Rotary Club and outcomes of this project are still being analyzed.

To date, six service learning projects grew out of teacher candidate initial wonderings. Teacher candidates began to realize that education is not something that merely exists within a classroom or school, but it exists also as a larger part of society (Schaffer et al., 2016). Externalizing their cognitive dissonance moved them to take action on the lack of inclusion and equity, and implement evidence based practices to further encourage diversity at the middle school.

Twenty-six teacher candidates, or 52% of the reflection papers included actions they *would pursue in the future* based on their experiences at the UPDS. They listed "closing the gap" activities such as standing up for what is right, educating other teachers and parents, collaborating with others, and making sure people knew about community resources and programs. A second group of teacher candidates *took some action steps* during the semester to help resolve their own cognitive dissonance. Sixteen teacher candidates, or 32% of the reflection papers suggested students participated in activities including the solicitation of local community donations for school projects, volunteering at organizations such as Special Olympics and The Boys and Girls Club, and attending school board meetings. Both groups of students do not appear to have yet crossed in the next stage of teaching for social justice, however we did find that the remaining, albeit few, did move in the final stage of cognitive dissonance.

Teaching for Social Justice

The final stage of cognitive dissonance is teaching for social justice. The extension of cognitive dissonance into a wider social and societal context is challenging and sometimes relentless work (Schaffer et al., 2016). Social justice is a philosophical perspective that encourages individuals to act and lead others to a more equitable world (Schaffer et al., 2016). This requires people to advocate and be committed to social action.

Eight teacher candidates, or 16% of reflection papers included narrative about inequities viewed through a social justice lens and challenging systems that had a negative impact on students with disabilities. The following excerpt is indicative of someone who has externalized his or her cognitive dissonance through a lens of social justice:

> Later in life I want to run for public office and even if I do not win a seat I will run with a stance based on public education reform. In addition to taking courses this semester, I chose to complete an independent internship with the school board. During my time I worked with several members to understand policy and help them make an informed decision for all. I designed a policy crosswalk for the school year and interacted with media to spread awareness of inclusive education for students with disabilities.

Other examples of social justice demonstrated by teacher candidates included writing grant proposals which were ultimately funded, advocating with the local Rotary Clubs to talk about the lack of assistive technology for students with autism, presenting at national conferences, and being hired as a student ambassador to promote community-based transformational learning experiences on a regional level.

Both the PDS model and the service-learning component appear to have had a positive impact on a smaller percentage of teacher candidates' commitment to action and social justice. The authentic learning environment provides an opportunity to implement evidence-based practices recommended for students with moderate and severe disabilities. For example, many schools in our district do not have peer support as an elective. Initiating the development of the peer support program gave teacher candidates a chance to collaborate with other professionals beyond the classroom to advocate and affect change for students with disabilities.

> Excerpt #1: This experience affected me professionally in ways I never thought about. It made me realize that I have the power and the ability to make change, and that change does not have to be in just one classroom but can be so much larger. Making a difference is more than what happens in one classroom with a small group of students but what happens in a whole school or in an entire community. This experience has motivated me to make

change in my community and get more people involved in advocacy for people with disabilities.

Excerpt #2: Before I came to LSMS I thought that inclusion was nothing more than a thinly veiled budget cut with a name designed to pull on the heartstrings of parents. I attributed inclusion to stripping individuals with disabilities of the specialized care and supports they needed and deserved. To put it mildly, I was not a fan. Thankfully this experience has shown me what inclusion can be and what it was designed to be. Our schools don't always get it right, there aren't always enough resources, and unfortunately some kids do get left behind. At least I can see now that we are headed in the right direction and the more of us that get on board the faster we'll get there. This has given me a new passion for the inclusion movement and collaborating with others to keep things moving in the right direction.

Persistent Dilemmas Teacher Candidates Face

While the shift to clinical practice offers great promise in preparing teachers for working with students in special education, it is not without challenges. Teacher candidates revealed in their reflections several dilemmas they faced in their preparation for teaching.

Teacher candidates must continue to work in a system that marginalizes students with disabilities. Candidates are challenged to learn how to navigate a system where students with disabilities are separated from and educated away from students without disabilities. These factors have great potential to foster in students a sense of marginalization and separation from the general population, often leading to isolation, lack of preparation for living in a diverse community, and other challenges. Marginalization persists with the high number of teacher shortages in special education. To fill shortages, available teaching positions to work with students with the most significant needs are often filled with unqualified or provisionally certified teachers.

Additionally, mentors and school-based educators do not always share the same beliefs/teaching practices as teacher candidates. Philosophical differences such teaching in self-contained versus inclusive settings may be difficult to navigate. Another issue presented in the data suggests that while teacher candidates may learn about content and are prepared to use evidence-based pedagogy in their clinical experiences, school partners are often conflicted due to district mandated curriculum and pacing guides. Mentor teachers are similarly challenged by mandates of restrictive accountability measures leading to linear views of teaching where scripted, one size fits all approaches are the norm.

Teacher candidates in special education also wrestle with the inability to change structures for more inclusive practices. General education teachers have limited training and preparation to not only work with students with disabilities but also to collaborate with their special education colleagues in inclusive settings. These persistent challenges often result in frustration, classroom management and academic challenges for teachers, communication issues and eventually the removal of student with disabilities to more restrictive settings.

DISCUSSION

Though, our PDS at LSMS is still in its infancy, we recognized the need to share our students experiences by extracting their thoughts and ideas from authentic learning opportunities embedded into redesigned coursework. Examining the outcomes from a framework of dissonance (Shaffer et al., 2016) was helpful in showing where teacher candidates fell along the various stages, and how they moved through those stages to make sense of their experiences. Excerpts from the reflections showed promise that teacher candidates were transformed by their experiences in this course, and prepared for dual lives as future educators and effective citizens. Teacher candidates authentically addressed challenges they faced while working in classrooms with students with disabilities. Several candidates' preconceived notions regarding the education of students with disabilities were challenged. Perspectives were broadened as their written reflections indicated they had a better understanding of the struggles of students with disabilities by the end of the semester.

More importantly, service learning is a valuable component to preparing teachers and provides opportunities for collaborative engagement from all stakeholders involved in the PDS. It is an opportunity for teacher candidates and faculty to develop relationships with others outside of the campus environment, engage more in curriculum development around the needs and interests of students, participate in inquiry, and ultimately prepare them for the future of education and transformational teacher preparation. However, additional studies are needed to further understand how service learning and reflection help inform teacher preparation in clinically rich settings. It would also be helpful to the field to look at how teacher candidate perceptions of working with students with disabilities evolve over time.

A shift in focus from traditional classroom teaching to service learning in the community offers promising and transformational results. Service learning within the context of a UPDS model opens the door for teacher candidates to gain a better understanding of the challenges facing students with moderate and severe disabilities in an authentic urban context. While this understanding is important, it is merely a small step toward improved outcomes for this marginalized group of students. Future collaborative work is necessary to ensure more actions are taken to increase quality outcomes for students with moderate and severe disabilities, teacher candidates and community partners. Far too often, we see students with disabilities in more restrictive settings, when inclusion in a less restrictive placement would be preferred. Our students were challenged by this dilemma and many shifted from approaching the issue as a deficit perspective to developing a social justice stance (Sawyer et al., 2016). Preparing teacher candidates for future advocacy work as civically engaged citizens is needed and can be powerful, especially in a society where education is changing rapidly, and students with disabilities remain vulnerable amidst those changes.

University faculty members are expected to provide students with transformational learning experiences. Service learning within a PDS model gave the PIR and RCF an opportunity to bring the text to life by offering teacher candidates meaningful examples of instructional practices for students with moderate to severe disabilities. It also provided a natural setting for inquiry and thoughts for future research. This study suggests that PDSs can offer a unique third space where teacher candidates, teachers, faculty, and students can come together and further transform practice through creativity in thinking and reflecting on practice (Sawyer et al., 2016). PDSs provide a powerful opportunity to develop teaching skills while addressing real life challenges in classrooms and school settings. Snow-Gerono (2005) found teachers work best in environments where they can question and maintain attitudes of openness to uncertainty and change. This experiences help transform the teaching profession to a culture of learning, growing and risk-taking, rather than one of defensiveness and isolation.

Further, Dana and Yendol-Hoppey (2014) maintain that qualitative work by university researchers related to issues of context is often intended for academic audiences, while school-based voices are limited. The study moves beyond this notion and can inform practitioners as it examines teacher candidates' perspectives and offers insight into how connecting theory to practice can enhance teacher candidate learning. In the future we need more research on classroom teachers' voices working in PDSs that were not reflected in this study. Moving forward and as the PDS relationship continues to evolve, it will be important to work closely with classroom teachers and other school professionals in transforming professional practice using teacher inquiry (Burns et al., 2015; Dana & Yendol-Hoppey, 2014).

In sum, colleges of education faculty must work together with our school-based partners to transform the way educators are prepared and expand clinically based preparation models. To prepare effective teachers, we must radically shift from traditional academic preparation and coursework to programs grounded in clinical practice (Darling-Hammond, 2012; NCATE, 2010; NAPDS, 2008). PDSs can and should be a vehicle for this change, especially in today's educational climate that mandates accountability and outcomes. To move clinical practice forward, PDS partnerships must stop viewing themselves as two separate entities and instead, form a true partnership with shared goals, purposes, common definitions, and consistent expectations and role identification (Baum & Korth, 2013).

REFERENCES

Anderson, J., & Erickson, J. (2003). Service-learning in preservice teacher education. *Academic Exchange Quarterly, 7*(2), 111–115.

Ash, S., Clayton, P., & Atkinson, M. (2005). Integrating reflection and assessment to capture and improve student learning. *Michigan Journal of Service Learning, 11*(2), 49–60.

Baum, A., & Korth, B. (2013). Preparing classroom teachers to be cooperating teachers: A report of current efforts, beliefs, challenges, and associated recommendations. *Journal of Early Childhood Teacher Education, 34*(2), 171–190.

Braun, V., & Clarke, V. (2006). Using thematic analysis in psychology. *Qualitative Research in Psychology, 3*(2), 77–101.

Bringle, R., & Hatcher, J. (2009). Innovative practices in service-learning and curricular engagement. *New Directions for Higher Education, 147*(Fall), 37–46.

Browder, D., & Spooner, F. (2011). *Teaching students with moderate and severe disabilities.* New York, NY: The Guilford Press.

Burns, R., Yendol-Hoppey, D., & Jacobs, J. (2015). High quality teaching requires collaboration: How partnerships can create a true continuum of professional learning for educators. *The Educational Forum, 79*(1), 53–67.

Council for the Accreditation of Educator Preparation. (2013). *Council for the Accreditation of Educator Preparation accreditation standards.* Washington, DC: Council for the Accreditation of Educator Preparation.

Carrington, S. (2011). Service-learning within higher education: Rhizomatic interconnections between university and the real world. *Australian Journal of Teacher Education, 36*(6), 1–14.

Carter, E., & Kennedy, C. (2006). Promoting access to the general curriculum using peer support strategies. *Research and Practice for Persons with Severe Disabilities, 31*(4), 284–292.

Dana, N. F., & Yendol-Hoppey, D. (2014). *The reflective educator's guide to classroom research: Learning to teach and teaching to learn through practitioner inquiry* (3rd ed.). Thousand Oaks, CA: Corwin.

Darling-Hammond, L. (2012, March). *Teacher education and teacher quality: What will it take to build a true profession?* Keynote address presented at the annual meeting of the National Association for Professional Development Schools, Las Vegas, NV.

Eyler, J., & Giles, J. (1999). *Where's the learning in service-learning?* San Francisco, CA: Jossey-Bass.

Gibson, M., Hauf, P., Long, B. S., & Sampson, G. (2011). Reflective practice in service learning: Possibilities and limitations. *Education and Training, 53*(4), 284–296.

Gutierrez, K.D. (2008). Developing a sociocritical literacy in the third space. *Reading Research Quarterly, 43*(2), 148–164.

Ikpeze, C., Broikou, K., Hildenbrand, S., & Gladstone-Brown, W. (2012). PDS collaboration as third space: An analysis of the quality of learning experiences in a PDS partnership. *Studying Teacher Education, 8*(3), 275–288.

Jackson, L., Ryndak, D., & Wehmeyer, M. (2010). The dynamic relationship between context, curriculum, and student learning: A case for inclusive education as a research-based practice. *Research and Practice for Persons with Severe Disabilities, 33*(4), 175–195.

Jenkins, A., & Sheehey, P. (2009). Implementing service learning in special education coursework: What we learned. *Education, 129*(4), 668–682.

National Association of Professional Development Schools. (2008). *What it means to be a professional development school.* National Association for Professional Development Schools. Author.

National Council for Accreditation of Teacher Education's Blue Ribbon Panel. (2010). *Transforming teacher education through clinical practice: A national strategy to prepare effective teachers.* Washington, DC: Author.

National Task Force on Civic Learning and Democratic Engagement. (2012). *A crucible moment: College learning and democracy's future.* Washington, DC: Association of American Colleges and Universities.

Ryndak, D., & Alper, S. (2003). *Curriculum and instruction for students with significant disabilities in inclusive settings* (2nd ed.). Boston, MA: Allyn & Bacon.

Sawyer, R., Neel, M., & Coulter, M. (2016). At the crossroads of clinical practice and teacher leadership: A changing paradigm for professional practice. *International Journal of Teacher Leadership, 7*(1), 17–36.

Schaffer, C., White, M., & Brown, C. (2016). *Questioning assumptions and challenging perceptions: Becoming an effective teacher in urban environments.* Lanham, MD: Rowman & Littlefield.

Sherman, R., & Webb, R. (1988). *Qualitative research in education: Focus and methods.* Bristol, PA: Falmer Press.

Snow-Gerono, J. (2005). Professional development in a culture of inquiry: PDS teachers identify the benefits of professional learning communities. *Teaching and Teacher Education, 21*(3), 241–256.

CHAPTER 9

UNDERSTANDING TEACHER CANDIDATES' PERSPECTIVES OF LEARNING TO TEACH DURING AN INNOVATIVE SUMMER PRACTICUM

David Hoppey
University of North Florida

David Allsopp, Michael W. Riley, Aimee Frier, and Stacy Hahn
University of South Florida

ABSTRACT

This qualitative study focused on how teacher candidates come to understand, develop, and construct meanings from the daily events and interactions of an alternative summer practicum experience that is tightly coupled with a methods course. Four assertions emerged from the data that informed the design of a summer practicum and important areas of learning on the part of teacher candidates. The importance of tightly coupling coursework

Outcomes of High-Quality Clinical Practice in Teacher Education, pages 171–194
Copyright © 2018 by Information Age Publishing
All rights of reproduction in any form reserved.

with rich clinical experiences as an important component of effective teacher preparation is discussed, including how the findings of this study contribute to the research base on effective teacher preparation practices.

With the call for increased accountability and improved teacher quality, teacher education programs must thoughtfully integrate opportunities for teacher candidates to demonstrate competencies reflective of highly effective teachers. Critics are increasingly scrutinizing colleges of education contending that traditional teacher preparation programs do not adequately prepare teachers for the realities of teaching in today's schools. Specifically, critics contend that teacher education programs do not adequately prepare teacher candidates' subject matter knowledge, as programs emphasize theoretical coursework over the application of knowledge and skills in practice (Greenburg & Walsh, 2008; Hess, 2002; Walsh, Glasser, & Wilcox, 2006). Further, one longstanding critique of teacher preparation programs has been the lack of connectedness between field experiences and coursework resulting in program fragmentation where information is delivered in compartmentalized topical chunks that are often devoid of any close associations to what candidates are experiencing in their field placements (Clift & Brady, 2005; Zeichner, 2010). In part, these critiques have led to the growth of alternative teacher education or fast track programs that minimize the role colleges of education play in training new teachers (McConney, Price, & Woods-McConney, 2012; Milner, 2013; Zeichner, 2010).

To address this dilemma and combat the mounting criticism, leading scholars and teacher education organizations have recently described how universities can strengthen teacher education and enhance teacher outcomes by creating clinically based teacher education programs in partnership with local schools (CAEP, 2013; Cochran-Smith & Lytle, 2009; NCATE, 2010; Rosaen & Florio-Ruane 2008; Zeichner, 2010). The National Research Council (2010) identified the development of strong field experiences as an essential teacher preparation characteristic that has the potential to improve teacher candidate learning and positively impact PK–12 student learning outcomes. Similarly, Standard 2 of the Council for the Accreditation of Educator Preparation (CAEP) requires that teacher education programs ensure that "effective partnerships and high-quality clinical practice are central to preparation so that candidates develop the knowledge, skills, and professional dispositions necessary to demonstrate positive impact on all P–12 students' learning and development" (CAEP, 2013). These standards were developed using research that suggests that programs that tightly couple methods and content coursework with field experiences positively influence teacher candidate outcomes (Darling-Hammond, Hammerness, Grossman, Rust, & Shulman, 2005; Leko, Brownell, Sindelar, & Murphy, 2012; Zeichner & Conklin, 2005). Thus, learning to teach occurs in a teacher education program where teacher candidates participate by working with students, curriculum, and evidence based teaching strategies while immersed in theory about learning, development, and subject matter (Darling-Hammond & Baratz-Snowden, 2007).

Innovative summer field experiences can provide an untapped opportunity to offer a clinically rich environment devoid of the accountability policies that often hinder teacher education programs interested in identifying quality and curricular flexible placements for teacher candidates to learn to teach. However, the data on the impact of alternative summer field experiences is scarce and primarily centers on teacher candidate involvement in short 1 to 2 week long camps (Cuddapah, Masci, Smallwood, & Holland, 2008; Green et al., 2011; Hanuscin & Musikul, 2007; Holmes, 2011). Though this research base is extremely limited, it is important to note that teacher candidates viewed these experiences as beneficial. Positives of summer field experiences included teacher candidate appreciation for hands-on lesson planning and curriculum development, focused on effective differentiated instruction, as well as evidence based instructional and classroom management strategies. On the other hand, candidates noted that they would have preferred more in depth experiences with more instructional coaching to support their work on specific teaching practices. It is interesting to note that none of the studies described how the summer experiences were integrated within the systematic development and implementation of a school–university partnership nor were visualized as an integral component of the overall teacher education program.

Given the importance of providing teacher candidates with well-designed clinically intensive experiences where they have the opportunity to emphasize the development and application of knowledge and skills in practice, the special education undergraduate program at the University of South Florida redesigned their program to include a sequence of clinical experiences across the five semesters of the program, including one summer semester. This program revision occurred with the help of a 325T grant from the U.S. Department of Education, Office of Special Education Programs.

To date, uncovering how specific teacher education components impact teacher candidate development remains elusive (Clift & Brady, 2005; Zeichner, 2010). Some empirical evidence suggests that programs that couple methods and content coursework with field experiences positively influence teacher candidate outcomes (Darling-Hammond et al., 2005; Leko et al., 2012; Zeichner & Conklin, 2005). In essence, tightly coupling coursework with fieldwork appears to be a possible proverbial bridge to link the theory to practice gap that often plagues teacher education programs (Hoppey, 2016).

In order to develop clinical experiences that incorporate the kinds of practices suggested by Leko et al. (2012), teacher educators must have access to school sites that can support the development of these practices. A major concern for teacher education programs is locating and cultivating school partnerships where this can be accomplished. There are multiple barriers that make enacting this vision difficult. Factors such as high stakes testing and accountability (Ledoux & McHenry, 2008), lack of well-trained clinical teachers (Clarke, Triggs, & Nielsen, 2014), school culture that promotes the perception of university teacher candidates as "free hands" as opposed to developing teachers, and universities that devalue faculty involving themselves in the time-intensive business of field supervision and mentoring are examples of the kinds of barriers that can make the development and sustainability of clinical experiences difficult (Yendol-Hoppey, Hoppey, Morewood, Hayes, & Graham, 2013).

Alternative summer field experiences held during summer session are often overlooked and untapped opportunities for teacher educators and school partners to consider to provide the types of experiences suggested within the literature. Most PK–12 schools are still in session well into June and run summer enrichment programs for their students. To date, the research on alternative summer field experiences is limited and focuses essentially on short duration camps or fairs that typically last a week or less (Hanuscin & Musikul, 2007; Holmes, 2011) or a few weeks at best (Cuddapah et al., 2008; Green et al., 2011), and may or may not be academically focused. An interesting finding from the limited research base is that even these brief teaching episodes provided teacher candidates with hands-on experiences that included lesson planning, curriculum development, utilization of instructional practices that needed to be differentiated for a variety of learners, and application of classroom management skills for small group and one-to-one instruction. Results from these studies suggest that teacher candidates viewed these experiences as beneficial to their development but would have preferred more in depth experiences and coaching to strengthen their teaching practices. It is interesting to note that none of the studies described how the summer experiences were (a) integrated with the systematic development and implementation of a school-university partnership, (b) academically focused, or (c) visualized as an integral component of the overall teacher education program. Given the importance of providing teacher candidates with well-designed clinical experiences where they have the opportunity to emphasize the development and application of knowledge and skills in practice, this study investigates participants' learning within a Summer Institute (SI). The SI is designed to explicitly support teacher candidate learning while challenging them to utilize their existing knowledge and skills to enact assessment and instruction practices.

STUDY CONTEXT

In response to the critique that teacher preparation programs fail to prepare effective teachers, we engaged in revising the scope and structure of our undergraduate special education preparation program. The program is structured so that all special education coursework and field experiences are organized according to 3–6 credit hour instructional blocks across five semesters. Each instructional block is closely aligned with an intentionally designed field experience. The instructional blocks build teacher candidate capacity to meet program goals in a developmental way. This is done by systematically moving teacher candidates from initial understandings to advanced understandings, to application, to proficiency, to mastery.

Each practica and the final internship are designed and implemented in concert with the focus of our curriculum and in collaboration with our school partners. Each of these field experiences have a particular focus that correlates with "content big ideas" emphasized in the associated instructional block. The field experiences build upon the content of previous semesters and we attempt to work with school partners to enact field experiences that integrate both the program curriculum with school partner needs and practices. This particular study occurs during the program's third semester where teacher candidates participate in a SI that occurs at one of our partner schools.

The SI is an innovative 6-week program implemented by the special education program and Pepin Academy which is a local charter school for students with disabilities. Pepin Academy is a tuition-free school serving approximately 600 third to 12th grade students with disabilities. Students attending are primarily identified as having learning disabilities, intellectual disabilities, or autism spectrum disorders. The two-fold purpose of the SI is to provide an alternative learning experience focused on developing reading and mathematics skills for K–12 students with disabilities when school is not is session. Simultaneously, the SI offers the opportunity for teacher candidates to implement evidence-based practices as the "teachers of record."

THE USF-PEPIN ACADEMY PARTNERSHIP: THE GENESIS OF THE SUMMER INSTITUTE

The genesis of the USF-Pepin partnership was a meeting at Pepin Academies between several school leaders (i.e., director/principal, assistant principals, and school founder) and two faculty members in USF's Department of Special Education. The purpose of the meeting was to explore a possible partnership that would be mutually beneficial to Pepin and to USF. A beginning list of potential partner activities was developed across several subsequent meetings. Initially, our partnership activities centered on USF providing support to Pepin related to several areas of need. For example, USF special education faculty facilitated a professional learning community (PLC) with a group of middle grades (4–8) teachers focused on mathematics instruction. The PLC was structured as a book study where two USF faculty members met with the teachers on a regular basis, discussed assigned readings, and worked with them to implement an inquiry project around a mathematics related question each teacher had with respect to their students. Another example of our initial partnership activities was USF supporting Pepin to evaluate the impact of a program they were implementing related to developing problem solving and self-regulation skills among students. This consisted of helping Pepin first identify relevant data sets the school had collected that might be helpful in gauging the impact to the program. A doctoral student in special education then worked with the school's data specialist to complete the analysis.

As the first year of our partnership progressed a Memorandum of Understanding (MOU) was developed between USF and Pepin that formalized our developing partnership. At the same time, USF undergraduate program faculty in special education were finalizing a major revision of the undergraduate program in special education (described in the previous section) through funding from a 325T grant from the U.S. Department of Education, Office of Special Education Programs. An important component of the revised program is the SI, where special education teacher candidates apply what they are learning about effective instruction, co-teaching, and classroom/behavior management in a summer school/extended day environment. The SI was scheduled to occur during the third of five semesters for each cohort of students. Of course, we needed to identify a partner school where the SI could occur. At the time, Pepin ran 1-week summer camps for students focusing on certain areas of interest but did not implement a summer school. The USF faculty shared the idea of the SI with Pepin's administration and they were very excited about the prospect of working collaboratively with us to implement the SI with their students. Primarily, Pepin agreed to provide classroom space and other physical resources (e.g., access to the school media center/library, copying machines, athletic equipment, sensory lab equipment for students with ASD who have sensory impairments, space for the seminars for teacher candidates led by USF faculty, etc.), organize the recruitment of students including necessary paperwork, and to assist USF faculty in grouping students based on needs. Additionally, particular administrators would be on campus during the summer and agreed to provide necessary student academic information including access to students' cumulative folders that included individualized education plans and other academic related information necessary for instructional planning by USF teacher candidates for Pepin students. The

USF Department of Special Education agreed to operate all other aspects of the SI. This includes preparing and supporting USF third semester special education teacher candidates to provide summer school instruction across a four week period of time, USF faculty administering the summer school, and USF faculty supporting the teacher candidates and Pepin students during the summer school through seminars, coaching, and mentorship of teacher candidates.

The SI experience integrates coursework with an intensive field experience. Prior to the field-based component, teacher candidates participate in a 2-week on-site course. This course focuses on revisiting and applying the knowledge and skills learned in literacy, mathematics, classroom management, and co-teaching from courses in previous semesters. After this, teacher candidates begin the SI as classroom teachers at Pepin Academy. Pepin Academy students attend the SI four mornings a week (Monday–Thursday) from 8:00 a.m. to 12:00 p.m. for 4 weeks. Pepin Academy provides in-kind support for the program such as classroom materials, copy machine access, and upfront consultation about the needs of students attending. School personnel collaborate with university faculty to design, implement, and monitor the students' progress as well as the institute itself.

The role of faculty and doctoral students during the SI is intensive. First, vertical staffing is used to coordinate the institute as faculty teach the coursework and simultaneously supervise the field experience daily (Tom, 1997). In traditional field placements, classroom teachers directly supervise teacher candidates (McIntyre, Byrd, & Foxx, 1996) and faculty visit classrooms to support and evaluate. However, since classroom teachers are not present during the SI, university faculty provide oversight and coaching. The supervision approach mirrors the model presented by Jacobs, Burns, and Yendol-Hoppey (2014) which includes: (a) direct assistance using the practices of fostering critical reflection, fostering adaptive expertise, and providing targeted instructional feedback; (b) individual support with research based practices including challenging PST to take risks and utilize their existing knowledge and apply it in practice, and helping PST teachers cope with stress; (c) creating learner-centered communities where PST have opportunities to support each other; (d) curriculum support with the practices of fostering theory and practice connections and strengthening curriculum planning; and (e) research for innovation where PST reflect on their own practice and innovating.

Direct supervision involved formal and informal teacher candidate observations as well as a summative evaluation. Additionally, faculty facilitated weekly seminars throughout the summer to discuss teacher candidate progress, instruction, and concerns. Moreover, faculty were also on-site to administer the SI, to provide coaching, to assist with behavioral situations that teacher candidates had difficulty addressing, and meet with co-teaching teams to problem solve as needed.

Between 75–85 Pepin students and 25–30 teacher candidates participate in the SI. A co-teaching model is used that typically pairs two teacher candidates together to teach a small group of approximately six to eight students with disabilities. The co-teaching model provides an opportunity for teacher candidates to collaborate together and tailor the curriculum to meet student needs. This structure provides teacher candidates the opportunity to move beyond mandated curriculum typically found in classrooms during the school year to learn how to plan, collaborate, and co-teach with one another. The SI faculty supported teacher candidates as they implement evidence-based instructional practices.

The SI is a unique experience that emphasizes teacher candidates providing research-based reading and mathematics instruction during for students with disabilities. In the SI, K–12 student participation is voluntarily and offered at no cost. Given this unique configuration including co-teaching, research-based practice, faculty supervision, and teacher candidate responsibility for instructional decision-making, this study investigates what teacher candidates perceive they learned within an alternative summer field experience designed to support teacher candidate learning within a university–school partnership. Since summer field experiences are a relatively unexplored topic in the general teacher education literature, and even less explored in the special education teacher education literature, we believed that investigating participants' learning within a SI would contribute to teacher educators understanding of the potential of alternative field experiences.

METHODOLOGY

Two research questions framed this study: "What SI design structures supported teacher candidates' learning?" and "What do teacher candidates learn as a result of participating in the SI?" The study was qualitative in nature and epistemologically grounded in constructivism (Lincoln & Guba, 2000). As a result, we acknowledge that as researchers' our interpretation of the studied phenomenon is a construction as was the participants' interpretation of their experience.

Data Collection and Analysis

Our research team was comprised of five researchers who participated in the data collection and analysis process over a 2-year period. These researchers included three faculty and two doctoral students who taught during two different years of the SI. Focus groups served as the primary data source. Participation included 62 students drawn from two cohorts of special education majors across two summer semesters. We conducted ten focus groups, comprised of six to eight students after each summer session was completed. Each focus group lasted approximately 60 minutes. During the focus groups, we gathered teacher candidate perspectives of their learning in relation to the content and structure of their experience. An open-ended survey served as a secondary data source. This data primarily served as a tool for identifying and crafting the questions that would be explored through the focus group.

We used a constant comparative method which required each researcher to take one piece of data at a time and compare it to all other pieces of data allowing for patterns to emerge (Strauss & Corbin, 1998). Data analysis began as our research team independently open coded the data by breaking down, examining, comparing, conceptualizing, and categorizing data in light of the research questions. After engaging in this initial independent open coding process, we met to share and discuss our codes. Together as a research team, we compared our initial independently identified codes in light of the research question and collaboratively identified a set of shared codes. Once we identified the shared codes, we collapsed the open codes and reached consensus on four themes. Each of these themes led to a corresponding assertion which informed our understanding of what teacher candidates' learned during the SI. Finally, we returned to the data to specifically "re-search" for challenges or threats some teacher candidates faced in relation to the four assertions. These challenges or threats to learning are included within each illustration to emphasize how those interested in engaging in this kind of teacher candidate development might guard against these challenges or threats.

Role of Researchers, Credibility, and Trustworthiness

Finally, our research group was comprised of special education faculty as well as doctoral students. All of us taught at least 1 year of the SI providing teacher candidates daily support. Researcher triangulation consisted of our initial independent analysis followed by our research team's collaborative analysis which enhanced the credibility and trustworthiness of this study (Patton, 2002). Finally, in addition to re-searching for challenges and threats, to guard against providing a "victory story," once we believed our analysis was complete, we asked a colleague who was not involved in the data analysis to review the data in light of the findings.

FINDINGS

In total, we present the four assertions that illustrate what we learned with respect to our research questions (Figure 9.1). Assertions 1 and 2 provide insight into the research question: "What SI design structures supported TCs' learning?" Assertions 3 and 4 offer insight into the research question: "What do TCs learn as a result of participating in the SI?" Each assertion and challenges to each assertion are discussed in this section.

> **Assertion 1:** *Through collaboration TCs learn to compromise and challenge, as well as, establish a professional relationship, hold each other accountable, and learn from others.*

Evidence of Assertion

During the SI, teacher candidates worked side-by-side and collaborated with faculty to plan, teach, and assess. As a result, most candidates began to recognize the power of working together. Comments indicating the strength of their co-teaching experience included: "We did everything together...we worked off each other's strengths and weaknesses, and we

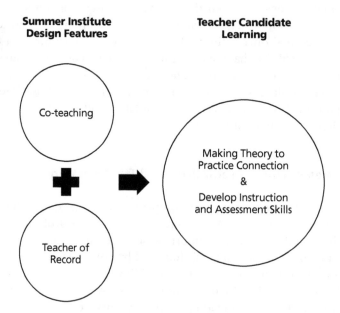

Figure 9.1 Design features (Assertions 1 & 2) and teacher candidate learning (Assertions 3 & 4).

were able to fill in the gaps that each of us had" (P3, 3:83) and "We constantly revised and fine tuned our interactions with the students. It was a fine example of a co-teach experience" (P4, 4:45). As a result, the SI became a laboratory for learning how to co-teach. Compromise between the teaching pairs became immediately important as the teacher candidates recognized having different ideas of what and how to do things in the classroom. Their differing approaches sometimes led to conflict that, early on, challenged their friendships. As a result, teacher candidates quickly realized that they needed to develop new ways of working together because of their responsibility to help their students' learn. One candidate said, we needed "to find a way to work together, to meet in the middle and make it work" (P2, 2:9). As their professional and personal relationships evolved, they indicated that they learned to challenge each other "by sitting down and saying 'why do you want that' or 'why do you think it's going to work,'" and then finding we understand each other better" (P2, 2:10). Candidates learned how to problem solve together, with other educators, and even with parents to challenge and compromise with each other to target instruction.

Teacher candidates also learned the importance of collaborative problem solving. This became particularly important as they responded to student behavior challenges. They learned that by sharing multiple perspectives of what causes certain student behaviors to arise and how to respond to these behaviors, allowing them to generate more constructive ideas than they might have constructed individually. For example, one pair of candidates was challenged by increasing instances and intensity of a student's aggression toward her peers. After working with their instructor to develop a plan, they "came together with her [the student's] grandmother, to try and address the issue" (P3, 3:7). Together with the grandparent, the candidates developed a successful action plan to prevent the antecedents to the student's aggressive behaviors. By the end of the SI, most candidates recognized the value of having multiple ideas and multiple experiences to draw on in resolving challenging behaviors among their students. Candidates learned how to problem solve together, with faculty, and even with parents to brainstorm, plan and administer behavior plans for students who were demonstrating disruptive behaviors. Similarly, one candidate discussed, when her students were not "getting on task, [my co-teaching partner] would kind of jump in to help me get them on task" (P3, 3:55). Or, as another candidate discussed, "when one of us reached our frustration level, the other one knew and jumped in" (P4, 4:61). In this case, teacher candidates learned how to be in touch with a partner's needs and respond when needed. Many candidates talked about being frustrated by challenging student behaviors or by students failing to respond to instruction. However, co-teaching provided problem-solving opportunities and support as teacher candidates experienced frustration with their students.

Although teacher candidates faced challenges related to collaboration, many still believed that co-teaching allowed them to learn from one another. Many candidates recognized experiencing a balance between partners in management, instruction, and, subject matter knowledge. One candidate explained that she was paired with "a person who was [her] yang." She illustrated what she meant by "yang" by comparing her own "controlling" management style with her partner's "laid back" approach to teaching and classroom management. She indicated that eventually their relationship developed into "just a great balance" that benefitted student learning (P6, 6:19). Other teacher candidates indicated that collaboration led to enhancing certain subject area content or instructional strategies by learning from a partner who, as one teacher candidate expressed, was "more knowledgeable" than her in certain areas, and reciprocating by supporting her partner's learning through her own strengths. By the end of the SI, these collaboration skills facilitated teacher candidates' collaborative decision making, as they planned and implemented instruction, assessment, and behavior management in their co-taught classrooms.

Important to note is that learning these important collaboration skills often required intensive support from the on-site faculty. In fact, teacher candidates regularly called upon faculty to help them enhance their ability to work together and to solve problems related to classroom management, instruction, and assessment. One teacher candidate shared, "The professors were there to help when ever we needed assistance" (P4, 4:202) and another explained that

> when we were confused about how to teach certain concepts and skills to the students, one of our supervisors actually taught us how to teach it. By him doing this it cleared up confusions that we had. Just by him teaching us, helped us to plan together how we were going to teach the math skills to the students the next day. (P4, 4:309)

The candidates recognized that the conversations and opportunities to work in the classroom with their professors generated specific ideas that strengthened their teaching and learning. For most candidates, the collaboration skills were the most important skills they identified learning during the SI. We really had "to learn to work with others who may not necessarily share [their] the same skills, work ethic, knowledge, beliefs, or sense of responsibility within the classroom. But I learned a lot" (P4, 4:60). In general, teacher candidates recognized that their collaboration extended beyond their co-teaching partner to include the faculty that were on-site to offer support.

Challenges to Assertion One

As a part of co-teaching, candidates sometimes needed to hold each other accountable. Specifically, candidates recognized that during the SI their level of involvement was uneven. For example, one candidate said that if she could experience the SI again, "she would have communicated more with her partner about planning and responsibility." She noted, "At the beginning, I think that it was up to me to do more, but overtime I began to really contribute" (P3, 3:11). Other times, the candidates believed they needed to exert themselves within their professional relationships in order to ensure student needs were met. For example, some candidates indicated that her partner needed to "be accountable to meet student needs should take precedence over any of their own personal goals, such as friendship or likeability." In these cases, professional responsibility was defined as "holding each other accountable to each other and to their students."

However, reaching this understanding of co-teaching benefits required time and practice. For example, some candidates emphasized the difference between learning about co-teaching during the pre-planning experience to doing co-teaching once the SI began. In instances where co-teaching partners did not initially get along well with each other, most learned to develop a professional relationship. Several candidates talked about having difficulty understanding what to expect from their partners. Some candidates struggled with understanding how to deal with "uncooperative partners" (P4, 4:48). Others were challenged by "not knowing each other's expectations" (P4, 4:46), and inexperience in "motivating others to work collaboratively together" (P4, 4:44). One TC used athletics as a metaphor for collaboration with her partner. She said, "Sometimes [I] needed to be separate, kind of like an athlete, like when you're on the field and your teammates are your teammates, not your friends" (P6, 6:11). This approach to collaboration required some candidates to "fake it till we make it" as a part of maintaining a professional relationship. One candidate explained that in the beginning we "put on a good show and [to] not let [our] students see [our] frustration, always respecting each other even when we couldn't stand each other" (P4, 4:118). In many, but not all, cases partners developed a greater sense of respect for and trust in their partners as they worked together. In sum, most candidates developed a set of productive co-teaching skills. The SI structure required the candidates to work through challenges on behalf of their students.

Assertion 2: *The teacher candidate's position as the "teacher of record" helped them assume responsibility for student learning.*

Evidence of Assertion

Serving as the classroom "teachers of record" was eye-opening to the candidates and the experience helped them begin to understand what their future role would be. The candidates talked about how the SI differed from earlier field experiences. One candidate shared, "I think this experience opened eyes to the role of the special educator, and the problems we'll be facing, and why the burnout rates are so high and why people get so frustrated." Another candidate explained:

> I think that because we were the teachers in the classroom, we weren't under somebody else, we had a greater appreciation for what goes into it. And we had to work a lot harder. I mean for my other experiences I was in a resource class where there wasn't really all that much I could do because my teacher was so thorough with everything that she did. I really only got to teach maybe five times during the whole semester. And two of those were for observation...In this one I could get to know my students. I can assign the work. I can do the assessments. And it gave me the hands on experience that I really need to make the connections. (P3, 3:43)

Teacher candidates also identified that the SI experiences caused them to consider the special education teacher's role in establishing the learning environment. As one candidate described, "It's so much more than just teaching them in the classroom and finding different strategies...I mean there's a lot of different things that I didn't really think about until I was actually in a classroom" (P2, 2:48). Almost all of the candidates noted that they felt a shift from student to teacher as a result of participating in the SI. One candidate explained:

> I learned more this semester than I did in the last two combined, hands down, like totally responsible in the actual classroom. I completely agree with that. Because we always say, like, you can get a 4.0 and graduate, but you're not going to learn half, anything, until you get in the classroom, like, that's not going to matter. And I appreciate that, I really do.... I don't suppose I was necessarily expecting it, because I was still going to be in my undergrad practicum that counts for a grade with eight other assessments combined. (P2, 2:73)

Another candidate explained:

> Having the opportunity to actually have my own classroom, my own students, and choosing my own curriculum was invaluable to aiding my development as a special educator. When in other people's classrooms, it is hard to get a real feel for how a classroom should be run with regards to implementing instruction based on individual student needs. We were allowed to review our students' files, assess them and make instructional decisions based on what

we felt were the most effective instructional practices for our students. I feel I am more prepared in the actual nuts and bolts of teaching due to my summer experience. (P4, 4:17)

And another candidate described why she felt more confident in her professional skills and abilities:

Being a primary figure in the classroom brought a sense of reality and responsibility to the experience. Instead of just being held accountable to an evaluation or to a project, I was accountable to my students. They were real, meaningful opportunities for independent application and exploration of my knowledge.

The candidates collectively indicated this SI design contributed to deeper and more complex understandings of their roles and responsibilities as special education teacher once they complete their program and begin their careers.

Challenges to Assertion Two

Although the candidates identified the learning opportunities that serving as the teacher of record brought them, many of them still identified challenges. Some candidates struggled with the amount of work they were asked to do. In many cases they described having too many assignments that kept them from focusing on any one assignment well. For example:

It's terrible to say, but you know, you do worry about your grade. And you have a student involved, so I think that needs to be your priority, the same time, you are worried about getting a good grade on the thing so you can get your grant or you get your scholarship or whatever. (P7, 7:37)

The candidates often experienced a tension between being a student and the teacher of record. The tension was a result of the assignments attached to the course. One candidate noted, "My co-teacher made sure she did the projects which was her grade. Other candidates emphasized they felt "overwhelmed by projects" and "the paperwork" associated with assignments. They felt that "having to do two projects on top of planning for everyday instruction" proved difficult.

Finally, some candidates identified a lack of curriculum materials and financial concerns related to assuming the classroom teacher role. For example, complications existed related to acquiring necessary teaching resources. One candidate noted that, "Not having an outline for curriculum to teach, we were just thrown in with very little experience" (P1, 1:32).

Another candidate indicated that "the school should provide materials just as they do to regular teachers. Especially if we are free" (P4, 4:221).

With respect to our first research question—"What SI design structures supported teacher candidates' learning?"—structuring the SI so that candidates co-taught as teachers of record were two SI design features that emerged as important. Our next two assertions emerged as we considered our second research question, "What do candidates learn as a result of participating in the SI?"

Assertion 3: *Tightly coupled coursework and fieldwork facilitated the merging of theory and practice.*

Evidence of Assertion

The candidates emphasized the role that the SI played in helping them merge theory to practice. Candidates were asked to collaboratively develop, deliver, and evaluate their instructional plans based on what they had learned during the past year of their teacher preparation program and with what they were learning and experiencing day to day during the SI. These candidates identified their appreciation for the opportunity to freely "experiment" applying theory to practice. This opportunity had not been available in previous field experiences as they followed the direction of their supervising teachers who were the teacher of record. The SI afforded the teacher candidates the time they needed to link theory to practice. One candidate explained, "Experiencing how abstract processes learned through course readings, lectures, and observations in the field really worked in practice. We had to make connections to specific strategies from courses" (P4, 4:147). Another described that "this took time but we were developing deeper understandings and skills in applying strategies that were unclear to me how to do" (P3, 3:97). Teacher candidates recognized that putting theory into practice was not an abstract exercise since they had "real world responsibility for our student outcomes" (P3, 3:9).

Over the course of the institute, candidates did develop deeper understandings and proficiency in applying specific instructional strategies learned through course lectures, activities, readings, and self-study. These instructional strategies ranged from broad concepts such as differentiated instruction to specific instructional techniques like using Elkonin boxes for word work. The opportunity to practice and develop their teaching skills in a real-world setting provided candidates with multiple opportunities to experiment with instructional strategies. They developed deeper understandings of differentiated instruction and individualized accommodation, discovering that what works for one may not work for or benefit another.

For this reason, candidates consistently echoed sentiments that "all of my students learned differently, so UDL (Universal Design for Learning) was essential" (P4, 4:77). Another candidate summarized, "I mean I guess you figure out that just because it's research supported doesn't mean it's going to work for every kid. Cause some things, you know, you have to differentiate for everybody" (P3, 3:28).

Challenges to Assertion Three

Teacher candidates also faced a challenge as they sought to tie theory from their coursework to their SI classroom practice. Many felt like they had the opportunity to make important connections between their coursework and fieldwork. As one candidate explained, "I learned that the strategies actually mean something and work. It's not just talk that the professors constantly throw at us. I found myself using strategies I didn't think I ever would use" (P1, 1:66). However, although the candidates noted that they felt fortunate to have the knowledge acquired during their methods courses and that many times the strategies did work, they were also challenged when the course knowledge did not readily transfer to their specific classroom with specific students. Even though the strategies seemed promising, sometimes candidates struggled to figure out how to use the strategies in their classrooms. One candidate who was trying to draw on classroom management coursework explained, "trying to use it [the Behavior Intervention Plan process] to get her to do stuff...I enjoy the challenge of trying to figure out what it is we need to do to tap into these kids to have them produce work. 'Cause they can produce work once you figure out what it is you need to tap into. It's just sometimes really hard...But you stay at it" (P6, 6:54). As a result, the candidates needed to understand that making theory to practice links requires patience. The candidates needed to learn how to implement the concepts from their courses as they taught but then recognize that their instruction must be adjusted to the specific context and students.

Assertion 4: *Expectations for teacher candidates to implement research-based instruction and assessment focused the teacher candidates on student learning.*

Evidence of Assertion

Planning for instruction during the SI moved far beyond the scaffolded planning opportunities offered in coursework and prior field experiences. In fact, candidates indicated that one of the greatest challenges during the SI involved planning research-based instruction that would engage students. In prior coursework and field experiences, candidates learned to develop lesson plans and deliver instruction under the direct supervision of special education faculty member and school based mentors. One candidate explained, "It was extremely useful to have the understanding about how to put instructional practices into play, utilize resources, collaborate with others, accommodate all students, incorporate various lesson representations" (P4, 4:360).

During the SI, the responsibility for planning and delivering the research-based instruction taught in the methods courses significantly expanded. For example, one candidate said, we had to "learn to plan for a whole day of instruction versus a 50 minute block" (P4, 4:6). The stakes had changed related to planning, "Instead of just being held accountable to an evaluation of a project, I was accountable to my students" (P4, 4:12). As candidates faced planning the students that they were responsible for, they had to figure out how to implement these strategies in light of identified student needs. This required developing "real world instructional decision-making skills" (P3, 3:9). They were "learning about students by working with them" (P5, 5:44), figuring out how to apply the knowledge and skills they acquired through previous coursework and prior field experiences, and gaining a deeper understanding of how to create a learning context that was responsive to all students' needs.

Although candidates learned a great deal about differentiating instruction to meet student needs during coursework, candidates credited learning about differentiated planning to working closely with their students. Many candidates described they were "learning about students with disabilities by working directly with them" (P4, 3:8). The hands-on, real world SI provided candidates with the opportunity to explore and experiment with their prior learning, and develop new professional understandings. With the responsibility for co-teaching a small group, candidates experienced a "wide range of ages and behaviors" (P4, 4:81), requiring them to draw on their previous experiences to make instructional decisions for their students.

Another candidate discussed how she learned to differentiate instruction for students who were more proficient in some skills than others in the class. In one instance, a particular student demonstrated math calculation skills well above those of her peers, finishing an assignment with complete accuracy long before her classmates. As the candidate said:

> She was also working on higher level math when she was home. So I [the candidate's learning] was trying to figure out that balance of being able to teach the other students basic addition while still working with her on multiplication. (P3, 3:20)

Assessment had always been heavily emphasized in program coursework. However, the SI experiences required the candidates to understand how assessment leads to instructional changes. For example, one candidate discussed her decision to reassess a student's reading skills in order to make learning activities in her class more relevant to his needs, saying she conducted the assessment to "figure out what was important" (P2, 2:30). Another candidate explained:

> Some of my students were still working on phonics and others were working on fluency, and others were working more on comprehension, and one student might be at a pre-primer level, while another was at maybe a second or third grade level. So, assessing where they are and learning how to differentiate instruction was really big for me. (P2, 2:24)

As the candidates used assessment to understand their students' needs, they recognized the importance of differentiating instruction.

Challenges to Assertion Four

The SI offered the candidates more time to implement research based instruction and assessment. Although candidates implemented instructional and assessment techniques taught in their courses, candidates still believed they needed more knowledge of math practices, and clearer explanation of how to use the reading and math interventions for students at different levels. Most candidates valued the help that they received from their professors during the SI:

> When we were confused about how to teach certain concepts and skills to the students, I remember one of our supervisors actually taught us how to teach it. By him doing it cleared up confusions that we had. Just by him teaching us, helped us to plan together how we were going to teach the math skills to the students the next day. (P4, 4:53)

However, given that the candidates were accountable for instruction many candidates wanted more coaching than they were given. "One thing that I felt is that I was not as experienced with the assessments for reading and math and needed more help" (P4, 4:202). Other candidates echoed, they needed "more daily feedback from the supervisors and professors on our teaching skills, practices, etc...." (P4, 4:200). Another candidate added that although she received informal feedback, she would have benefited by "meeting weekly with the co-teaching partner and a professor" (P4, 4:215). Even with the faculty present each day, teacher candidates seem to have wanted more support as they worked towards developing instructional and assessment practices.

In sum, the SI provided the candidates opportunities to practice what they had learned in their coursework related to planning, assessment, and differentiate instruction. However, many candidates wanted even more support with instruction and assessment.

DISCUSSION

The SI enabled our candidates to experience several of the features that Leko et al. (2012) suggest are effective teacher education program practices. First, Leko et al. (2012) discuss systematically integrating coursework and field experiences within university-school partnerships and integrating subject matter and instructional practice knowledge to address the learning and behavioral needs of students with disabilities. Without the strong partnership with the school, this would not have been possible. Teacher candidates, working together under faculty supervision, assumed full responsibility for their students. Teacher candidates organized their classroom environments, developed and implemented classroom management plans, planned for daily reading and math instruction, conducted assessments, evaluated student needs and achievement, and modified their plans and practices based on assessments of students' needs. The result is a specific tailored field experience that allows teacher candidates to experience first-hand the complexities of teaching and provide opportunities to practice the application of practices they are learning. This aligns with a third suggestion by Leko et al. (2012), the need to extend the amount of practice opportunities teacher candidates have to apply the knowledge and skills they are developing across their teacher preparation program. As high-stakes testing drives and often limit teachers' instruction, more effort needs to be made to find opportunities where teacher candidates can have the flexibility to implement and perfect research-based instruction.

Another suggestion offered by Leko et al. (2012) is that teacher educators should utilize data to inform the assessment of their preparation program and make programmatic decisions to improve the outcomes of PK–12 students. Further, the SI allows the program to start collecting data about the impact teacher candidates have on student learning when they are engaged in clinical experiences (CAEP, 2013). In all, this research illustrates the importance of designing field experiences in ways that support teacher candidate's ability to design and implement targeted instruction with scaffolded support from faculty/university supervisors. Although designs like the SI offer potential for teacher candidate learning, broad scale implementation of this type of clinical based model faces many challenges.

One issue confronting most schools today is the summer slide for students in terms of learning loss during the summer break, which can be particularly problematic for students at-risk for failure or who are struggling academically (see Borman & Boulay, 2004 for a comprehensive discussion of summer learning loss). Therefore, partnerships like the SI must find ways to better examine student achievement data longitudinally in conjunction with partner school student performance benchmarks to determine the extent to which students' participation reduces the summer slide effect.

Another challenge is that the SI requires a great deal of faculty resources which are often not provided to support field experiences in teacher education (e.g., faculty were on-site for 25–30 hours each week for a 6-week period of time). Making sure that faculty are adequately compensated for this level of engagement further complicates this dilemma. Even when faculty are adequately compensated, another challenge is the fact that those faculty and doctoral students need to possess effective instructional practices, coaching skills, and the ability to develop strong partnerships with schools. Finally, with respect to the SI, we also need a better understanding of how to move candidates from seeing teaching tasks as assignments for grades toward seeing them as processes for helping them develop their teaching skills.

Future research needs to go beyond this study's findings, which were based on teacher candidates' perceptions. Future studies of alternative experiences could include direct observation data of candidate practice, reflections on their teaching practice, and evaluation of student outcome data. Future research might also explore different forms of coaching that facilitate candidate theory to practice connections (e.g., research supported reading and mathematics instructional as well as assessment practices).

LIMITATIONS

This qualitative study examined the perceptions of two cohorts of teacher candidates participation in an alternative summer clinical experience. Data was collected through focus group interviews. As such, the findings in this study are reflective of this particular teacher candidate group. The extent to which future candidates in the same program or candidates in other programs and other areas of certification would have the same perceptions cannot be asserted. Triangulation of the data was accomplished through a constant comparison process including coding and checks at the individual and group (research team) levels with an external reviewer who evaluated the findings in connection with the coded data. Nevertheless, each member of the research team served as faculty and/or clinical supervisor during at least one of the two SIs where data were collected. Therefore, although there is merit in the participatory quality of this study, there is always possibility that bias contributed to our interpretation of the data.

CONCLUSION

This study investigated the impact that an alternative practicum during the summer had on the professional development of special education teacher candidates. Two design features, an emphasis on co-teaching/collaboration and an emphasis on teacher candidates being the teacher of record, were most important to these teacher candidates with respect to their professional development. Two learning outcomes appear to be most important to these teacher candidates including the ability to make theory to practice connections and the ability to focus on student learning through the use of research supported instructional practices. This study recognizes the power of a school-university partnership that created an alternative summer experience. The study contributes to and expands a growing body of literature on teacher education and the importance of tightly coupling coursework with rich clinical experiences.

REFERENCES

Borman, G. D., & Boulay, M. (Eds.). (2004). *Summer learning: Research, policies, and programs*. New York, NY: Routledge.

Clarke, A., Triggs, V., & Nielsen, W. (2014). Cooperating teacher participation in teacher education: A review of the literature. *Review of Educational Research, 84*(2), 163–202. doi:10.3102/0034654313499618

Clift, R. T., & Brady, P. (2005). Research on methods courses and field experiences. In M. Cochran-Smith & K. M. Zeichner (Eds.), *Studying teacher education: The report of the American Educational Research Association panel on research and teacher education* (pp. 309–424). Washington, DC: American Educational Research Association.

Cochran-Smith, M., & Lytle, S. L. (2009). *Inquiry as stance: Practitioner research for the next generation*. New York, NY: Teachers College Press.

Council for the Accreditation of Educator Preparation. (2013). *Council for the Accreditation of Educator Preparation accreditation standards*. Washington, DC: Author.

Cuddapah, J. L., Masci, F. J., Smallwood, J. E., & Holland, J. (2008). A professional development school-sponsored summer program for at-risk secondary students. *NASSP Bulletin, 92*(4), 261–275.

Darling-Hammond, L., & Baratz-Snowden, J. (2007). A good teacher in every classroom: Preparing the highly qualified teachers our children deserve. *Educational Horizons, 85*(2), 111–132.

Darling-Hammond, L., Hammerness, K., Grossman, P., Rust, F., & Shulman, L. (2005). The design of teacher education programs. In L. Darling-Hammond and J. Bransford (Eds.), *Preparing teachers for a changing world: What teachers should learn and be able to do* (pp. 390–441). San Francisco, CA: Jossey-Bass.

Green, A. M., Kent, A. M., Lewis, J., Feldman, P., Motley, M. R., Baggett, P. V.,...& Simpson, J. (2011). Experiences of elementary pre-service teachers in an urban summer enrichment program. *The Western Journal of Black Studies, 35*(4), 227–239.

Greenburg, J., & Walsh, K. (2008). *No common denominator: The preparation of elementary teachers in mathematics by America's education schools.* Washington, DC: National Council on Teacher Quality. Retrieved from https://www.nctq.org/publications/No-Common-Denominator:-The-Preparation-of-Elementary-Teachers-in-Mathematics-by-Americas-Education-Schools

Hanuscin, D. L., & Musikul, K. (2007). School's IN for summer: An alternative field experience for elementary science methods students. *Journal of Elementary Science Education, 19*(1), 57–68.

Hess, F. M. (2002). Tear down the wall: The case for a radical overhaul of teacher certification. *Educational Horizons, 80*(4), 169–183.

Holmes, J. A. (2011). Math fair: Meeting the challenge of meaningful summer field experiences for elementary mathematics methodology students. *Literacy Information and Computer Education Journal, 2*(2), 356–361.

Hoppey, D. (2016). Developing educators for inclusive classrooms through a rural school-university partnership. *Rural Special Education Quarterly, 35*(1), 13–22.

Jacobs, J., Burns, R. W., & Yendol-Hoppey, D. (2014, April). *What do we know about preservice teacher supervision since the release of the NCATE PDS Standards and the NCATE Blue Ribbon Report? A Meta-Analysis.* Paper presented at the annual meeting of the American Education Research Association in Philadelphia, PA.

Ledoux, M. W., & McHenry, N. (2008). Pitfalls of school-university partnerships. *Clearing House, 81*(4), 155–160.

Leko, M. M., Brownell, M. T., Sindelar, P. T., & Murphy, K. (2012). Promoting preservice special education expertise. *Focus on Exceptional Children, 44*(7), 1–16.

Lincoln, Y. S., & Guba, E. G. (2000). Paradigmatic controversies, contradictions, and emerging confluences. In N. Denzin & Y. Lincoln (Eds.), *Handbook of qualitative research* (pp.163–188). London, England: SAGE.

McConney, A., Price, A., & Woods-McConney, A. (2012). *Fast track teacher education: A review of the research literature on Teach For All schemes.* Perth, Australia: Murdoch University, Centre for Learning, Change and Development.

McIntyre, D. J., Byrd, D. M., & Foxx, S. M. (1996). Field and laboratory experiences. In J. Sikula, T. J. Buttery, & E. Guyton (Eds.), *Handbook of research on teacher education* (2nd ed., pp. 171–193). New York, NY: Macmillan.

Milner, H. R. (2013). *Policy Reforms and De-professionalization of Teaching.* Boulder, CO: National Education Policy Center. Retrieved from http://nepc.colorado.edu/publication/policy-reforms-deprofessionalization.

National Council for the Accreditation of Teacher Education. (2010). *Transforming teacher education through clinical practice: A national strategy to prepare effective teachers.* Retrieved from http://www.caepnet.org/~/media/Files/caep/accreditation-resources/blue-ribbon-panel.pdf

National Research Council. (2010). *Preparing teachers: Building evidence for sound policy.* Washington, DC: National Academy of Sciences.

Patton, M. Q. (2002). *Qualitative research and evaluation methods* (3rd ed.). Thousand Oaks, CA: SAGE.

Rosaen, C., & Florio-Ruane, S. (2008). The metaphors by which we teach: Experience, metaphor and culture in teacher education. In M. Cochran-Smith, S. Nemser, & D. J. McIntyre (Eds.), *Handbook of research on teacher education* (pp. 706–731). New York, NY: Routledge.

Strauss, A., & Corbin, J. (1998). *Basics of qualitative research: Techniques and procedures for developing grounded theory* (2nd ed.). Thousand Oaks, CA: SAGE.

Tom, A. R. (1997). *Redesigning teacher education.* Albany: State University of New York Press.

Walsh, K., Glasser, D., & Wilcox, D. D. (2006). *What education schools aren't teaching about reading and what elementary teachers aren't learning.* Washington, DC: National Council on Teacher Quality. Retrieved from http://www.readingrockets.org/article/what-education-schools-arent-teaching-about-reading-and-what-elementary-teachers-arent

Yendol-Hoppey, D., Hoppey, D., Morewood, A., Hayes, S., & Graham, M. (2013). Micropolitical and identity challenges influencing new faculty participation in teacher education reform: When will we learn? *Teachers College Record, 115*(7), 1–31.

Zeichner, K. (2010). Rethinking the connections between campus courses and field experiences in college- and university-based teacher education. *Journal of Teacher Education, 61*(1–2), 89–99.

Zeichner, K., & Conklin, H. (2005). Teacher education programs. In M. Cochran-Smith & K. Zeichner (Eds.), *Studying teacher education: The report of the AERA panel on research and teacher education,* (pp. 645–736). Washington, DC: American Educational Research Association.

SECTION IV

OUTCOMES OF NEW PROGRAM CONFIGURATIONS

CHAPTER 10

RESTRUCTURING TEACHER PREPARATION WITH CULTURALLY RELEVANT PRINCIPLES

A Best Practice for Clinically Rich Teacher Preparation and 21st Century Learners

**Janice Bell Underwood, Gail K. Dickinson,
and Diana V. Cantu**
Old Dominion University

ABSTRACT

The student population of the United States is becoming more ethnically and racially diverse than ever before. Yet, the teaching workforce remains mostly White and female (Aud et al., 2011). Research suggests new teachers feel ill-prepared to address the growing needs of diverse classrooms and teacher education is culpable for lack of student achievement; and thus, must reform preparation programs to meet the needs of diverse learners (Ladson-Billings, 2000). In order to address these growing concerns, the Darden College of

Outcomes of High-Quality Clinical Practice in Teacher Education, pages 197–218
Copyright © 2018 by Information Age Publishing

Education (DCOE) at Old Dominion University (ODU) has implemented a non-traditional teacher preparation program, the Teacher in Residence (TIR) that uniquely and skillfully prepares pre-service STEM teachers to work in today's classrooms, while actively engaging diverse 21st century learners in urban schools. This chapter provides a discussion of this clinically rich program to include, an in-depth analysis regarding the use of critical autobiography for teacher candidates and discourse on implications the TIR program has for teacher education.

Today many critics are challenging teacher preparation programs to take the lead in transforming how preservice teachers (PST) are prepared, so that not only hegemonic beliefs, curriculum, and practices are eradicated from education, but also that learning becomes contextualized and academic achievement increases for all students (Ladson-Billings, 2000; Mensah, 2011, 2013). In order for this to occur though, PreK–12 classroom teachers are expected to remain highly knowledgeable and capable of delivering high quality instruction to all learners. Thus, to achieve this, teacher education is called to foster clinically intensive programs that marry academic learning and practitioner expertise in a way that mitigates a deep divide between theory and practice. Hence, many suggest the implementation of the culturally relevant pedagogy (CRP) framework into preparation programs to teach PSTs how to increase student engagement and achievement among PreK–12 students (Mensah, 2011, 2013; Morrison et al., 2008; Parsons 2008; Ruiz & Cantú, 2013).

PROBLEM

Many researchers believe the missing piece in improving academic achievement is the lack of critical teaching (Atwater, Lance, Woodard, & Johnson, 2013; Cherian, 2006; Mensah, 2013). Critical teaching is a pedagogy style whereby a teacher acknowledges the dominant culture's power on systems of education and seeks to reform unjust social structures and teaching practices to benefit both underserved and privileged students (Mensah, 2013). These same researchers suggest many educators and policy makers regard critical teaching as unrealistic theoretical abstractions that are inconsequential to the accountability movement. Consequently, many PreK–12 students of color exist marginally in the classroom (Morrison et al., 2008; Ruiz & Cantú, 2013) and particularly in the science classroom (Curran & Kellogg, 2016; Mensah, 2013; Parsons, 2008). Curran and Kellogg (2016) provide evidence of this marginalization in their study that looked at science, mathematics, and reading gaps of early elementary students. Their study showed that although some achievement gaps are noted in reading and mathematics early on, science achievement gaps were by far more significant. They proffer this could be attributed to both in and out of school factors, such as socioeconomic status, increased segregation of students across schools, and also that lack of quality teachers not being uniformly distributed across schools.

Because teacher education faculty have a trickle-down effect over all areas of PreK–16 education, many scholars conclude that the system of teacher education is partially culpable for the problems in PreK–12 classrooms (Ladson-Billings, 2000; Lin, Lake, & Rice, 2008; Prater & Devereaux, 2009; Mensah, 2013). Specifically, some of those problems, like the White–Black achievement gap (Oats, 2009), disproportionate discipline referrals for students of color (Bickel & O'Neil, 1982), the hidden curriculum (Margolis, Soldatenko, Acku, & Gair, 2001), and the over representation of African Americans in special education (Harry & Anderson, 1994) continue to grow. Ladson-Billings (1998) says these trends are both unconsciously and deliberately orchestrated by the dominant culture to disenfranchise and marginalize students who are not taught the rules of power (Delpit, 1988).

Many of the aforementioned racially-charged inequities are usually not ones for which teacher educators accept blame (Atwater et al., 2013; Prater & Devereaux, 2009); yet, some say teacher educators in preparation programs (Sobel, Gutierrez, Zion, & Blanchett, 2011) should at the very least examine the snowball effect their actions have on PreK–12 outcomes. Consequently, Buehler, Gere, Dallavis, and Haviland (2009) say all teacher educators must examine: (a) what perpetuates racial inequity, (b) solutions to eliminating racial and social injustices in education, and (c) the role teacher educators play in exonerating the school systems of these and other blatant injustices. More specifically, Bryan and Atwater (2002) and Mutegi (2011) suggest science teacher educators have a significant role to play as they prepare the next generations of science teachers to contemplate the pedagogical changes necessary to meet the needs of African American and other diverse learners in 21st century classrooms. For example, Bryan and Atwater suggest that teacher educators and PreK–12 teachers must personally examine and resolve their own biases and prejudices, so that teaching and learning can be maximized for all students. In a focused study regarding Black racial identities, Zirkel and Johnson (2016) argue that despite a multitude of studies, teachers remain unmoved in their own personal beliefs about Black racial identities. Yet many others (viz. Curran & Kellogg, 2016; Hernandez, Morales, & Shroyer, 2013; Mensah, 2013; Mutegi, 2011) suggest alternative approaches in teaching to address issues of equity and access through the use of transformative methodologies, such as CRP. Therefore, it is imperative to design CRP centered preparation programs with clinically rich field experiences to better explore the outcomes CRP programs may have over time.

THE CRP FRAMEWORK EXPLAINED

Culturally relevant pedagogy (CRP), a term created by Gloria Ladson-Billings (1995) describes a kind of anti-racist teaching where teachers empower students intellectually, socially, emotionally, and politically. Ladson Billings distinguishes her CRP model as one that critically mitigates an awareness-to-action model, so that teachers and students feel empowered to confront injustices they experience in their lives or the lives of marginalized people. Therefore, culturally relevant teaching begins with reflection of personal biases and hegemonic injustices, and ultimately leads to teachers strengthening their and their students' cultural identity and pride to improve academic achievement (Benson, 2003; Brown-Jeffy & Cooper, 2011). Accordingly, Ladson-Billings (2000) calls for teacher education leaders to improve preparation programs by restructuring field experiences, whereby there is a return to the classrooms of diverse experts, restructuring course work with enriched clinical experiences, and with the integration of personal reflection or autobiography—all of which are supported by the CRP framework. Also, she calls for diversifying teacher preparation programs with faculty of color to interrupt the narrative that people of color are not capable of leadership positions in teacher education. CRP rests on three criteria: (a) teachers must have high expectations for students to experience academic success, (b) teachers must develop and maintain cultural competence for themselves and their students, and (c) teachers must foster a critical consciousness through which they help their students to challenge the status quo (Brown-Jeffy & Cooper, 2011; Ladson-Billings, 1995).

Academic Success

To develop and maintain academic success, setting high expectations for all students has been shown to be an effective strategy for developing an intrinsic motivation to succeed (Berryman, 2015; Ladson-Billings, 2000). Specifically, teachers must use high quality research-based instructional practices that foster a sense of personal motivation, such as with direct instruction, inquiry approaches to learning, and problem-based learning. When teachers learn to facilitate structured learning using these evidenced based strategies, they are able to capture students' attention, interest, and confidence by purposefully scaffolding instruction to meet the needs of students. Thus, once students realize their capacity for achieving academic success, they may feel that they are taking less of a risk with increasingly more challenging tasks.

Cultural Competence

Teachers who purposefully encourage students to learn about and maintain their own cultural integrity as well as to help students uncover the rules of the dominant culture are developing cultural competence (Ladson-Billings, 1995). Interestingly, Ladson-Billings contends that cultural competence is not simply advancing awareness about different cultures; instead, cultural competence is fostered when teachers link students' home values, language, and traditions with curricula and subject matter. Examples of how one could foster cultural competence would be to reveal missing narratives or contributions within the curriculum of a particular content area, interrupt the cycle of inferiority with counter-stories of achievement, encourage and value the epistemological input of all students by incorporating student ideas and experiences into instruction, or to expose blatant social injustices in past or current events. For example, a Eurocentric account of history neglects the many contributions in science by African Americans in the curriculum and collective conscious. Specifically, many elementary students learn that Thomas Edison invented the light bulb; yet, it is not often shared that it was Lewis Latimer, the son of a Virginia slave, who provided Edison with the impetus for this invention (Krapp, 1999). It is information like this that teachers committed to building cultural competence must expose, so that students of all races and backgrounds develop a more accurate account of the contributions of African Americans in STEM fields. Secondly, teachers can provide the development and maintenance of cultural competence by involving the wisdom and expertise of parents and other honored family members in the classroom (Ladson-Billings, 1995). By privileging the skills and knowledge of community stakeholders, teachers create learning opportunities for students to study more about local contributions made by people representing varied cultures; thus, providing a counter narrative to a one sided account of history (Morrison et al., 2008).

Critical Consciousness

Ladson-Billings (1995) says, "students must develop a broader sociopolitical consciousness that allows them to critique the cultural norms, values, morals, and institutions that produce and maintain social inequities" (p. 162). This sense of critical consciousness, the most misunderstood tenant of CRP (Young, 2010) posits that once social injustices are uncovered, teachers must help students confront those injustices. So, to build a critical consciousness teachers use the curriculum in a way that engages students critically with each other, their communities, and the world. Thus, teaching and learning changes from memorizing content-related facts to a more advanced democratic process of learning, where students apply the content of what they have learned to critique society and change oppressive structures for themselves or others. Examples of how teachers can help students build a critical consciousness in action-oriented ways would be to facilitate projects or initiatives that explicitly engage areas of student interest in the academic content and social equality, such as holding class debates, creating online blogs or petitions, or conducting a letter writing campaign. Lastly, when thinking about building a critical consciousness, it is important to note that *how* a teacher facilitates an awareness-to-action process varies greatly because curriculum needs, student interests, and the cultures represented in each classroom differ from year to year. So, facilitating a critical consciousness requires that teachers keep the relationship between themselves and their students "fluid and equitable" (Ladson-Billings, 1995, p. 162) as they encourage students to think and act as leaders. This action-oriented role of students becoming a sort of co-teacher helps students become more confident and proficient with increasingly challenging academic rigor (Morrison et al., 2008).

RESTRUCTURED TEACHER PREPARATION

In reaction to Ladson-Billings' (2000) and many others' (Mensah, 2013; Morrison et al., 2008; Mutegi, 2011; Rodriguez, 1998) call for reform in teacher preparation, Old Dominion University (ODU) has led the way in implementing an innovative and clinically intense teacher preparation program. This program incorporates the principles of CRP and anti-racist teacher preparation (Ladson-Billings, 2000; Lin et al., 2008) in an effort to improve the academic achievement and engagement of math and science students in an urban school district. The Teacher in Residence (TIR) program at ODU demonstrates how academic success can be achieved when the conventional model of teacher preparation is restructured with anti-racist teacher preparation strategies, which include innovative field experiences in highly diverse classrooms, reformed course work and professional development to include comprehensive instruction on CRP, and ongoing personal reflections, while at the same time working directly with diverse students.

Restructured Clinical Experiences

Ladson-Billings (2000) argues that traditional teacher preparation programs and the antiquated clinical experiences within these programs have perpetuated the inability of teachers to engage diverse students. She suggests that teacher education must reimagine their preparation of PreK–12 teachers, so that teachers are better equipped to meet the needs of 21st century classrooms. Accordingly, one of Old Dominion's teacher preparation programs, TIR, not only strives toward what Ladson-Billings calls restructured field experiences with classrooms of experts, but in doing so, has taken the lead by also restructuring admission procedures and access to faculty of color.

ODU's programs are in partnership with school division educators in a unique way that helps our PSTs to better understand the legitimacy and complexities of the urban populations of PreK–12 students served by our partnering school district. The Darden College of Education purposefully and exclusively partners with this specific urban school district for these innovative programs so that our PSTs are adequately prepared to collaborate with diverse professionals and engage all diverse children. In particular, ODU's teacher preparation programs, such as the TIR program are purposely staffed with diverse university and school district faculty in terms of race and language preference to allow teacher candidates in these programs to experience faculty of color in a way that may help to deconstruct biased notions of Black or Brown faculty and the urban communities served by the TIR program.

Specifically, the TIR program is designed for graduate students with a math or science undergraduate degree who are highly motivated to devote full-time study to becoming a culturally relevant math or science middle school teacher. TIR candidates are prepared in a partnership with a local urban school division adjacent to the university, with a supervising classroom teacher and university faculty sharing the responsibility for development over the span of approximately 9 months. Thus, when admitted into the program, in lieu of a traditional clinical experience, the students are immersed into a middle school within the school district near the university for a period of 8 months. During this *teacher candidate internship*, the TIR student works alongside a supervising mentor teacher, while simultaneously matriculating through course work with university faculty. This supervising mentor teacher, selected because he or she is regarded as a highly qualified expert in the teaching profession, eventually scaffolds the TIRs into full classroom teaching after 2 months of classroom observations and small group instruction. During this teaching residency, the TIR university faculty provides close guidance, support, and supervision by providing the students with 24-hour access to email, video conferencing, professional development, and in class observations/evaluations. Faculty and supervising mentor teachers work collaboratively to help TIR candidates plan culturally relevant instruction, conduct classroom observations, and provide timely feedback to the TIR candidate. They continuously meet and maintain an open dialog with the TIR candidate to address any of the candidates' or schools' needs. In return for the TIRs participation, TIRs are provided a living stipend for 8 months (up to $25,000) and full tuition and fees for a master's degree in secondary education with full licensure. After completion of the academic and clinical parts of the program, if the TIR candidate is recommended for hire by the participating school district, they are contracted to spend 3 years teaching in that school division, or may have to repay their costs to the program.

Restructured Recruitment and Course Work

The TIR program, a grant-funded graduate initiative at ODU is based on attracting graduate students who have a content-rich baccalaureate degree and want a rigorously fast-paced track into teaching. TIR is based on teachers becoming a part of the school community, as well as the local culture. Because of that, special attention is paid to recruiting teachers who already live in or are familiar with the community. These students are recruited from the Colleges of Sciences and Mathematics from ODU as well as neighboring institutions of higher learning in southeastern Virginia. Prospective students are also recruited from community events and through online social media. These students, who already possess an undergraduate degree in a math or science content area, are carefully vetted to determine if they possess the necessary dispositions and interest for teaching in the urban schools near the university. For example, the structured interview process, which is led by both ODU and school district stakeholders, includes but is not limited to carefully crafted questions about culturally affirming classroom management, the many different types of diversity, the lack of parental involvement in certain schools, and bullying. Accordingly, the traditional coursework needed for a teaching credential is realigned by competencies within the eight courses and the internship for the TIR program. For example, in this program, the course work is directly shaped around the school culture and K–12 students the TIR teacher candidates work with during their internship; therefore, in this way, coursework becomes contextualized with the clinical experience as opposed to theoretical abstractions from a textbook. The specific course names they participate in with university faculty are described in Table 10.1.

CRP is embedded into TIR course work and professional development. For example, soon after admission in December, the TIRs participate in a one credit *Seminar in Teacher Education* during the winter session, where they are introduced to the basics of teaching and scholarship regarding CRP. During this time, the candidates are given time to reflect and confront themselves about statements or beliefs shared in the interview process and participate in intense, yet safe discussions about the influences of racism in teaching. Then, for the entire month of January (before the beginning the

TABLE 10.1 Teacher in Residence Program Curriculum	
Teachers in Residence Curriculum (31 hours)	
Seminar in Teacher Education (4 Credit Hours) (Winter (1) and Summer Semester (3))	Teacher Candidate Internship (9 Credit Hours) (Entire Spring and Summer Semester)
Behavior Change in Classrooms (3 Credit Hours) (Spring 1 Semester)	Culturally Relevant Science and Math Classrooms (3 Credit Hours) (Spring 1 Semester)
Human Development and Student Learning (3 Credit Hours) (Spring 2 Semester)	Literacy for Diverse Learners (3 Credit Hours) (Maymester Semester)
Assessment and Evaluation of Student Learning (3 Credit Hours) (Summer 2 Semester)	Evolution of Education (3 Credit Hours) (Summer 3 Semester)

internship), the TIRs participate in *Human Development and Student Learning*, affectionately called, "bootcamp," because the TIR candidates participate five days a week from 8:00 a.m. to 5:00 p.m. This workshop style instruction focuses on understanding children's and adolescents' physical, social, emotional, intellectual, and speech/language development, integrating and incorporating children and adolescent differences (economic, social, racial, ethnic, religious, physical, and mental) into understanding developmental issues as they relate to instruction, including the identification and instruction of students with exceptionalities as well as special needs. Research and best practices regarding how to apply information from learning theories into culturally affirming teaching, assessment, technology, special education, classroom management, lesson planning, and rapport building for middle school aged children is examined.

By February 1 and until August 1, the TIR candidates are immersed into the teacher candidate internship with their assigned mentor teacher in a highly diverse middle school classroom. During the internship, the TIR candidate works alongside the mentor teacher to deliver high quality instruction to diverse students, many of who are African American and Hispanic American. Concurrent to the internship, from January to May, the TIRs take two more courses. First, they take *Culturally Relevant Science and Math Classrooms* in the evenings after the school day. In this class, TIRs gain an understanding of discipline specific content and methodologies to create culturally relevant unit plans, using inquiry based teaching strategies to motivate and challenge reluctant learners and focuses on best practices in working with the diverse students they are currently serving in the middle schools in which they are placed. Secondly, the TIRs take *Behavior Change in Classrooms* where they learn to embrace culturally affirming classroom management and how to work with students with and without special needs to increase student learning. For example, this course addresses the overrepresentation of students of color being referred for special education and the proactive strategies necessary to prevent cultural misunderstandings between students and teachers when addressing behavior issues. Next, in the Maymester, which is from May 1 to May 31, the TIRs who remain in their daytime placements, also take *Literacy Across the Content for Diverse Learners* in the evening, three nights a week for 3 hours each meeting. In this course, the TIR candidates learn how to incorporate reading and writing into their science and math curriculum. This course focuses on the metacognitive development and implementation of strategies that will accommodate how language and cultural differences affect communication and learning; knowledge of the impact of language-based curriculum skills such as listening, speaking, reading, and writing; instructional techniques needed to assist individuals identified as culturally, linguistically, and academically diverse in achieving reading and comprehension skills; comprehension strategies; and an understanding of reading across the math and science. In particular, the TIR candidates create writing projects or initiatives whereby their middle school students can address STEM related issues in their communities. By June, the TIR candidates take *Assessment and Evaluation of Student Learning*, which is a course designed to teach the candidates how to assess student learning. In this course, TIRs begin an "Impact on Student Learning Project," which includes instruction about formative and summative assessment practices that are nurturing to students and how to construct and use a variety of formal and informal teacher assessment procedures.

Once the traditional school year has ended, the TIRs with the close support of a mentor teacher and ODU faculty, lead a summer school class from approximately the last week in June to the first week in August, whereby the TIRs are fully responsible to deliver instruction and assess student learning. During this same time period, the TIRs also take *Evolution of Education*. This course focuses on the foundations of the U.S. education system, the legal aspects for educational delivery in the United States and Virginia, the contributions of technology integration to learning outcomes, and evidence-based ways for improving learning outcomes of urban children and youth. Within the scope of this class, the TIRs also critique and confront hegemonic practices in American schooling, such as the tracking students of color into less rigorous STEM courses. Additionally, during this summer semester, TIR candidates take the last three credits in the program for the *Seminar in Teacher Education*. In this final course, the TIR candidates examine instructional problems or concerns and complete the "Impact on Student Learning" project by demonstrating achievement from their summer school class students. Also, during this class, the TIRs participate in a comprehensive exam.

Professional development is also provided periodically throughout the clinical experience with an annual field trip to a nearby university's commemoration to Dr. Martin Luther King program in January, weekly 1-hour seminars for the entire internship, and a culminating 2-day 8-hour summer institute about working with diverse students. These experiences include time for reflection of personal bias and addressing instructional concerns with regard to differences in race, gender, socioeconomic status, and sexual orientation and how these factors may impact the classroom. During this ongoing process, TIRs meet with local and national leaders committed to social justice learning and attempt to implement what they have learned into their lesson plans within their various middle schools around the city. Thus, the TIRs emerge from the program more confident to engage diverse students, parents, and community members because they have confronted their own biases and are equipped with the essential skills to empower diverse students in math and science, and African American students in particular.

AUTOBIOGRAPHY

Ladson-Billings (2000) calls for teacher education programs to include intensive autobiography components in both field and course work. Accordingly, the TIR program uniquely integrates autobiography components into the entire 9-month experience. Specifically, the TIR program incorporates several and ongoing reflective assignments as students matriculate through the course work and clinical experiences. In particular, the TIR teacher candidates are required to compose reflections during and after each course, professional development offering, and teaching experiences, to process their thoughts about themselves, their diverse students, and the supervising teachers they interact with in terms of equity of classroom management procedures, diversity and race, instructional practices, and ethical and responsible assessment of student learning. For example, during the internship, the TIR teacher candidates strategically confront their own ideas of identity and how personal experiences and American socialization may have created personal bias, which is a paramount first step toward becoming a culturally relevant pedagogues.

METHODOLOGY

The structured reflections that are embedded throughout the TIR clinical experience call for the TIR teacher candidates, all of who have little to no prior teaching experience, to devote dedicated time to thinking about their thinking, while gleaning expertise from each other in the cohort and a select group of teacher experts who have been identified by their school administration as exemplars for working with beginning teachers and diverse students.

Therefore, since autobiography or reflection assignments were used throughout the TIR program, the research question we addressed was: *How does autobiographical reflection capture the TIRs' development as culturally relevant pedagogues?*

The 2015–2016 cohort began with ten teacher candidates. These candidates included two men and eight women. Of the ten candidates, three self-identified as Black, six as White, and one as a White Hispanic. Additionally, four were emerging math teachers and six were emerging science teachers. One of the teacher candidates requested to be removed from the program due to extenuating personal circumstances; thus, nine completed coursework for teacher licensure and are currently working full time with our partnering school district.

For this qualitative study, we used a multi-part approach to the integration of clinically rich teacher preparation for the 2015–2016 cohort of the CRP integrated TIR program. A qualitative design was appropriate for this investigation because the outcomes of this clinical immersion process allowed the TIR candidates to provide in depth descriptions of their lived experiences and intentional thinking about how they and their students related to the concepts they were learning throughout the program.

First, we presented the ten TIR teacher candidates with instruction on how to conduct reflective action research on their journey. Secondly, through an iterative process of writing, reflection, and return to writing, we presented a model where the candidates reflected not only on their immediate thoughts and actions, but also on how their thoughts as emerging culturally relevant teachers changed as they matriculated through their coursework and internship. This high level of reflection was purposefully threaded in the program with both structured prompts during their course work and teaching, as well as with open autobiography during intense professional development experiences. This was done as they confronted their own personal ethnicity and ideas of the situated pedagogies regarding how ethnicity, race, class, gender, and sexual orientation is represented in their classrooms. During the 8-month clinical period, the TIR candidates worked alongside a mentor teacher in a Norfolk middle school classroom, co-planned lessons, and eventually independently delivered instruction. The TIRs were observed many times by the mentor teachers, ODU faculty, and the first author of this study. The first author directly supervised the process of autobiographical reflection.

The first author reviewed the journal entries across all course work, the teaching experience, the TIRs participation in a guest lecture with a leading multicultural education researcher, and an intense summer professional development about culturally relevant pedagogy to ensure that a longitudinal view of the TIRs' journey was captured. In addition, when the TIR candidates first entered the program, they crafted a description of an initial teaching philosophy. After participating in the continuum of autobiographical experiences during their coursework and the internship, the TIRs composed a final draft of their teaching philosophy. Thus, the evolution of these teaching philosophies was analyzed.

Given the exhaustive amounts of descriptive data, the first author used a thematic approach (Aronson, 1994) based on narrative inquiry (Connelly & Clandinin, 1990) to guide the analysis and discover themes. Specifically, the first author read all of the autobiographies and narratives several times, while making notes to determine commonalities among initial categories. The data were reexamined several times to substantiate the categories and allow the eventual themes to naturally emerge. The first author shared this process with the second author to establish trustworthiness of the analysis.

FINDINGS

With the research question in mind, the themes that emerged in this study were: (a) growing respect and affirmation for otherness, (b) because race matters, specific strategies must be used to engage students of color, and (c) there is institutional resistance to implementing culturally relevant instruction.

Growing Respect and Affirmation for Otherness

During the scope of the program, the TIR faculty purposefully uncovered and helped the TIRs confront hegemonic influences in society and in American schooling. And in doing so, the TIRs were exposed to a host of resources and experiences to either establish awareness of or critique otherness. For example, during the first course, a one credit *Seminar in Teacher Education*, the TIRs held discussions about internet video clips, such as *Race: A Girl Like Me* (Davis, 2007) and wrote personal reflections about what they saw. For example, in reaction to the clip, *Race: A Girl Like Me* (Davis, 2007), TIR 2, one of the Black female TIR candidates, said, "I was hurt at what the little girls in the video said about the White and Black dolls, but I realize I was probably socialized the same way. I didn't even have any Black dolls when I was growing up." Similarly, in reaction to *Race: A Girl Like Me*, a male TIR candidate shared:

> I am a White privileged male who has little to no experience with what this video is talking about. I was not taught to care about these issues. I had no idea this was even a thing. But I can totally see how if I was their teacher, I would miss opportunities to either connect what I was teaching to what they cared about or might have said something that could have been viewed as insensitive. (TIR 7)

During a professional development experience a TIR reported:

> The fishbowl activity and discussion gave insight into a racial and cultural perspective I have never seen before. I think it was a learning experience that is unique to this program. I loved hearing all of the participants speak and felt safe... We really dug in deeply about our personal experiences and biases concerning gender, race, and social status. (TIR 1)

Similarly, the initial teaching philosophies written at the start of the program did not contain any dimensions of diversity; however, the final teaching philosophies written toward the end of the program revealed a growing respect and affirmation for diversity. Specifically, these final teaching philosophies identified a respect for diverse students and principles of teaching math and science in culturally relevant ways. For example, TIR 4's initial teaching statement reflected, "I believe that all students can learn and it is my job to encourage every child to their highest potential"; however, TIR 4's final teaching statement indicated, "Children learn best when they can relate what they are learning about in science to their lives, experiences, and culture." Similarly, TIR 5's initial teaching statement noted, "All educators must maximize learning for all students using the best strategies," but the same TIR's final teaching statement was: "We must affirm student diversity so that learning becomes relevant and students are engaged in math on deeper metacognitive levels.

Thus, in tandem with the intentional activities that fostered a safe space to think about otherness, the TIRs gained a genuine, yet cursory respect and affirmation for otherness that we believe will continue to grow and increase as they further their educational careers.

Because Race Matters, Specific Strategies Must Be Used to Engage Students of Color

One of the sub themes that emerged in the data, was that race matters in education and science and math education in particular. Across the autobiographical narratives, the TIR candidates overwhelmingly shared their awareness of racial and cultural bias in science education, but more importantly identified ways or teaching practices to address the learning needs of their mostly African American and Hispanic American students. This call to action by the TIRs to implement a move from theory to practice is evidenced as one TIR recognized the need to focus on culturally relevant strategies:

> Successful teaching must use practices that mitigate factors which hinder learning, such as stereotype threat for my Black students especially . . . teachers should incorporate diversity within the content area, lessons should not only be student centered, but related directly to the students' lives, and we must encourage students with positive affirmations, study groups, collaborative learning, and although the practice of remediation has the good intention of helping struggling students to understand the content, it can perpetuate stereotype threat . . . so one way to avoid stigmatizing the struggling students is to differentiate lesson plans to accommodate individual needs with authentic tasks that make them feel good about themselves . . . not just more worksheets. (TIR 6)

Similarly, another TIR shared concerns about some teachers' instruction that she had noticed:

> I hate to have to say this because it is a sad reality, but I have seen when teachers only call on the White kids or pick the White students for important class jobs or roles. Educators must find ways to get all students involved in the school . . . I want my Black students to feel supported in the school settings. The ones who don't get asked to help around the school or classroom, don't perform to their potential. (TIR 5)

Finally, another TIR indicated that

> issues of race and racism affect my science classroom . . . I know this . . . I have seen and felt it as a student and as a teacher . . . but we as teachers must always try to bring the world outside into the classroom, we should try to bring openness and understanding into our own lives and families as well. I am learning to use special projects that peak my kids' interest . . . many of their other teachers just think they are bad and won't sit still . . . it's because they don't care about what is being taught in those classes. I show my students what is going on and why they should care. . . . (TIR 10)

Together, these data reveal an acknowledgement by the TIRs that issues of race affect teaching and learning; and as a result, the TIRs recognize that their students of color must be engaged in specific ways. Further, from their experience in their course work and internship, they identify best practices to engage their students.

There Is Institutional Resistance to Implementing Culturally Relevant Instruction

Across the narratives, while the TIRs often noted that teaching in culturally relevant ways was a best practice, they identified barriers to its implementation in their internship and in general. Most notable however, were the solutions documented in the reflections. This theory to practice gap was never more obvious than in the TIRs reflections about their mentor teachers. For example, TIR 4 noted, "Time is always a challenge, especially when trying to implement culturally relevant practices. I think I will achieve better results if I have a teaching partner or a team to collaborate with who also is committed to this type of teaching." Other statements that reflected institutional resistance included:

> I feel my own experience with my academic career created stereotype threat in me . . . this is a challenge because the influence is subconscious and I really don't know how it might affect how I implement principles of CRP into my own teaching. I wonder if I hold myself back because I am not confident that I will be received well by the teachers and administrators in my school. (TIR 2)

Another TIR stated:

> My students are very unreceptive of learning because they have already been frustrated by their experiences in school, especially with teachers who don't understand them. I expect a challenge when trying to change these behaviors and thought patterns . . . I will have to dig through several mental blocks before being able to apply culturally relevant methods. (TIR 3)

This final theme illustrates the idea that despite the success they experience with implementing CRP during their internship, the TIRs report barriers to implementing CRP in their classrooms. Further, they predict institutional barriers and possible consequences will exist beyond their internship and into their own classrooms when they assume the full-time teacher role.

CONCLUSION

The TIR graduate program at ODU is an example of a clinically rich alternative teacher preparation program that relies heavily on the use of critical autobiography to help teacher candidates develop their identity as educators who embrace CRP principles in an effort to foster increased K–12 student engagement and achievement. The advantage of this program is that the use of critical autobiography that links the coursework to the internships helps the TIR teacher candidates avoid the lapse in theory to practice, often experienced in traditional preparation programs, because the TIR students are able to reflect about the course content simultaneously with the students they serve throughout the clinical experience. Based on the reflective assignments given throughout the 9-month graduate program, the 2015–2016 TIR teacher candidates have begun their process toward assuming a culturally relevant teaching platform. Specifically, they collectively suggested they acquired a growing respect and affirmation for otherness, indicated specific strategies must be used to engage students of color, and reported there is intuitional resistance to implementing the CRP model in their internship classrooms.

Ladson-Billings (1998) argues that culturally relevant teaching empowers students' ability to critically examine educational content and the learning process, which develops students' voice and sense of democratic citizenship (Benson, 2003). CRP in general aims to ensure that educators acknowledge and honor the diverse viewpoints of their student population and refrain from promoting homogeneous perspectives as universal beliefs (Berryman, 2015; Glanzer, 2008; Morrison et al., 2008). Further, the purpose of addressing teaching and learning through a CRP lens is to foster academic achievement by responding to and confronting the status quo that create and sustain structural inequities (Schmeichel, 2012), which until now, teacher education programs have largely ignored (Ladson-Billings, 2000; Mensah, 2013).

Another largely ignored facet in teacher preparation is the implementation of clinical experiences, particularly internships in urban school districts that require emerging teachers to work with multicultural and multiracial students. Not surprisingly, usually in urban schools, new teachers report they feel ill-prepared to address the growing needs of diverse classrooms. So, to address these growing concerns, the Darden College of Education at ODU implemented a non-traditional teacher preparation program, TIR. This program uniquely and skillfully prepares preservice science and mathematics teachers by embedding autobiographical reflection throughout an intense eight-month clinical internship to strategically foster the use of CRP and help these emerging educators better engage diverse 21st century learners in urban schools.

Evidence from this study suggests that the use of a critical autobiography process enriches the clinical experiences within teacher preparation programs, especially those that deliberately encourage PSTs to work with PreK–12 students who represent cultural and racial otherness. So, clinically rich programs, such as the TIR program that purposely facilitate an authentic process for identity development and the use of CRP, provides a benchmark for transforming clinical experiences among teacher preparation programs. Specifically, the TIR program provides teacher education an exemplar whereby critical autobiography is explicitly embedded in the coursework and in concert with the simultaneous teaching internship to foster the teacher candidates' identity as a culturally relevant teacher, to both explore teacher beliefs and perceptions, and help guide PST behaviors and dispositions, while working with diverse PreK–12 students in urban settings.

Implications for Teacher Education

Increasing emphasis in the use of critical autobiography to foster CRP in teacher preparation programs involves closer collaborations and interactions with all educational partners during the teaching internship. Teacher preparation programs, particularly those accredited by the Council for the Accreditation of Educator Preparation (CAEP) must respond to standards that call for genuine in-roads for issues surrounding diversity and equity and collaborative relationships with PreK–16 partners in the field. In the continuing quest to meet these accreditation standards, the Darden College of Education at ODU hears the same plea from all its school partners. One of the strongest ways that teacher preparation programs can prepare teachers for such a broad spectrum of teaching possibilities is to focus on and strengthen the use clinically rich alternative routes to teacher licensure that foster the use of CRP, so that all students learn to read, write, and problem solve in a way that legitimizes their participation in our democratic discourse and decision-making. Consequently, more research is needed that links the use of these interventions to student achievement data.

Of critical importance, which is also substantiated in the findings from the TIR project is the need to remove institutional barriers to implementing CRP, so that PSTs feel confident and supported to apply this framework in classrooms as opposed to promoting an inoculated version of multicultural education. It has been widely established that teachers teach how they were taught; thus, the institutional barriers PST experience at the PreK–12 level begin at the university level. Hence, it is important that teacher education faculty model good teaching practices, such as the use of CRP, or this framework will see little to no inroads in the PreK–12 settings. Further, underrepresented students often seek guidance and mentorship from professors of color because they are seen as role models, allies, and evidence that higher education can be fruitful (Griffin, Perez, Holmes, & Mayo, 2010). Therefore, it is important for institutions of higher education to both recruit and retain faculty of color, particularly in STEM fields. This can help to diversify the often-privileged voices in teacher education (Delpit, 1988) and deconstruct the notions of inferiority of faculty who are members of marginalized groups. Moreover, advertisements for educator preparation faculty should also include a requirement for CRP. One possible strategy to legitimately increase faculty diversity would be to include this dimension in the reporting and ranking of U.S. colleges and universities.

The restructuring of traditional teacher education is critical to meet the needs of 21st century teachers and students because today's learner requires more than content specific knowledge; he or she requires a process whereby learning is contextualized in meaningful ways. As the Darden College of Education at ODU moves forward in the pursuit of continuous program improvement and the use of clinically rich preparation programs with the use of autobiography and CRP, the following are other lessons learned with the implementation of the TIR program:

- All teacher educators must be explicitly trained to implement CRP principles in teacher education curriculum and during the internship, to include an intentional process for reflection of bias and racism.
- Coursework and clinical experiences must be restructured to use a competency-based framework, so that PSTs are provided a genuine theory to practice approach to simultaneously address the real learning needs of their students with theoretical evidence based strategies, such as CRP to engage diverse students.
- Teacher education must recruit top teacher candidates, who express an interest in working in urban school systems by specifically offering incentives, such as full tuition reimbursement and legitimate living stipends.
- Provide professional development for school division personnel to further support knowledge and use of CRP, especially with mentor or supervising teachers.

Final Thoughts

Regarding the TIR program, data collection is ongoing across the 2015–2016 cohort and other successive cohorts. The first graduates of the CRP infused TIR program were in 2015 and current data collection is intended to investigate potential impacts the program had on these and other teachers in the TIR pipeline and their subsequent students as they transition into the 3-year teaching commitment. As the 2015–2016 cohort and subsequent cohorts graduate, we are interested in following these novice educators to determine their use of and the impact of their CRP training in clinically rich contexts.

Lastly, it is important to share, we admittedly see a strong need to more thoroughly educate all of our colleagues with the use of critical autobiography and CRP as a tool to develop a clinically rich preparation program as many across the other teacher preparation programs are not familiar with this kind of teaching. We realize that we must all actively model this good teaching framework, so that not only teaching and learning is enhanced at the university level, but our intention is that this teaching philosophy trickles down to the PreK–12 settings. So, in conjunction with efforts to strengthen CRP (Paris, 2012), we urge teacher education leaders to seek support in both understanding and implementing the merits of critical reflection in clinically rich preparation programs because we believe this measured process helps PSTs to prepare to work with multi-culturally and racially diverse students in urban classrooms. On a final note, we are pleased to share the most notable outcome of the TIR graduate program is that we are producing viable and productive graduates in STEM teaching areas for the hard to staff schools for the urban school district our university serves. Evidence of the success of our work lies in the fact that for the first time the critical shortages in the area of science and mathematics education appear to be closing with our school district partner.

REFERENCES

Aronson, J. (1994). A pragmatic view of thematic analysis. *The Qualitative Report, 2*(1). Retrieved from http://nsuworks.nova.edu/tqr/vol2/iss1/3/

Atwater, M. M., Lance, J., Woodard, U., & Johnson, H. (2013). Race and ethnicity: Powerful cultural forecasters of science learning and performance. *Theory into Practice, 52*(1), 6–13.

Aud, S., Hussar, W., Kena, G., Bianco, K., Frohlich, L., Kemp, J., & Tahan, K. (2011). *The Condition of Education 2011* (NCES 2011-033). U.S. Department of Education, National Center for Education Statistics. Washington, DC: U.S. Government Printing Office.

Benson, B. E. (2003). Framing culture within classroom practice: Culturally relevant teaching. *Action in Teacher Education, 25*(2), 16–22.

Berryman, M. (2015). Editorial: Culturally responsive pedagogies as transformative praxis. *Waikato Journal of Education, 18*(2), 3–10.

Bickel, F., & O'Neil, M. (1982). Reducing disproportionate suspension in a selected secondary school: A case study. *The Clearing House, 55*(6), 269–272.

Brown-Jeffy, S., & Cooper, J. E. (2011). Toward a conceptual framework of culturally relevant pedagogy: An overview of the conceptual and theoretical literature. *Teacher Education Quarterly, 38*(1), 65–84.

Bryan, L. A., & Atwater, M. M. (2002). Teacher beliefs and cultural models: A challenge for science teacher preparation programs. *Science Teacher Education, 86*(6), 821–839.

Buehler, J., Gere, A. R., Dallavis, C., & Haviland, V. S. (2009). Normalizing the fraughtness: How emotion, race, and school context complicate cultural competence. *Journal of Teacher Education, 60*(4), 408–418.

Cherian, F. (2006). Can you spare some social change: Preparing new teachers to teach social justice in times of educational reform and standardized curriculum. In A. Salhi (Ed.), *Excellence in teaching and learning* (pp. 125–135). New York, NY: Rowman & Littlefield Education.

Connelly, M., & Clandinin, D. J. (1990). Stories of experience and narrative inquiry. *Educational Researcher, 19*(5), 2–14.

Curran, C., & Kellogg, A. (2016). Understanding science achievement gaps by race/ethnicity and gender in kindergarten and first grade. *Educational Researcher, 45*(5), 273–282.

Davis, K. (2007). Race: A girl like me. *Reel Works Teen Filmmaking.* Internet. Retrieved from http://www.understandingrace.org/lived/video/

Delpit, L. (1988). The silenced dialogue: Power and pedagogy in educating other people's children. *Harvard Educational Review, 58*(3), 280–298.

Glanzer, P. L. (2008). Harry Potter's provocative moral world: Is there a place for good and evil in moral education. *Kappan, 89*(7), 525–528.

Griffin, K. A., Pérez, D., Holmes, A. P. E., & Mayo, C. E. P. (2010). Investing in the future: The importance of faculty mentoring in the development of students of color in STEM. *New Directions for Institutional Research, 148,* 95–103.

Harry, B., & Anderson, M. G. (1994). The disproportionate placement of African American males in special education programs: A critique of the process. *The Journal of Negro Education, 63*(4), 602–619.

Hernandez, C. M., Morales, A. R., & Shroyer, G. M. (2013). The development of a model of culturally responsive science and mathematics teaching. *Studies of Science Education, 8*(4), 803–820.

Krapp, C. (1999). *Notable Black American scientists.* Farmington Hills, MI: Gale Research.

Ladson-Billings, G. (1995). But that's just good teaching! The case for culturally relevant pedagogy. *Theory into practice, 34*(3), 159–165.

Ladson-Billings, G. (1998). Preparing teachers for diverse student populations: A critical race theory perspective. *Review of Research in Education, 24,* 211–247.

Ladson-Billings, G. (2000). Fighting for our lives: Preparing teachers to teach African American students. *Journal of Teacher Education, 51*(3), 206–214.

Lin, M., Lake, V. E., & Rice, D. (2008). Teaching anti-bias curriculum in teacher education programs: What and how. *Teacher Education Quarterly, 35*(2), 28–51.

Margolis, E., Soldatenko, M., Acku, S., & Gair, M. (2001). Peekaboo: Hiding and outing the curriculum. In E. Margolis (Ed.), *The hidden curriculum in higher education,* (pp. 1–20). New York, NY: Routledge.

Mensah, F. M. (2011). A case for culturally relevant teaching in science education and lessons learned for teacher education. *The Journal of Negro Education, 80*(3), 296–309.

Mensah, F. M. (2013). Theoretically and practically speaking: What is needed in diversity and equity in science teaching and learning? *Theory Into Practice, 52*(1), 66–72.

Morrison, K. A., Robbins, H. H., & Rose, D. G. (2008). Operationalizing culturally relevant pedagogy: A synthesis of classroom-based research. *Equity & Excellence in Education, 41*(4), 433–452.

Mutegi, J. (2011). The inadequacies of "Science-for-All" and the necessity and nature of a socially transformative curriculum approach for African American science education. *Journal of Research in Science Teaching, 248*(3), 301–316. doi:10.1002/tea.20410

Oats, G. L. C. (2009). An empirical test of five prominent explanations for the Black–White achievement gap. *Social Psychology and Education, 12*(4), 415–441.

Paris, D. (2012). Culturally sustaining pedagogy: A needed change in stance, terminology, and practice. *Educational Researcher, 41*(3), 93–97.

Parsons, E. C. (2008). Learning contexts, Black cultural ethos, and the science achievement of African American students in an urban middle school. *Journal of Research in Science Teaching, 45*(6), 663–683.

Prater, M. A., & Devereaux, T. H. (2009). Culturally responsive training of teacher educators. *Action in Teacher Education, 31*(3), 19–27.

Rodriguez, A. J. (1998). Strategies for counterresistance: Toward sociotransformative constructivism and learning to teach science for diversity and understanding. *Journal of Research in Science Teaching, 35*(6), 589–622.

Ruiz, E. C., & Cantú, N. E. (2013). Teaching the teachers: Dismantling racism and teaching for social change. *The Urban Review, 45*(1), 74–88.

Schmeichel, M. (2012). Good teaching? An examination of culturally relevant teaching as an equity practice. *Journal of Curriculum Studies, 44*(2), 211–231.

Sobel, D. M., Guiterrez, C., Zion, S., & Blanchett, W. (2011). Deepening culturally responsive understandings within a teacher preparation program: It's a process! *Teacher Development, 15*(4), 435–452.

Young, E. Y. (2010). Challenges to conceptualizing and actualizing culturally relevant pedagogy: How viable is the theory in classroom practice? *Journal of Teacher Education, 61*(3), 248–260.

Zirkel, S., & Johnson, T. (2016). Mirror, mirror on the wall: A critical examination of the conceptualization of the study of Black racial identity in education. *Educational Researcher, 45*(5), 301–311.

CHAPTER 11

PERCEPTIONS OF PREPAREDNESS

Reflections of Deaf Education Program Graduates

Jennifer Renée Kilpatrick
University of North Florida

Emily Headrick-Hall and Kimberly A. Wolbers
University of Tennessee

ABSTRACT

Over the last 40 years, legislation and technological advances have led to significant changes in the field of deaf education. The roles and responsibilities for which deaf education teacher preparation programs are preparing graduates are changing. While studies have documented that there have been changes in deaf education program requirements, little is known about the preparedness of program graduates or about which program components impact their preparedness. The purpose of this chapter is to examine these topics from the perspectives of beginning teachers of the deaf. We share the findings of a qualitative interview study of graduates ($N = 13$) of one deaf edu-

Outcomes of High-Quality Clinical Practice in Teacher Education, pages 219–248
Copyright © 2018 by Information Age Publishing

cation teacher preparation program and conclude by providing implications for the design of deaf education teacher preparation programs.

The field of deaf education has changed dramatically over the last several decades. Prior to the passing of the 1975 Education of the Handicapped Act, most deaf and hard of hearing (d/hh) students were educated in residential schools and self-contained classrooms; however, this is no longer the case. An increasing percentage of d/hh students are being educated in general education classrooms for the majority of their day (Gallaudet Research Institute, 2000, 2010). Education policies, as well as additional developments, such as universal newborn hearing screenings, early intervention services, and cochlear implants, have led to significant changes in the field (Lenihan, 2010). The number of students enrolled in early intervention (i.e., birth to three and special education preschool) programs serving d/hh students has increased (Gallaudet Research Institute, 2000, 2010), resulting in a greater need for teachers of the deaf prepared to meet the needs of these young students. Additionally, the percentage of students with cochlear implants, as well as the percentage of students served in programs that provide instruction primarily through spoken language (i.e., without sign language communication), has increased significantly (Gallaudet Research Institute, 2000, 2010). The teachers who work with these students must have knowledge of cochlear implants and other listening technologies (e.g., FM systems). The 1988 "Deaf President Now" protest at Gallaudet University has been credited with an increased interest in American Sign Language (ASL) and issues of deaf culture (Dolman, 2008). As a result, an increasing percentage of d/hh students are also enrolled in schools and programs that have adopted a bilingual-bicultural philosophy (Gallaudet Research Institute, 2000, 2010). In schools with a bilingual-bicultural philosophy, the emphasis is on developing both ASL and English. Therefore, teachers in ASL-English bilingual settings, must be highly proficient in ASL.

These recent, rapid developments in the education of d/hh students have led to an undeniable shift in the roles and responsibilities of today's teachers of the deaf, who provide services to the estimated 77,000 d/hh students receiving special education services (National Center for Education Statistics, 2016). Teachers of the deaf must be prepared to meet the needs of d/hh students across the wide continuum of placements and communication philosophies. One deaf educator's role may be to support general education teachers and to facilitate the development of listening and spoken language and self-advocacy skills of d/hh students educated primarily in a general education setting, while another deaf educator's role may be to provide ASL/English bilingual instruction for d/hh students attending a residential school for the deaf. Deaf education programs are charged with providing graduates for these (and many other) very different positions.

The purpose of this study was to gain insight into the roles and responsibilities of teachers of the deaf in the field by interviewing beginning teachers of the deaf in a variety of placements. We focused on the self-perceptions of preparedness from graduates of one clinically rich teacher preparation program. The study was guided by the following research questions: (a) How do graduates of the program describe their perceptions of preparedness for the responsibilities of the positions they obtain after graduation?; and (b) How do the graduates describe the relationship between their perceptions of preparedness for the responsibilities of the positions they obtain after graduation and their clinical experiences (practicum courses and internship)? Identifying the components of teacher preparation that positively impact graduates' perceptions of preparedness is essential to informing the design of deaf education teacher preparation programs.

REVIEW OF THE LITERATURE

We briefly summarize three bodies of literature that inform our research: (a) literature that informed the design of the program discussed in this chapter, (b) literature that examines the relationship between the clinical experiences of teacher preparation programs and graduates' self-perceptions of preparedness, and (c) literature that describes and supports the typical requirements of deaf education teacher preparation programs.

Design of the Program

The participants of this study were graduates of a deaf education program at a university member of the Holmes Partnership, a national network of partnerships between major research universities and local public K–12 schools and national affiliate organizations involved in the reform of teacher education. This partnership grew out of the work of The Holmes' Group (1986, 1990, 1995), a consortium of leaders in higher education who advocated for a transformation of teaching from an occupation to a true profession. The group was organized with the goals of reforming teacher education and the teaching profession. In their three seminal works known as *The Holmes' Group Trilogy*, the group outlined a vision for collaboration, through which universities and schools could achieve common goals by combining available resources. The partnership marked the beginning of a new way of looking at the design of teacher preparation programs by focusing on the purpose and outcomes of clinical experiences, a central component of university and school partnerships.

Teacher preparation programs must be thoughtful about the design and use of clinical experiences. The clinical experiences should be designed with a focus on simultaneous renewal (Auton, Berry, Mullen, & Cochran, 2002; Darling-Hammond, Berry, Haselkorn, & Fideler, 1999; Goodlad, 1994) and situated learning (Brown, Collins, & Duguid, 1989; Clancey, 1994; Lave & Wegner, 1991; Pitri, 2004). In *Educating School Teachers,* Arthur Levine (2006) describes four exemplar teacher preparation programs, each of which integrate coursework with a clinical experience component that is "sustained, begins early, and provides immediate application of theory to real classroom situations" (p. 81). Additionally, intentional and systematic coordination of theory and methods courses and clinical experiences strengthens teacher preparation by providing an avenue for teacher preparation programs to bridge theory to practice through necessary guided practice (Griffin, 1999) supported by experienced, knowledgeable mentor teachers (Davis, Higdon, Resta, & Latiolais, 2001).

Beginning in the 1990s, in response to the efforts of several teacher preparation and education reform groups, including the Holmes Group, some programs have made structural changes, including moving to a 5-year program model. Since that time some research has shown that teachers prepared in 5-year programs enter and remain in teaching at higher rates than teachers prepared in 4-year programs (Andrew, 1990). Additionally, graduates of these programs have been viewed by supervisors as being more competent (Andrew & Schwab, 1995), and they have reported feeling better prepared (Andrew, 1990). Thus, it comes as no surprise that, Levine (2006) recommends that universities "make five-year teacher education programs the norm" (p. 106). Five-year programs provide flexibility that allows preservice teachers additional time to take additional courses that focus on the development of both subject area knowledge and pedagogical knowledge. This model also allows preservice teachers to begin clinical experiences earlier in their programs and to spend a greater amount of time in classrooms prior to graduation.

Perceptions of Preparedness

Turning to the literature that examines self-perceptions of preparedness, several survey studies have examined the relationship between teachers' self-perceptions of preparedness and the clinical experiences of teacher preparation programs from which they graduated. In one such study, Ronfeldt and Reininger (2012) found that the duration of student teaching positively predicted self-perceived instructional preparedness. In a subsequent survey study, however, Ronfeldt, Reininger, and Kwok (2013) found that the duration of student teaching was not related to self-perceptions of preparedness among the participants. In this study, they found two other characteristics of student teaching that were positive predictors of preparedness: mentor teacher quality and amount of autonomy preservice teachers were given to make instructional decisions during their student teaching. Boe, Shin, and Cook (2007) surveyed beginning general education teachers and special education teachers and found a positive correlation between the amount of preservice clinical experience and indicators of preparedness to teach when clinical experiences were aligned with teaching position. Dodd and Scheetz (2003) surveyed 110 beginning teachers of d/hh students and found the majority of teachers reported feeling their programs had prepared them for their positions, and the majority also reported spending more hours in their clinical experience settings than was required by their programs.

Deaf Education Teacher Preparation

There has been very little research on the design and duration of preservice clinical experiences in deaf education teacher preparation programs; however, we do know that the Council on the Education of the Deaf (CED), the national accrediting body in the field of deaf education, requires programs to incorporate a minimum of 150 classroom hours during practicum placements and 250 classroom hours during student teaching placements. Additionally, Dolman (2008) found that d/hh teacher preparation programs during the 2006–2007 school year required students to complete a mean of 3.86 practicum credit hours and 12.54 student teaching credit hours. In comparison, the program discussed in this chapter requires a minimum of approximately 174 classroom hours (6 credit hours) during practicum placements and 840 classroom hours (12 credit hours) during student teaching placements.

One unique challenge of deaf education teacher preparation programs is the responsibility of preparing teachers for a field that requires them to be proficient in ASL, which is not the native language of the majority of preservice teachers of the deaf. Because spoken language is neither the chosen nor the appropriate communication modality for every d/hh student, teachers of d/hh students must be prepared to provide instruction via ASL. As a result, deaf education teacher preparation programs must focus on facilitating the development of communicative competency in ASL in addition to typical teacher preparation competencies. Dolman (2008) found that d/hh teacher preparation programs in 2006–2007 required a mean of 10 credit hours in ASL, while the program discussed in this chapter requires a minimum of 15 credit hours in ASL. Although CED does not provide guidelines regarding ASL credit hours, it does require that the program prepare candidates to meet the unique language and communication needs of d/hh children in accordance with the institution's philosophy. Research in the foreign languages suggests that taking foreign language courses alone is insufficient in developing native speaker-like fluency (Freed, Segalowitz, & Dewey, 2004; Isabelli-Garcia & Lacorte, 2016). Freed et al. (2004) found that immersion with native speakers is the most useful method. This suggests that the preservice teachers of the deaf need opportunities for immersion in ASL during clinical experiences.

RESEARCH CONTEXT

This chapter explores the perspectives of graduates from one clinically rich deaf education teacher preparation program in the southeastern United States. This program has a history of preparing teachers of the deaf for the field for more than 80 years. It is one of only 33 programs nationwide accredited by the CED. Graduates of CED accredited programs are eligible for CED Individual Certification, which represents the highest national standard of quality for teachers of d/hh students. CED accredits teacher preparation programs in accordance with Council for Exceptional Children (CEC) core standards, as well as its own standards, which have been designed specifically for programs that are preparing teachers of d/hh students.

At the time that the participants in this study graduated from this program, the communication philosophy of the program was *comprehensive.* This term is used to indicate that a program is designed to prepare preservice teachers to teach d/hh students in a variety of communication philosophy settings. Such programs are intended to address each of the various communication philosophies in the field, which include listening and spoken language, total communication, and ASL-English bilingual, meaning the coursework and field experiences in a comprehensive program are designed to guide preservice teachers in the development of the knowledge, skills, and dispositions needed to work with students who use any/all mode(s) of communication (i.e., spoken and/or signed languages).

Required Coursework and Clinical Experiences

The students in this master's degree program are seeking initial licensure through a 5-year program. Students spend their first 4 years completing undergraduate coursework to earn a Bachelor of Science (BS) degree in Special Education with a concentration in education of the deaf and hard of hearing. As a part of this undergraduate degree, preservice teachers take 50 credit hours of general education requirements, 12 credit hours of teacher licensure core requirements, 6 credit hours of educational methods, 12–15 credit hours of professional electives, and 40 credit hours of courses in ASL, deaf education, audiology, and speech pathology. The educational methods courses and professional electives courses that preservice teachers take vary according to the additional endorsement area they selected (i.e., elementary general education or a secondary content area). After preservice teachers obtain the BS degree, they complete a year-long internship along with additional graduate-level coursework in deaf education (e.g., literacy methods, content methods, research methods) to earn a Master of Science in Teacher Education.

Throughout the program, preservice teachers complete multiple clinical experiences, during which they observe and are mentored by experienced teachers. University supervisors facilitate these clinical experiences by establishing and maintaining open lines of communication with mentor teachers, conducting informal and formal observations of preservice teachers' instruction, reviewing weekly evaluations that have been completed by mentor teachers, and meeting with preservice teachers to discuss both the observations and evaluations. Undergraduate clinical experiences are tied to practicum coursework that preservice teachers take during the third and fourth years. Placements are determined based on a preservice teacher's selected area of endorsement. Preservice teachers are given the opportunity to express preferences (e.g., grade level, communication modality, setting) for the placements; however, placements do not always align with preferences. This may be due to availability of placements or to provide preservice teachers with a range of experiences (e.g., various grade levels, communication modalities, settings) within their selected endorsement area. During two of the clinical experiences, preservice teachers observe teachers and support and teach lessons in a deaf education setting for 6 hours per week for a full semester. During the third clinical experience, preservice teachers observe individual and group therapy sessions in a speech and hearing clinic for 6 hours per week for a full semester. Typically, two to three additional placements are assigned to preservice teachers during the full-year internship. They spend the majority of the year in placements with d/hh students; however, they spend one quarter of the year in a general education placement in order to complete requirements for their additional endorsement area. All practicum and internship courses are taken along with co-requisite methods courses. This allows the preservice teacher to engage in cyclical learning through application and reflection. Theory and methods course assignments are integrated into the clinical experiences by requiring preservice teachers to apply what they are learning in class to assessment, lesson planning, and instruction in their placements. For example, in a literacy methods course, preservice teachers learn methods for assessing students' reading and writing performance, setting appropriate objectives, and designing literacy lesson plans with evidence-based instructional approaches. Then, they implement these strategies with the students in their placements. Post-assignment reflections are brought back to class so that preservice teachers can engage in discussions with peers, creating opportunities for further learning and additional mentoring from university faculty.

Because graduates of a comprehensive deaf education teacher preparation program must be prepared to provide instruction via ASL, the program requires preservice teachers take 15 credits of ASL and also requires preservice teachers obtain a minimum intermediate rating on the Sign Language Proficiency Interview (SLPI) prior to the fifth year internship placement in a signing environment. Additionally, several courses taken during the fourth year and all classes taken during the fifth year are taught via ASL. This immersion experience allows preservice teachers to continue to develop their receptive and expressive proficiency in the language.

METHODS

The sole source of data for this study was semi-structured qualitative interviews with graduates of the program. Over the course of 3 years, graduates were invited to participate in interviews approximately 1 year after they graduated. The purpose of these interviews was both to evaluate the teacher preparation program and to collect data on the perceptions of beginning teachers of the deaf regarding their current roles and corresponding responsibilities; therefore, only graduates who were currently teaching d/hh students were eligible to participate. The participant recruitment process entailed emailing recent graduates from the program an invitation detailing the purpose of the study, the informed consent, and interview process. Of the 23 graduates invited to participate, 13 met the criteria and consented to participation. These participants had been hired to teach d/hh students ranging in age from 3–21 in various programs and schools in four different states located in the Northwestern, Midwestern, and Southeastern United States. The positions obtained by these graduates were representative of the wide range of teaching positions for which deaf education teacher preparation program graduates are typically hired. They included positions ranging from pre-school to post-secondary transition and all communication philosophies (total communication, listening and spoken language, and ASL-English bilingual) and settings (itinerant, self-contained classrooms, resource classrooms, and classrooms at residential schools for the deaf).

We met with each participant for one 30–60 minute interview session. During the interviews, participants were asked to reflect on their experiences in the program and during their first year of teaching. Using semi-structured interview protocols, the researchers asked questions regarding participants' perceptions in the following four areas of interest: roles and responsibilities of their current positions, competencies needed in their current position, competencies developed through the program, and identification of competencies needed in current position but not adequately developed by the program. Iterative questioning was used as an initial strategy for ensuring trustworthiness (Guba, 1981; Schwandt, Lincoln, & Guba, 2007; Shenton, 2004). Eleven of the interviews were conducted in spoken English and audio-recorded; two interviews were conducted in ASL and video-recorded. Next, each interview was transcribed by a member of the research team or by a hired transcriber who signed a confidentiality agreement. The interviews that were conducted in ASL were transcribed using a written English translation.

Data Analysis

Coding was a collaborative process between the first and second authors, using the qualitative data analysis software, NVivo. We began with using open coding (Strauss, 1987; Strauss & Corbin, 1990) to identify the areas of the transcripts in which participants responded to the two research questions. We each listened to or watched the recordings to familiarize ourselves with the data, generating initial codes based on the participants words. On subsequent rounds of analysis we searched for patterns (Miles & Huberman, 1994) among the codes, collapsing them into themes. Throughout the coding process, we used frequent debriefing sessions as a strategy to deepen our analysis, develop and expand our ideas and interpretations, and recognize our own biases (Guba, 1981; Schwandt et al., 2007; Shenton, 2004). All experiences and codes were considered relevant and were used to identify themes in the data. In other words, our analysis and findings were not influenced by quantity and include relevant unique, or deviant, cases because we valued equally the data provided by each participant. The third author reviewed the analysis and participated in some of the debriefing strategies, adding a fresh perspective.

FINDINGS

Our examination of the participants' words revealed several themes that respond to our research questions. While some themes were mentioned by several of the participants, other themes were mentioned by only one to two of the participants. Participants indicated they perceived they were most prepared for the following responsibilities: facilitating language and literacy development, planning and implementing instruction, and providing instruction via ASL, while they perceived they were less prepared for the following responsibilities: managing behavior, developing and implementing IEPs, managing hearing equipment, and interpreting and communicating via Simultaneous Communication. They indicated that the components of the program that positively influenced their perceptions of preparedness for these responsibilities were focus on application in methods courses, quantity and diversity of clinical experiences, and influence of mentors.

Research Question 1

Our first research question was: *How do graduates of the program describe their perceptions of preparedness for the responsibilities of the positions they obtain after graduation?* As the participants talked about their roles and responsibilities in the positions they accepted after graduation, the participants indicated that they felt the program had prepared them for the primary responsibilities of their current positions when those positions aligned with their area of endorsement. However, there were some responsibilities for which the participants felt unprepared. In the sections that follow, we provide a summary of each of these themes (i.e., responsibilities for which they felt prepared/unprepared) and include representative quotes selected from the interviews.

Facilitating Language and Literacy Development

When asked about what was the most beneficial part of their teacher preparation, some of the graduates spoke of the program's emphasis on facilitating language and literacy development. Research indicates that d/hh students lag behind their hearing peers in language and literacy development (Albertini & Schley, 2003; Apel & Masterson, 2015; Sirois, Boisclair, & Giasson, 2008; Traxler, 2000), making it vital for teachers of the deaf to know how to facilitate language and literacy development. The program emphasizes the importance of effective language and literacy instruction throughout the course sequence; students are assigned readings and application-based projects focused on the best practices for facilitating language and literacy development.

Some participants stressed that the program's focus on language development was the most beneficial part of their preparation. Morgan said,

> I always think back to how important [my professor] would say language development is. I think people forget that with deaf kids—that it's so important to just focus on language development. I'm always trying to do stuff based around developing their language first because they're not going to be able to read or to write until they have a primary language. I try to really stick with that when I work with my Pre-K kids, especially because they're so little right

now. That's probably the thing that has been the most helpful from the program, but everything was really helpful!

Tim echoed Morgan's reflection, saying, "Understanding the language development of d/hh children—I think that was the most beneficial thing [I learned in the program]. Just understanding [that] makes your job so much easier." Morgan and Tim's comments suggest the program provided a strong foundation for understanding language development theory.

Throughout the program, there is an intentional emphasis on language development. Preservice teachers in the program take a three course sequence in language and literacy development and methods specific to d/hh students; this sequence is double the number of credit hours that is average for deaf education teacher preparation programs (Dolman, 2008) and must implement lessons in their placements that focus on both language development and content area objectives. This provides an opportunity to practice focusing on language development in addition to content, regardless of grade-level or subject area. Anna spoke about one of these assignments during her interview. She said,

> We had an [interactive writing] project that I remember being very helpful because it actually forced me to use that writing instruction [strategy] and really examine what the students' needs were based on their IEP goals and the standards. Teaching an [interactive writing] lesson and having to go back and reflect was super beneficial for me.

Rich also spoke about his experiences using interactive writing during his internship and first year of teaching, saying "I really feel like it gave me not just a tool, but almost like a utility belt of instruction for writing." He emphasized that he felt "really prepared for literacy instruction." He said,

> I wasn't freaking out about how to teach writing. I knew exactly what I was going to do. I knew exactly how to do it. I had experience doing it. I knew how to make progress in it.

In addition to feeling prepared to facilitate language and literacy development through instruction, participants also indicated that they perceived they were prepared for planning and implementing instruction in general.

Planning and Implementing Instruction

Participants spoke of planning and implementing instruction in general, and some participants specifically referenced the challenge of differentiated instruction. Their reflections indicated that lesson planning was a key component of many of their methods courses, as well as their practicum courses and internships. When asked which responsibilities of her position she felt most prepared for, Haley concisely replied, "I think they prepared us well as far as lesson plans" indicating that this is an area of strength for the program.

The participants discussed learning how to write lesson plans early in their coursework and continuing to develop the skill of planning instruction throughout the third, fourth, and fifth years of the program. Jane provided a detailed description of her memories of writing lesson plans during her time in the program and her retrospective appreciation for how those experiences prepared her for the responsibilities of her current position. She also said, "At the time it was annoying, but really, really practicing lesson plans was helpful, and I feel like has given me a really good foundation." Sarah also indicated that she felt prepared for planning and implementing instruction. She said, "I felt comfortable and prepared for teaching the content. I also felt prepared for teaching deaf students. I feel good about that because of my internship experience and knowing how to write lesson plans." Her words indicate that her internship provided her with an opportunity to practice planning and implementing lessons in an authentic instructional setting.

As participants spoke about planning and implementing instruction, some specifically mentioned differentiated instruction. They stressed the heterogeneity of their classes or caseloads and indicated that much of their job responsibilities are related to finding and/or modifying materials and selecting and/or designing assessments for students of varying developmental levels with a wide range of needs. They expressed that this task was one of their most difficult primary responsibilities, yet most of them stated that they felt the program had prepared them to do this well. Francis reflected, "I feel like I know how to change what I'm teaching based on my students. Individualized instruction. That was a big focus [of the program]. Differentiated instruction." Tim said, "Differentiating instruction. Just knowing how to do that, I feel pretty comfortable with it . . . I had a pretty good understanding of it." When he was asked how he thought he learned this, he emphasized the importance of the opportunity to engage in "hands on learning" during practicum and internship experiences. Participants indicated that in addition to planning and implementing (and differentiating) instruction, they felt prepared to provide that instruction via ASL.

Providing Instruction via ASL

All of the graduates who participated in the study, were hired for positions that required them to be proficient in sign language. In fact, the majority of the participants provide instruction for students via ASL and mentioned that this was an essential competency for their positions. Participants indicated that they felt well prepared for this responsibility and discussed how they developed these skills in several ways during the program. Interestingly, the participants did not reference their ASL courses. Instead, they talked about the opportunities they had during the program to use ASL for authentic communication purposes both in university classes and in their clinical experiences.

Students take ASL I–IV early in their studies. This may be why they did not mention these courses. It may also be that these classes did not provide (as many) authentic opportunities to communicate in ASL. Preservice teachers are presumed to have basic communicative proficiency in ASL when they begin taking deaf education courses. Throughout the third and fourth years the amount of instruction provided in ASL gradually increases, and by the fifth year, all classroom discourse occurs in ASL. Rich said,

> I was really happy that we had classes in ASL; it really benefited me . . . Being able to just "voice off" and understand that I was going to be signing today all day with my class—that helped. I think [having classes in ASL] helped everyone become more comfortable with their sign skills, especially receptively . . . ASL is going to help any kind of instruction that you're going to be providing, so that was a big thing.

While the majority of participants were hired for positions in which they were required to provide instruction via ASL, Haley was not. She is the only participant who does not use ASL substantially in her position; however, she still mentioned feeling prepared for this responsibility, saying,

> As far as preparing me to be in the classroom signing and everything, I think they did a great job . . . being able to go to a residential school for our internship . . . you're forced to use it everyday . . . and the classes that are taught fully in sign language. As terrifying as that is when you first go into it, it's a good thing . . . You realize students are actually having to read sign language all day for everything, and it's work [for them] to actually do that.

Haley's reflection indicates that not only did these opportunities to use ASL in their courses and clinical experiences prepare them to communicate through ASL, it also helped them consider the perspective of a d/hh student who communicates through ASL. While Haley only uses ASL minimally in her position, she still mentions the fact that the program prepared her for this responsibility, indicating that she perceives ASL competency to be an important skill for preservice teachers of the deaf to develop during their program.

While participants indicated that they felt prepared to facilitate language and literacy development, plan and implement instruction, and provide instruction via ASL, there were also some responsibilities for which they did not feel fully prepared. These responsibilities are discussed in the following sections.

Managing Behavior

Two participants specifically mentioned managing the behavior of their students as a responsibility for which they did not feel fully prepared. Although both participants attribute their unpreparedness in classroom and behavior management to their preparation, they attribute to different aspects of behavior management. Bartholomew mentioned that he had received limited instruction in behaviors related to various (additional) disabilities. He explained, "We had our stereotypical special education classes that involved deafness, but it was pretty surface [level regarding] all of the other disabilities and specific behaviors related to those disabilities. I just don't have much training at all." His course of study prepared him for a position in secondary science; however, he accepted a position in a post-secondary program, which requires him to provide transition instruction for students, many of whom have additional disabilities.

Anna, like Bartholomew, accepted a position outside of her endorsement area. While she studied elementary education during the program, she was hired to teach high school math. She described classroom and behavior management as being more challenging with high school students. She said, "I was not prepared for high school. It was a lot more difficult than I was expecting. It's a whole different type of education in how you interact with the students' [and with] behavior management." She also mentioned that all of her practicum and internship experiences were in elementary settings. While both students had opportunities to practice behavior management during their clinical experiences, the skills they developed did not generalize to all settings. Behavior management is a responsibility for which all beginning teachers need to be prepared; however, the other responsibilities the participants mentioned are responsibilities unique to special education and deaf education.

Developing and Implementing IEPs

While some participants mentioned feeling prepared for IEP related responsibilities, others mentioned feeling less prepared. Bartholomew said, "I feel like I wasn't necessarily prepared for the IEP process. I sat in an IEP meeting in internship. And we had to do a mock IEP (in class), but it wasn't anything close to the real deal." As he notes, the IEP process was taught in his program. He observed a real IEP meeting during his internship, and he wrote a mock IEP and participated in a mock IEP meeting during a course. However, he still did not feel prepared to take on this responsibility independently during his first year as a teacher. Molly also mentioned that she recalled writing an IEP during the program, but that the experience of writing an IEP in the position for which she was hired seemed different. She explained,

> I remember writing an IEP, but I don't remember it being like what I have to do now... We use Easy IEP... if there's a way to show them how to do it [in Easy IEP]... Maybe I just needed it step-by-step, but it's way different than what I thought it would be.

Her explanation emphasizes that developing IEPs requires that beginning teachers of the deaf need to know not only how to write goals and objectives, but also how to use specific software (in her case, Easy IEP) to do so.

On the other hand, Rich discussed IEP responsibilities. He mentioned that the responsibilities with IEPs go beyond the development of IEPs. He explained,

> IEPs. We probably could have spent some more time [on them]... One of the things that I'm still struggling with in my job right now is practical use of an IEP and documenting progress. I have 28 students, and, for a lot of them, I didn't write their goals and objectives. I have 28 students times three objectives, and I have to figure out how to address them and how to document that they're making progress on them. So progress monitoring for IEP objectives would be something that I could have learned a little more about before I left [the program].

Rich's explanation emphasizes that implementing IEPs requires teachers of the deaf to monitor and document student progress on their IEP objectives. It is unclear to what extent the participants were involved with IEP progress monitoring during their internships because none of them mentioned this activity when reflecting on their experiences in the program. It's likely that this was not a task that directing teachers expected the preservice teachers to take responsibility for during their internship. While developing and implementing IEPs is a primary job responsibility for all teachers of students with disabilities, managing hearing equipment is a job responsibility that is unique to only some teachers of the deaf.

Managing Hearing Equipment

According to the Gallaudet Research Institute (2010), 63.5% of d/hh students use cochlear implants and/or hearing aids, and 45% use assistive listening devices. At schools for the deaf, audiologists often take primary responsibility for managing these hearing equipment. But in mainstream settings, there may or may not be audiologists available to take on this task, and beginning teachers of the deaf can be expected to take on this responsibility. The teachers who mentioned feeling unprepared for this responsibility were hired as teachers in mainstream settings.

Morgan explained, "I don't feel like I knew enough about [hearing amplification devices] when I accepted this job." Similarly, Haley stated that her greatest area of unpreparedness was not "knowing more about hearing aids, FM [systems], and cochlear [implants]." She explained,

> [With cochlear implants] it's pretty much straight forward, as far as the lights and the battery. You can pretty much reset it just by undoing the battery and putting it back in. But as far as the hearing aids, I've called Phonak for that. Probably a month into my position I had ordered a FM system for a student, and I was trying to set up this FM system. And I had no clue how to set up an FM system. We didn't go over that [in the program]. I know how to turn it on and off. At [the school where I did my internship] the FM systems just mounted on the wall. If they didn't sync, the student walked back out and back in. So I had to call Phonak and figure out how to do it, and they told me [the student] has to take the hearing aids to the audiologist first and get it programmed. They basically just have to flip a switch on the program, and then you can hook it up together. You have to put the pieces on and take off the battery door and put on a new battery door, and it's a lot more detail than you realize.

The language the participants used, such as needing to know "more" or not knowing "enough," indicates that these topics were addressed in their program, but that they felt could have had additional preparation. The participants took several courses in audiology; however, these courses were not taught in the college of education. Instead, they were housed in the college of health. The courses were intended to provide students with a comprehensive knowledge of hearing science, but they did not include practicum components. The participants also took a course in speech development that was housed in the college of education. This course did have a practicum component, but was focused primarily on speech and language therapy, not on hearing equipment management. The majority of preservice practicum and internship experiences are completed at the school for the deaf. At these schools, the teachers are typically not the primary professionals managing the equipment. As a result, the participants likely had minimal opportunities to practice hearing equipment management skills during the program. In addition to minimal opportunities to practice hearing equipment management, participants also reported minimal opportunities to practice some skills related to working with some students who use sign language.

Interpreting and Communicating via Simultaneous Communication

Although participants identified providing instruction via ASL as a responsibility for which they felt prepared, multiple participants identified additional responsibilities related to ASL use, for which they felt unprepared.

On of these responsibilities was interpreting. The program does not specifically require students to take interpreting classes, as the preservice teachers are not intended to be prepared as interpreters. Jane provided some insight into some of the reasons that a beginning teacher of the deaf might need to develop interpreting skills. She said,

> I think interpreting would be a really important skill for us...learning how to have interpreting skills for when you go on field trips, when you need to interpret videos in the classroom, or when someone else who doesn't know sign language comes into the classroom...There are so many opportunities where we have to interpret so that would be a really important skill.

While there are interpreters available to interpret for d/hh students in some settings, beginning teachers of the deaf, like Jane, may be responsible for interpreting in other settings.

Students in the program do have the option of taking interpreting courses as electives. Some of the participants, including Molly, did. When she mentioned the interpreting classes that she took during the program, she said,

> I think [we could have taken] more interpreting classes. I had Sign to Voice and Voice to Sign, and that was it. Those were the only two interpreting classes, and I feel my signing lacks a little. I'm good in the deaf ed setting, but I wish I was better. I wish I had more group activities with deaf people as a part of the interpreting classes and ASL I–IV. I didn't learn nearly as much sign language in those classes as I did my first semester teaching in a deaf setting.

Although she suggests taking additional courses in interpreting, she also acknowledges that her own proficiency was acquired through authentic opportunities to use ASL.

Another responsibility related to sign language that participants mentioned was using simultaneous communication (simcom). Simcom is communication in which a person uses both spoken and signed language simultaneously. When a person uses simcom, the sign language that is used is not ASL, but rather contact sign language, which elements of both ASL and English and does not strictly adhere to the grammar of either language. Jane, who accepted a position that required her to use simcom mentioned that she wished she had learned to simcom better. Tim also mentioned simcom. He said,

> [We had] very strict ASL teachers in college who wanted [us to use] ASL. I really enjoyed...but some people might not have felt prepared to switch from voice off [ASL] to simcom...We really focused on [ASL only] so I don't know what I would have done if I'd taken an itinerant position where there was some spoken language, some simcomming, and a little bit of ASL...I don't think I would have been ready for that.

Tim's comments highlight the diversity of the field and the difficult task teacher preparation programs face in preparing beginning teachers of the deaf for the wide range of positions in the various settings.

In response to our first research question, participants described feeling most prepared to facilitate language and literacy development, plan and implement instruction, and provide instruction via ASL, while they described feeling least prepared to manage behavior, write and implement IEPs, manage hearing equipment, and interpret and communicate via simcom. In the next section we relate these area of preparedness and unpreparedness to the students' reflections on their clinical experiences.

Research Question 2

Our second research question was: *How do the graduates describe the relationship between their perceptions of preparedness for the responsibilities of the positions they obtain after graduation and their clinical experiences (practicum courses and internship)?* When the graduates discussed their perceptions of preparedness they also discussed several components of the program; these components were almost always connected to some type of practical application or clinical experience. The themes we identified in response to this question were: focus on application in methods courses, quantity and diversity of clinical experiences, and influence of mentors.

Focus on Application During Methods Courses

While our second research question was focused on their reflections of their clinical experiences, it is important to mention that participants mentioned that the heavy focus on application in their methods courses was beneficial. As we previously described, the program intentionally coordinates coursework and clinical experiences. When students reflected on how they learned to facilitate language and literacy development, plan and implement instruction and provide instruction via ASL they talked about the opportunities they had to practice those skills in both their methods courses and their clinical experiences.

Participants also mentioned the use of practical examples in their courses. Bartholomew said of her coursework,

> It was helpful because it wasn't just, "Here are a bunch of vocab words. Go memorize them all." It was, "These are case studies." And if you can pretend it's something that's real and applicable to you . . . that is beneficial.

Similarly, Erin reflected,

Experience is the biggest thing that you can give beginning deaf educators. Just experience. Different experiences. All kinds. And just throwing out random scenarios—This is what you might get. And this is what might happen to you, so be prepared. I definitely feel like I was well prepared.

These participants indicated that the use of case studies and scenarios in their courses stuck with them and helped them feel prepared. Professors used this strategy to make the information more authentic and allowed students to apply the theories and methods they were learning through guided and shared practice. Another way that professors connected theory and practice was through guided discussions of the preservice teachers' experiences in their practicum and internship placements.

Participants explained that during practicum courses and internship they were given time during classes to discuss their experiences and they found these opportunities to be beneficial. Anna noted,

I really liked classes that were discussion classes about our experiences...the practicum classes and the classes that you were really actually able to do hands on experience were the most beneficial. And coming back and talking as a group...other professionals...these are things that work well or these are the things I saw. And talking through that helps the most.

Anna and others indicated that the opportunity to talk with and to seek advice from peers who are experiencing similar challenges can be helpful. They explained that when they were not sure what to do in a particular situation, their peers often had ideas and/or examples of strategies that had worked for them.

Hearing about each other's experiences also allowed the participants to extend their learning opportunities beyond their own experiences to a broader variety of settings, grade levels, and subjects. Becky explained that reflecting on what she had learned from her peers helped her in the position for which she was hired after graduation. While her selected endorsement area was Elementary Education K–6, she was hired as a long-term substitute for high school mathematics.

After we taught all week [in our internship], we all came back [to classes] on Fridays. When I interned in preschool, I would talk about my experiences and other people would talk about their experiences...hearing other people's experiences was interesting. And then once I got the maternity leave position...hearing those stories from other students helped me in my job...I was able to relate back to what they had said happened and what had worked for them. I tried to do [what worked for them] too, and that helped.

Although the program cannot create opportunities for preservice teachers to experience every possible job in the field while still allowing them time to become highly qualified in an endorsement area, participants provided insight into how the program took advantage of the collective diverse practicum and internship placements of the preservice teachers. As a result, when participants encountered challenges in their first year of teaching they were able to apply what they learned from not only their own clinical experiences, but also their peers' clinical experiences. This strategy allows the preservice teachers to benefits from the diversity of the program's array of practicum and internship placements.

Quantity and Diversity of Clinical Experiences

A main component of the program is the clinical experiences that preservice teachers complete throughout Years 3, 4, and 5. The participants mentioned both quantity and diversity of clinical experiences in their reflections. All participants' clinical experiences were the same in terms of quantity, but they were placed in a wide variety of settings. These placements were determined based on their selected endorsement area, their preferences, and availability.

Some participants described a wide variety of placements throughout their time in the program. For example, Bartholomew mentioned clinical experiences with a speech language pathologist, an elementary school teacher, a middle school reading remediation teacher, and a high school math teacher. In addition to these experiences with d/hh students, she also had the opportunity to work with hearing students in a middle school language arts class. Haley also had a wide variety of placements; one of those placements pushed her out of her comfort zone. She explained,

> I did a practicum in the high school, and I'm personally geared more towards the younger kids. So going into the residential school in the high school and being put in that classroom was kind of terrifying. Not gonna lie! But once I was in there…the teacher was deaf, so…. "Okay I have to sign." And there's no way around it…I guess it was completely out of my comfort zone. But by the time you get into it a little bit, you start getting more comfortable, and answering questions for the kids, and helping a little bit more.

While some participants did have a variety of placements, others did not. Becky, indicated that she did not have a wide variety of clinical experiences. She earned an endorsement in elementary education; therefore, she requested and received all of her placements in elementary school settings. However, upon graduation she was not immediately hired for an elementary school position. Instead, she was hired as a long-term substitute in a residential school, and her first placement was substituting for a high school math teacher who was on maternity leave. She said,

> I did my practicums in elementary...and I kind of look back and I wish I would have done—which they told me I should have done—a practicum in a different grade level. Middle school or high school. But I was always just like, "I'm never going to teach them," but I did...I had [placements in] what I thought it was going to be like [after graduation], but then it was different. So I should have done a practicum in a different grade level, just to get that different experience.

Her words emphasize that, although preservice teachers plan and hope for a specific position after graduation, they often accept positions outside of their selected endorsement area. As we previously mentioned, when graduates accept positions outside of their selected endorsement area, this influences their perceptions of preparedness.

In addition to the variety of placements, participants also emphasized the impact of the full year internship. They stressed that it was important because it gave them an extended amount of time to apply what they learned in their classes, it provided them with an opportunity to experience multiple placements, and it allowed them to experience a school year from the beginning to the end of the year. Erin, like most participants, did three placements during her internship year. She began the year in a preschool program for d/hh students who use listening and spoken language. Next, she did a placement in a Kindergarten class with hearing children. Her final internship placement was at a residential school for the deaf with 1st and 2nd graders who used ASL. As she reflected on her experiences, she noted,

> I am just so thankful...talked to a lot of people who have come from programs where they are not in the classroom all day most of the week. Just that time of being there all day and getting to see what the whole day for four days out of the week was invaluable. And I had a whole year of it. I needed all the experience I could get. I liked having three different experiences. I think that really helped a lot. Having the regular ed experience really was helpful to me, especially now that I am in inclusion.

She stresses the benefits of both having multiple experiences and doing "a whole year," calling her experiences "invaluable." Molly also mentioned the impact of her internship experience. She reflected,

> I felt like my deaf ed internship was huge. I had an awesome [experience]...I mean I just learned so much and to have that hands-on work everyday was probably the biggest aspect of college for me. Getting that hands on experience with real kids everyday from the beginning of the year.

When she uses the word "real" she emphasizes a key component of clinical experiences to provide preservice teachers with authentic opportunities to apply what they have learned in guided, collaborative, and independent practice opportunities (Fisher & Frey, 2008). The information learned in classes is essential, but clinical experiences provide the opportunity for preservice teachers to develop competency in the skills needed for the responsibilities of the positions that await them. By beginning with practicum courses and culminating in a year-long internship, the program is able to use a true gradual release of responsibility model (Fisher & Frey, 2008; Pearson & Gallagher,1983; Vygotsky, 1978) for facilitating the development of these competencies. An important part of this model is the influence of the mentor teachers who provide guidance and feedback to students throughout their clinical experiences.

Influence of Mentors

During clinical experiences, participants had an opportunity to learn from both their university supervisors and their mentor teachers in the clinical experience placements. After observing exemplary instruction provided by their mentors, preservice teachers are given a chance to apply what they have learned in the classroom. They are observed multiple times, both formally and informally, by their mentors and their supervisor and provided feedback. The supervisor collaborates with mentors by establishing and maintaining communication regarding preservice teachers, which includes reviewing the mentors' weekly evaluations and inviting the mentors to join in post-observation conferences. Participants commented on the influence of mentors throughout their clinical experiences. Anna discussed both the university supervisor and mentor teacher in her reflections. She said,

> I had some really good mentors [from the university] ... they were observing frequently and giving feedback on teaching or other feedback on writing and things. My mentor teacher in [one practicum] was really awesome. She gave me plenty of time to try teaching myself ... that was really beneficial to get her feedback at such an early stage of learning how to teach.

She specifically mentions how both her university supervisors and her mentor teachers provided feedback early in the program. This helped her to begin developing her teaching skills prior to her internship and graduation. Anna explained that it was beneficial that her practicum teacher allow her ample time to teach lessons. Similarly, Tim explained that it was important that he had that opportunity during his practicum courses and internship. He said,

> The mentor teacher itself is probably the most important part ... I had a sink or swim teacher and some people may not have liked that. I enjoyed it because I had more control. I could learn [through] my own mistakes. And I had someone there who would support me, but they weren't going to just take over automatically. All three of my mentor teachers were that way.

His words stress the importance of having support while still being given full responsibility and control of the classroom.

In addition to having the opportunity to get feedback and support while teaching, participants also expressed that it was helpful to have a person whom they could go to with questions. Molly did the majority of her internship in another state. She met with her university supervisor regularly and joined her peers in class virtually each week; however, her mentor was the one whom she mentioned going to with questions. Molly reflected,

> I felt like my deaf ed internship was huge...I had an awesome mentor...I mean I just learned so much...Seeing how she does her assessments and her lessons and having someone to answer questions while you're figuring out what you're doing. That was really helpful.

In response to our second research question, participants indicated that the focus on application in methods courses, quantity and diversity of clinical experiences, and influence of mentors influenced their perceptions of preparedness for the responsibilities of the positions they obtained after graduation. In the next section, we discuss our findings and the implications they carry for future research and for the design of deaf education teacher preparation.

DISCUSSION

The purpose of this study was to serve as a starting point for research in the area of deaf education teacher preparation. We sought to better understand the demands of the field by documenting the perspectives of beginning teachers of the deaf who graduated from one clinically rich deaf education teacher preparation program. Although the participants were hired in a wide variety of positions after graduation, the themes that emerged from the data provided insight into how the program prepares its graduates for the positions available in the field. We found that the participants perceived themselves to be prepared for the major responsibilities of the positions for which they were hired; however, they perceived themselves to be less prepared for some of the responsibilities of those positions. They also identified the components of the program that influenced their perceptions of preparedness. These findings hold implications for the design of this particular program and other deaf education teacher preparation programs, as well as the broader context of teacher preparation.

Participants' reflections focused primarily on the hands-on experiences afforded to them in their clinical experiences, but they did mention their coursework as well. Liston, Whitcomb, and Borko (2006) found that teachers complain that the theories and methods they learn in their university coursework do not help them with their actual practice. Our participants did not echo these complaints. In fact, they mentioned course activities that allowed them to apply what they were learning. They specifically mentioned the use of case studies and scenarios in their classes as contributing to their preparedness. Richman (2015) found the use of case studies demonstrate a significant, measurable change in teacher learning. The use of case studies facilitates the transfer of learning from one situation to another by providing students with the opportunity to reason critically about classroom dilemmas, to develop the ability to be more metacognitive about their own teaching, to examine their teaching beliefs, and to have their learning influenced by social interaction with others (Lundeberg, 1999). Participants also mentioned opportunities to learn from their peers during discussions about their internship experiences. This is similar to the use of case studies because it provides additional opportunities for transferring learning from one situation to another. Teacher preparation programs can use case studies and guided discussion about clinical experiences during courses to provide opportunities for preservice teachers to begin applying theories and methods. The gradual release of responsibility can then continue through careful alignment and progression of practicum and internship experiences.

Although the program is designed to intentionally coordinate coursework and clinical experiences, participants in this study seemed to distinctly separate their coursework and their clinical experiences (Feiman-Nemser, 2001; Griffin, 1999; Levine, 2006; Zeichner, 2010). This finding was interesting because they did indicate that there was coordination between their courses and clinical experiences. In fact, with all of the responsibilities for which they reported feeling most prepared (facilitating language and literacy development, planning and implementing instruction, and providing instruction via ASL), they acknowledged that they had first learned these skills in courses and then had ample opportunity to develop them through clinical experiences. The participants reflections indicated that the program was clearly designed to gradually release responsibility (Fisher & Frey, 2008; Pearson & Gallagher, 1983; Vygotsky, 1978) and provide them with authentic opportunities to apply the theories and methods learned in courses through guided, collaborative, and independent practice opportunities (Fisher & Frey, 2008) in their clinical experiences as they reflected on their preparedness for these responsibilities. However, with the responsibilities for which they reported feeling least prepared (managing behavior, developing and implementing IEPs, managing hearing equipment, and interpreting and communicating via Simultaneous Communication), the intentional gradual release of responsibility was less clear and there were fewer opportunities for practice of these responsibilities in clinical settings.

We found that the quantity and diversity of clinical experiences had a positive impact on their perceptions of preparedness. Like Andrew (1990), we found that the 5-year model produced graduates who reported feeling prepared. By using a 5-year model, the program was able to incorporate a year-long internship, which participants indicated contributed to their preparedness. This supports studies that have found that increasing the duration of internships positively influences beginning teachers' perceptions of preparedness (Ronfeldt & Reininger, 2012). Additionally, students were able to have several different placements. Like Boe et al. (2007), we found that beginning teachers were more prepared for the responsibilities of their position when their clinical experiences aligned with the positions for which they were hired. Having several placements increases the likelihood that at least one of their clinical experiences would be similar to the position for which they were hired after graduation. It also allows preservice teachers to work with a variety of mentor teachers. Participants indicated that their mentor teachers positively impacted their perceptions of preparedness, supporting the findings of Ronfeldt et al. (2013). These findings emphasize the importance of the intentional design of clinical experiences and careful selection of high quality mentor teachers and are relevant for all teacher preparation programs.

Some of our findings, however, were unique to special education and/or deaf education teacher preparation. The development and implementation of IEPs is a responsibility for which special education and deaf education beginning teachers must be prepared. Our findings indicate that preservice teachers need multiple opportunities to practice writing IEPs and to engage in this process with their mentor teachers in clinical settings. Moreover, when possible they should be given opportunities to practice writing IEPs using common software available for this function. Because language and literacy development is especially complex and important with d/hh students, this is an important component of deaf education teacher preparation programs. The program in this study required 9 credit hours of coursework and opportunities for practice in both their practicum and internship experiences; this design positively influenced the participants' perceptions of preparedness. Preservice teachers of the deaf need extensive and integrated coursework and clinical practice in language and literacy assessment and instruction for d/hh students.

Providing instruction in ASL, managing hearing equipment, and interpreting and communicating via simcom were responsibilities expected of some of the teachers of the deaf in this study. Unlike the skill of developing IEPs, which is widely needed by deaf education graduates, the need for these skills depended heavily on teaching context. Additionally, in order to comprehensively develop skills sets for the responsibilities of managing hearing equipment and interpreting, one needs substantial coursework and practical experience, as these are each programs of study in their own right. With credit hour limitations for degrees, it is not possible to address all topics in depth. With the exception of providing instruction via ASL, these topics were integrated into the coursework on an introductory level and were not always integrated into clinical experiences. For example, the participants learned about hearing equipment during their speech and language course. While it was briefly taught, they did not have substantial hands-on experiences with hearing aids, cochlear implants, and FM systems. Acknowledging the challenge of addressing all potential responsibilities thoroughly in coursework and clinical experiences, it may be beneficial for preservice teachers to develop professional skills in how to collaborate with varied professionals to best serve students, cultivate networks of support, and locate resources within and outside of their school systems.

In the introduction, we discussed the extreme diversity of positions in the field of deaf education. We found that when clinical experiences aligned with the positions for which graduates were hired, they perceived themselves to be more prepared for the responsibilities they were given. We question whether this is also the case with responsibilities that require specialized knowledge (e.g., ASL, interpreting, and audiology). All of the participants had an extensive amount of coursework in and practical experience with ASL. This was not the case with interpreting and audiology. The preservice teachers in the program were able to choose 12–15 of professional electives. The preservice teachers who chose elementary education as their selected endorsement area were able to use these electives to take courses in interpreting or audiology. Although many participants did provide details regarding their individual program, we did not specifically ask which endorsement area they had selected or which professional electives they had taken. Therefore, we do not know whether the participants who mentioned these areas of unpreparedness took related electives. It is possible that students who chose to take electives in specialized knowledge areas felt more prepared for the related responsibilities. Without knowing which positions preservice teachers will accept after graduation, it is challenging to plan a corresponding program of study (i.e., courses and clinical experiences) for preservice teachers.

Further, the aim of comprehensive teacher preparation programs is to prepare teachers of the deaf who can work in any deaf education teaching context, yet the feasibility of that ideal must be questioned. Preparing teachers for diverse educational settings, philosophies, and communication approaches may spread a deaf education teacher preparation program too thin, and not allow sufficient depth in all potential areas of responsibility. The participants in the study reported feeling well prepared to provide instruction via ASL. Not only did they take a greater number of required credit hours in ASL than is average for deaf education teacher preparation programs (Dolman, 2008), they were also immersed in the language in both courses and clinical experiences. Participants credited these immersion experiences with their competency in ASL, supporting the findings of Freed et al. (2004). It should be noted that since the time of the study, the program has decided to build on this strength and transition from a comprehensive program to an ASL-English bilingual program. Instead of attempting to prepare teachers for every teaching context, they have decided to focus their preservice teacher preparation to allow deeper and richer experiences in bilingual contexts.

CONCLUSION

This study examined the perceptions of a small group of beginning teachers, who graduated from one deaf education teacher preparation program. The small sample size ($N = 13$) of this study is a limitation. We acknowledge that the participants knew the researchers and this likely impacted their responses to the interview questions in some way. For example, it is possible that because we are associated with the program, they were not comfortable sharing some of their perceptions and/or reflections with us, particularly if those perceptions and/or reflections could be perceived as critical of the program. Additionally, our own relationships to the program and perspectives of the field may have led us to focus our analysis on certain responsibilities or components of the program that we perceived to be most relevant. Despite these limitations, our findings make an important contribution to the field, shedding light on gaps in research examining the responsibilities of beginning teachers of the deaf as well as deaf education teacher preparation. It is important that future research continue to identify the roles and responsibilities of teachers of the deaf by including the experiences of a larger and more diverse group of participants. Furthermore it should seek to include additional measures of preparedness, beyond self-perceptions.

REFERENCES

Albertini, J. A., & Schley, S. (2003). Writing. In M. Marschark & P. E. Spencer (Eds.), *Oxford handbook of deaf studies, language, and education* (pp. 123–135). New York, NY: Oxford University Press.

Andrew, M. D. (1990). Differences between graduates of 4-year and 5-year teacher preparation programs. *Journal of Teacher Education, 41*(2), 45–51.

Andrew, M. D., & Schwab, R. L. (1995). Has reform in teacher education influenced teacher performance? An outcome assessment of graduates of an eleven-university consortium. *Action in teacher education, 17*(3), 43–53.

Apel, K., & Masterson, J. (2015). Comparing the spelling and reading abilities of students with cochlear implants and students with typical hearing. *Journal of Deaf Studies and Deaf Education, 20*(2), 125–135.

Auton, S., Berry, D., Mullen, S., & Cochran, R. (2002). Induction program for beginners benefits veteran teachers, too. *Journal of Staff Development, 23*(4), 77–92.

Boe, E., Shin, S., & Cook, L. H. (2007). Does teacher preparation matter for beginning teachers in either special or general education? *Journal of Special Education, 41*(3), 158–170.

Brown, J. S., Collins, A., & Duguid, P. (1989). Situated cognition and the culture of learning. *Educational Researcher, 18*(1), 32–42.

Clancey, W. J. (1994). Situated cognition: How representations are created and given meaning. In R. Lewis & P. Mendelsohn (Eds.), *Lessons from Learning, IFIP Transactions A-46* (pp. 231–242), Amsterdam, Netherlands: North-Holland.

Darling-Hammond, L., Berry, B. T., Haselkorn, D., & Fideler, E. (1999). Teacher recruitment, selection, and induction: Policy influences on the supply and quality of teachers. In L. Darling-Hammond & G. Sykes (Eds.), *Teaching as the learning profession: Handbook of policy and practice* (pp. 183–232). San Francisco, CA: Jossey-Bass.

Davis, B. H., Higdon, K. A., Resta, V. K., & Latiolais, L. L. (2001). Teacher fellows: A graduate program for beginning teachers. *Action in Teacher Education, 23*(2), 43–49.

Dodd, E. E., & Scheetz, N. A. (2003). Preparing today's teachers of the deaf and hard of hearing to work with tomorrow's students: A statewide needs assessment. *American Annals of the Deaf, 148*(1), 25–30.

Dolman, D. (2008). College and university requirements for teachers of the deaf at the undergraduate level: A twenty-year comparison. *American Annals of the Deaf, 153*(3), 322–327.

Feiman-Nemser, S. (2001). From preparation to practice: Designing a continuum to strengthen and sustain teaching. *Teachers College Record, 103*(6), 1013–1055.

Fisher, D., & Frey, N. (2008). Releasing responsibility. *Educational Leadership, 66*(3), 32–37.

Freed, B. F., Segalowitz, N., & Dewey, D. P. (2004). Context of learning and second language fluency in French: Comparing regular classroom, study abroad, and intensive domestic immersion programs. *Studies in Second Language Acquisition, 26*(2), 275–301.

Gallaudet Research Institute. (2000). *Annual survey of deaf and hard of hearing children & youth.* Washington, DC: Author. Retrieved from https://research .gallaudet.edu/Demographics/

Gallaudet Research Institute. (2010). *Annual survey of deaf and hard of hearing children & youth.* Washington, DC: Author. Retrieved from https://research .gallaudet.edu/Demographics/

Goodlad, J. I. (1994). The national network for educational renewal. *Phi Delta Kappan, 75*(8), 632–639.

Griffin, G. A. (Ed.). (1999). *The education of teachers: Ninety-eighth yearbook of the National Society for the Study of Education.* Chicago, IL: University of Chicago Press.

Guba, E. G. (1981). Criteria for assessing the trustworthiness of naturalistic inquiries. *Educational Technology Research and Development, 29*(2), 75–91.

Holmes Group. (1986). *Tomorrow's teachers*. East Lansing, MI: Holmes Group.

Holmes Group. (1990). *Tomorrow's schools*. East Lansing, MI: Holmes Group.

Holmes Group. (1995). *Tomorrow's schools of education*. East Lansing, MI: Holmes Group.

Isabelli-Garcia, C., & Lacorte, M. (2016). Language learners' characteristics, target language use, and linguistic development in a domestic immersion context. *Foreign Language Annals, 49*(3), 544–556.

Lave, J., & Wegner, E. (1991). *Situated learning: Legitimate peripheral participation*. Cambridge, England: Cambridge University Press.

Lenihan, S. (2010). Trends and challenges in teacher preparation in deaf education. *The Volta Review, 110*(2), 117–128.

Levine, A. (2005). *Educating school leaders*. Washington, DC: The Education Schools Project. Retrieved from http://edschools.org/reports_leaders.htm

Liston, D., Whitcomb, J., & Borko, H. (2006). Too little or too much: Teacher preparation and the first years of teaching. *Journal of Teacher Education, 57*(4), 351–358.

Lundeberg, M. A. 1999. Discovering teaching and learning through cases. In M. A. Lundeberg,, B. A. Levin, & H. Harrington. (Eds.), *Who learns what from cases and how: The research base for teaching and learning with cases* (pp. 3–24). Mahwah, NJ: Erlbaum.

Miles, M. B., & Huberman, A. M. (1994). *Qualitative data analysis: A sourcebook of new methods*. Newbury Park, CA: SAGE.

National Center for Education Statistics. (2016, December). Elementary and secondary education (NCES 2016-014). In *Digest of Education Statistics: 2015*. Retrieved from https://nces.ed.gov/programs/digest/d15/ch_2.asp

Pearson, P. D., & Gallagher, M. C. (1983). The instruction of reading comprehension, *Contemporary Educational Psychology, 8*, 317–344.

Pitri, E. (2004). Situated learning in a classroom community. *Art Education, 57*(6), 6–12.

Richman, L. (2015). Using online case studies to enhance teacher preparation. *Journal of Technology and Teacher Education, 23*(4), 535–559.

Ronfeldt, M., & Reininger, M. (2012). More or better student teaching? *Teaching and Teacher Education, 28*(8), 1091–1106.

Ronfeldt, M., Reininger, M., & Kwok, A. (2013). Recruitment or Preparation? Investigating the effects of teacher characteristics and student teaching. *Journal of Teacher Education, 64*(4), 319–337.

Schwandt, T. A., Lincoln, Y. S., & Guba, E. G. (2007). Judging interpretations: But is it rigorous? Trustworthiness and authenticity in naturalistic evaluation. *New Directions for Evaluation, 2007*(114), 11–25.

Shenton, A. K. (2004). Strategies for ensuring trustworthiness in qualitative research projects. *Education for Information, 22*(2), 63–75.

Sirois, P., Boisclair, A., & Giasson, J. (2008). Understanding of the alphabetic principle through invented spelling among hearing-impaired children learning to read and write: Experimentation with a pedagogical approach. *Journal of Research in Reading, 31*(4), 339–358.

Strauss, A. L. (1987). *Qualitative analysis for social scientists*. Cambridge, England: Cambridge University Press.

Strauss, A. L., & Corbin, J. (1990). *Basics of qualitative research: Grounded theory procedures and techniques.* Newberry Park, CA: SAGE.

Traxler, C. B. (2000). The Stanford achievement test, 9th edition: National norming and performance standards for deaf and hard-of-hearing students. *Journal of Deaf Studies and Deaf Education, 5*(4), 337–348.

Vygotsky, L. S. (1978). *Mind in society: The development of higher psychological processes.* Cambridge, MA: Harvard University Press.

Zeichner, K. (2010). Rethinking connections between campus courses and field experiences in college and university-based teacher education. *Journal of Teacher Education, 61*(1–2), 89–99.

CHAPTER 12

LOOKING ACROSS THE CHAPTERS
Reflections and Enduring Questions

Rebecca West Burns
University of South Florida

As the editors mention in the introduction, the authors in the book are truly courageous in sharing stories and research about the work they are living on a daily basis. Their descriptions of outcomes are essential in identifying and articulating the impact of clinical practice. Equally courageous are the editors who challenged the authors to identify and write about the outcomes of their work because knowing and being able to communicate outcomes of clinically based teacher education will be imperative for scholars and practitioners as they design, implement, resource, and research clinically based teacher education programs.

In looking across the chapters of this book, it becomes clear that teacher education scholars are studying the work they are doing to reshape teacher education programs to reflect the calls for positioning the clinical component as central to learning to teach. What is unclear, however, is the complexity and nature of the work that led to the outcomes. That murkiness

Outcomes of High-Quality Clinical Practice in Teacher Education, pages 249–262
Copyright © 2018 by Information Age Publishing

most likely arises from the long-standing woes of a lack of common terminology, definitions, and conceptual framework for understanding clinically based teacher education (Zeichner, 2005). Yendol-Hoppey's (2013) continuum of models of teacher education (clinically limited, clinically accomplished, clinically intensive, clinically centered, and only clinical) is helpful in distinguishing teacher education programs, but the intricacies of developing the necessary and intentional school-university partnerships needed to successfully enact clinically intensive and clinically centered models of teacher preparation have yet to be deeply understood. The heuristic introduced in the first chapter also attempts to highlight the complexities and particulars of moving forward with reform that is centered on developing high quality clinical practices in teacher education and the need for studying these efforts (Yendol-Hoppey et al., 2017). Below, I will further the discussion of the clinical program practices framework and attempt to provide language to describe the nature of the work that led to the outcomes found in this book. Next, I discuss the importance of the framework in connection to outcomes for clinically based teacher education, and I describe two chapters as examples of the connection between the framework and the outcomes described in those chapters. Finally, I end the chapter with enduring questions for those working in clinically based teacher education.

SETS OF CORE PRACTICES OF SUCCESSFUL CLINICALLY BASED TEACHER EDUCATION PROGRAMS

One promising framework for clinically based teacher education is emerging from the work of Yendol-Hoppey et al. (2017), who have identified and named six core sets of practices for successful clinically rich and clinically centered teacher education programs. Those six core sets of practices are identified as: (a) teacher candidate evaluation practices, (b) teacher candidate coaching practices, (c) methods instruction practices, (d) partnership development practices, (e) program leadership practices, and (f) research practices (Table 12.1). In this section, I summarize these core sets of practices and explain how they can be coupled to foster meaningful outcomes in clinically based teacher education.

Core Set 1: Clinical Evaluation Practices

The first category, Clinical Evaluation Practices, includes the activities associated with assessing and rendering evidence-based judgment on a teacher candidate's performance. Activities in this category may include facilitating periodic evaluation conferences, documenting progress, developing

TABLE 12.1 Clinical Practices for University- and School-Based Teacher Educators

Clinical Evaluation Practices *Assessing Candidate Quality*	Clinical Coaching Practices *Supporting and Strengthening Candidate Performance*	Partnership Practices *Facilitating SBTE[a] & UBTE[b] Shared Responsibility for Teacher Education*	Methods and Foundation Course Practices *Creating Strong Course-to-Field and Field-to-Course Connection*	Educator Preparation Leadership Practices *Overseeing Clinically Intensive Programs*	Research Practices *Engaging in Teacher Education Research Practices*
• Conduct UBTE evaluations • Conduct SBTE evaluations • Review Candidate self evaluation • Conduct evaluation conference(s) with candidate and SBTE • When necessary collaborate as triad[c] to create and support a plan for continual improvement • Review professional standards concerns and participate in student initiated grievance processes	• Conduct observations to gather evidence for shared inquiry into candidate practice • Implement a range of signature pedagogies that focus on supporting candidate learning (e.g., inquiry, clinical supervision, content coaching, PLCs, teaching rounds, co-teaching) • Identify goals with candidate • Conduct coaching pre and post conferences with candidate and, when appropriate triad	• Establish a culture of shared responsibility for educator • Co-construct a shared understanding of candidate field experience expectations • Communicate regularly across stakeholders • Share feedback regarding coursework and fieldwork • Provide professional development support to strengthen learning of both UBTE & SBTE • Collaborate with stakeholders to	• Understand the clinical context including: curriculum, resources, and common pedagogical (core) practices • Work with school partners to design and revise curriculum and performance tasks • Facilitate candidate development of ability to negotiate curriculum and instructional tensions between course and field • Assure candidate understanding of the content needed for application of	• Bring together all faculty involved to develop program coherence • Facilitate on-going self-study • Collect, review, analyze, and share program related data • Collaborate with department chair on scheduling and staffing arrangement (including across departments) • Assure UBTE & SBTE credentials (e.g., effective, recency, relevancy) • Oversee professional standards	• Studying Teacher Education Program & Practices (e.g., evaluation, coaching, partnerships, course instruction, leadership) • Conducting Program Evaluation • Valuing a wide-range of paradigmatic (e.g., translational, applied, engaged scholarship) and methodological approaches (e.g., including self-study, action research) • Collaborative scholarship

(continued)

TABLE 12.1 Clinical Practices for University- and School-Based Teacher Educators (continued)

Clinical Evaluation Practices *Assessing Candidate Quality*	Clinical Coaching Practices *Supporting and Strengthening Candidate Performance*	Partnership Practices *Facilitating SBTE[a] & UBTE[b] Shared Responsibility for Teacher Education*	Methods and Foundation Course Practices *Creating Strong Course-to-Field and Field-to-Course Connection*	Educator Preparation Leadership Practices *Overseeing Clinically Intensive Programs*	Research Practices *Engaging in Teacher Education Research Practices*
• Conduct additional evaluations if educator candidate is on action plan • Maintain evaluation records and submit identified components as critical tasks • Write letters of recommendation for potential employers for candidates	• Maintain on-going communication related to candidate's growth • Plan and teach seminars designed to link theory and practice • Problem solve • Maintain regular contact with other program UBTE & SBTE to enhance coherence • Develop an understanding of course content that should be "performed" • Attend supervisory meetings	• problem solve • Create communication tools • Co-select placements • Engage in collaborative curriculum building, co-teaching, and research • Participate in on-going partnership assessment	knowledge • Develop SBTE and UBTE knowledge of subject-specific course instruction • Provide representations of practice, opportunities, deconstruction of practice, and opportunities for approximations of practice within course • Integrate coursework with field work through linked assignments • Participate in program coherence meetings	concerns and student grievances • Maintain evaluation records • Develop and implement program orientations each fall • Work with school partners to identifying partnership schools/placements for practicums and final internships • Recruit new partnership teachers for mentor training • Coordinate fingerprinting • Collaborate with advising	• Educator preparation grant writing activities

(continued)

TABLE 12.1 Clinical Practices for University- and School-Based Teacher Educators (continued)

Clinical Evaluation Practices *Assessing Candidate Quality*	Clinical Coaching Practices *Supporting and Strengthening Candidate Performance*	Partnership Practices *Facilitating SBTE[a] & UBTE[b] Shared Responsibility for Teacher Education*	Methods and Foundation Course Practices *Creating Strong Course-to-Field and Field-to-Course Connection*	Educator Preparation Leadership Practices *Overseeing Clinically Intensive Programs*	Research Practices *Engaging in Teacher Education Research Practices*
	• Conduct regular informal visits with candidates to support candidate learning		• Faculty Course Leads provide leadership across sections (e.g., adjuncts) • Revise and update syllabi, which may include preparing undergraduate/graduate program committee	• Collaborate with enrollment services on recruiting efforts	

a SBTE- School-based Teacher Educator

b UBTE- University-based Teacher Educator (Course/Field)

c Triad- SBTE, UBTE, teacher candidate

action plans as needed to guide candidate improvement, and maintaining candidate records. Whereas these activities may traditionally have been the sole responsibility of the university supervisor, in clinically intensive and clinically centered teacher education, teacher candidate evaluation should be a shared responsibility of school- and university-based teacher educators and it should be separate and distinguished from the next set of practices aimed at supporting candidate professional learning.

Core Set 2: Clinical Coaching Practices

The second category, Clinical Coaching Practices, includes developmentally appropriate activities associated with supporting candidate learning and enhancing candidate effectiveness in facilitating the learning of K–12 students in the clinical context. Much like the models of clinical supervision of inservice teachers (e.g., Cogan, 1973; Glickman, Gordon, & Ross-Gordon, 2014), coaching practices involve the design and use of data gathering tools to facilitate data-based conversations about candidates' teaching practice and its impact on K–12 student performance. Activities in this category may include peer observations, data collection while watching candidates work with K–12 students, pre- and post-observation conferences, co-teaching, and real-time coaching. Clinical Coaching Practices can be conducted individually but they should also be a shared responsibility of school- and university-based teacher educators.

Core Set 3: Partnership Practices

The third category, Partnership Practices, includes activities that nurture a culture of shared responsibility for teacher education between school- and university-based teacher educators. Developing shared expectations of candidates, collaborating on curriculum and research, engaging in ongoing collaborative problem solving, and establishing strong placements for candidates are all key activities in developing and maintaining school-university partnerships necessary to successfully enact clinically based teacher education. At the heart of Partnership Development Practices is the ability to establish and maintain relationships among stakeholders. Facilitation, negotiation, and conflict resolution skills are critical for school- and university-based teacher educators in order to successfully enact Partnership Practices.

Core Set 4: Methods and Foundations Course Practices

The fourth category, Methods and Foundations Course Practices, involves the reconceptualization of course instruction in clinically based teacher education programs to assure strong course-to-field and field-to-course connections. School- and university-based teacher educators (both methods instructors and field instructors) must collaboratively construct course content and develop performance tasks that match course goals while also honoring school curricula and the realities of classroom spaces. The results of integrating coursework with fieldwork provide multiple opportunities for candidates to apply what they have learned in their methods courses in a theory-to-practice approach. On the other hand, they also may allow for the reverse where candidates can engage in a practice-to-theory approach by noticing key incidents and naming them by connecting the incidents to theory learned in course instruction. When school- and university-based teacher educators engage in reconceptualized methods instruction practices, their knowledge of each other's professional contexts is strengthened and program coherence is improved.

Core Set 5: Educator Preparation Leadership Practices

The fifth category, Educator Preparation Leadership Practices, involves a shift in the mindset and enactment of school and university leaders. Leadership in clinically based teacher education must be collaborative with a shared focus on K–12 student learning that drives all decision-making. Collaboration should be inter-institutional and intra-institutional. Inter-institutional collaboration must occur among college department chairs, school building administrators, and district leaders to determine staffing arrangements, recruit teacher candidates, identify mentor teachers, select partnership schools, secure candidate placements, coordinate course offerings, and identify and allocate appropriate resources. Intra-institutional collaboration must occur between college deans to collaborate on course offerings. Intra-institutional collaboration must also occur between district leaders and building administrators to recognize, value, and reward the time and other resources needed for teachers to serve as school-based teacher educators.

Core Set 6: Research Practices

The sixth and final category, Research Practices, includes activities that guide program improvement and capture program outcomes. Such activities should include collecting, reviewing, and analyzing of program data to facilitate ongoing program evaluation and self study efforts. Much like the other categories, research activities in clinically based teacher education should be collaborative and utilize a wide range of methodological approaches. Engaging practitioners as coresearchers not only honors the voice and role of practitioners in the research process, but it will also likely challenge traditional academic perceptions and norms. The prestige of sole-authored publications and writing research only for other researcher audiences must change to value collaborative research and multiple publications outlets to have a greater impact on practice. Research is essential to understanding the benefits, persistent challenges, and impact of engaging in clinically based teacher education. This book is one attempt to synthesize data across individual studies with the goal of improving outcomes when using high quality clinical practices in teacher education programs. Each chapter contributes to the core set of research practices by designing innovative research and sharing results to help build the literature base.

Coupling Core Sets of Practices

The six sets of core practices are essential for successful clinically based teacher education. Together, they are the perfect unification of knowledge and skills development and learning environment development. Meaning, in schools, teachers are required daily to develop the knowledge and skills of K–12 students in mathematics, science, language arts, reading, writing, and social studies. In clinically based teacher education, the parallel is the coupling of teacher candidate coaching practices and methods instruction practices to develop teacher candidates' pedagogical content knowledge for teaching K–12 students. Secondly, just as teachers of K–12 students are asked to create classroom environments where students feel connected to part of a community, the same is true for school- and university-based teacher educators in clinically based teacher education. They must couple partnership practices and leadership practices to cultivate an environment where teacher candidates can take risks as they develop as emerging practitioners. In addition, school- and university-based teacher educators need an environment where they are resourced appropriately to support the time-intensive nature of clinically based teacher preparation. Finally, teacher candidate evaluation practices and research practices can be coupled to act as a gatekeeper for the education profession and as a mechanism for innovation where data is continually gathered and analyzed to foster meaningful assessment and evaluation of programs and individuals. Zeichner (2010) called for the rethinking of methods courses and field experiences to create a third hybrid space for preparing teachers. Today this third space should exist as clinically based teacher education through the coupling of core sets of practices.

Core Sets of Practices and Outcomes in Action

While I enjoyed reading all of the chapters, two of them particularly struck me that can be used as illustrations of the core sets of practices for clinically based teacher education. The first was Chapter 5, "Creating Spaces for Becoming: Interrogating the Voices that Arise in Clinical Practice," by Hayes and Bolyard. These authors discussed how stakeholders in clinically based teacher education position one another despite efforts to create a space of collegiality that challenged the status quo. The authors found that despite their efforts to encourage teacher candidate agency, they, as faculty, were continually positioned as "knowledgeable others" and "experts" thwarting their attempts to empower candidates through collegiality. They also recognized that the voices of practicing teachers were missing from their conversations, which may have contributed to the issues of positionality that they faced. While they desperately wanted to include practicing teachers, structures in schools that inhibited teachers' time from being school-based teacher educators and structures in universities that inhibited faculty from prioritizing working across boundaries over research and having time and space in their schedules to adjust to teachers' limited time served as barriers. Their quest to rethink the seminar course in clinically based teacher education curriculum to become a professional learning community that values all voices and challenges the status quo is worthy. By drawing upon the concepts found in the methods instruction practices, leadership practices, and research practices, perhaps Hayes and Boyland now could have language to advocate for the essential resources to support them in their resistance of being positioned in ways that perpetuate hierarchy and minimize collegiality.

The second chapter that particularly struck me was Chapter 2, "Understanding Mentoring Practices in a Professional Development School Partnership: Collaborating with the Professional Development Associate" by Mark and Nolan. These authors found that mentor teachers developed as school-based teacher educators because they collaborated with their Professional Development Associates, who were university-based teacher educators in their professional development school context. Unlike the previous example where the teacher educators' efforts were thwarted, this chapter illustrates how a context that unites the core sets of practices for clinically based teacher education through a professional development school model can have powerful outcomes for supporting teacher candidate learning AND teacher learning. The Mark and Nolan study debunks claims of the lack of importance of the university supervisor (e.g., Rodgers & Keil, 2007) and instead stands alongside many other studies that illustrate the importance of the university supervisor (e.g., Bates, Dritz, & Ramirez, 2011; Gimbert & Nolan, 2003). The findings of the Mark and Nolan study not only show that the university-based teacher educator is important in teacher candidate development but that the university-based teacher educator has perhaps an even more important role than just focusing on teacher candidate development—the university based teacher educator must support the classroom teacher in his/her development as a school-based teacher educator. Mark and Nolan may find the concepts and language of the core sets of practices of clinically based teacher education helpful in advocating for sustained resources that support the work happening in their professional development school.

The key for teacher educators interested in moving toward embedding clinical practices into programs is to discuss the ideas shared in the framework with colleagues and peers. This work is multifaceted, complex, and political. The goal should be to improve teacher candidates' knowledge and skills, but this will only occur if teacher educators share responsibility and study outcomes of clinical practices to inform the research base.

THE IMPORTANCE OF CORE PRACTICES FOR OUTCOMES OF CLINICALLY BASED TEACHER EDUCATION

Yendol-Hoppey and colleagues' (2017) framework of core practices for clinically based teacher education can enhance outcomes for clinically based teacher preparation. First, a core set of practices provides the field of teacher education language to describe the nature of the complex work that is often hidden from outsiders but well understood from insiders working in clinically based teacher education. Scholars have written about the struggles associated with teaching in the clinical context, formerly known as supervising clinical experiences (e.g., Bullough & Draper, 2004) but even less may be known about the challenges associated with coordinating clinically based teacher preparation. By naming the nature of the work, practitioners (both school- and university-based) can use the framework to guide the activities within their contexts to develop or enhance their clinically based teacher preparation programs.

Second, the framework provides ample opportunity for conducting research related to clinically based teacher education and particularly how outcomes are connected to the sophisticated, or unsophisticated, ways in which activities in the core sets of practices are enacted. A framework demystifies the artistry of designing and coordinating clinically based teacher education programs so that evidence-based practices can be fine-tuned to produce positive outcomes for candidates and K–12 students.

ENDURING QUESTIONS

As I reflect on what I learned from reading the chapters in this book and writing Chapter 12, I am left with a few enduring questions. Recently, supervision scholars have started discussing whether supervision is an endangered or an emerging field of study (e.g., Butler et al., 2017; Butler, Burns, & Willey, 2016). On one hand, the move towards clinically based teacher preparation situates supervision as emerging, offering ample opportunity to understand how to design meaningful clinically based teacher education programs to create an environment that facilitates teacher candidate learning. On the other hand, supervision may be endangered as clinically based teacher education programs may face a shortage (and perhaps even a crisis) of scholars who understand and can enact the core sets of practices of successful clinically based teacher education programs. Historically, the field of supervision has been divided between those who supervise inservice teachers in schools and those who supervise teacher candidates in teacher education programs. Rarely do scholars draw upon either literature base even those schools serve as the sites for clinical preparation and many parallels can be drawn between inservice teacher learning and preservice teacher learning. This begs the question—to what extent are doctoral students today being prepared to understand the knowledge base and skill set not only of teacher education, known as a pedagogy of teacher education (Loughran, 2006), but also the unique knowledge base and skill set found in the clinical context of teacher education, known as clinical pedagogy (Burns & Badiali, 2016)? How might the core sets of practices serve as a common framework for preparing the next generation of school- and university-based teacher educators who can successfully enact clinically based teacher education?

In addition to the preparation of the next generation of teacher educators, I think about outcomes identified in this book and the role and importance of research in clinically based teacher education. In the Introduction, editors, Hoppey and Yendol-Hoppey described Boyer's (1990) notion of engaged scholarship as the blending of four kinds of scholarship. They stated,

> Specifically, Boyer (1990) defined Engaged Scholarship as blending: (1) the *scholarship of discovery*, which contributes to the search for new knowledge through collaborative inquiry, (2) the *scholarship of integration*, which makes connections across contexts and disciplines, places specialized knowledge in larger contexts, and advances knowledge through synthesis, 3) the *scholarship of application* through which scholars ask how knowledge can be applied to educational dilemmas, address school needs, as well as test, inspire, and challenge theory, and (4) the *scholarship of teaching*, which includes working with partners to create, transform, and extend knowledge of teaching beyond the university walls. (p. 5, emphasis in original)

The editors argue that the chapters in this book are examples of engaged scholarship, and I concur with the editors—the outcomes described in this book are powerful, and engaged scholarship may be uniquely poised to be an important approach for clinically based teacher education. However, when

I think about the research practices as a core set of practices for clinically based teacher education and engaged scholarship as a critical approach for research in and on clinically based teacher education, I wonder to what extent current and future teacher educators are prepared and equipped to enact engaged scholarship. I also wonder to what extent engaged scholarship is considered acceptable in the academy and to what extent such practices may affect the hiring and tenure and promotion of scholars of teacher education. If teacher education is moving toward centering clinical practice in the curriculum, can teacher preparation afford to have teacher educators who cannot conduct or are not conducting engaged scholarship? It seems that as schools and universities work more closely and intentionally, the way in which research is conceptualized and enacted in schools AND in universities needs to be reconsidered. For teacher education scholars to be successful in the academy, practice-based research and engaged scholarship must become accepted and resourced appropriately at research institutions.

CONCLUSION

In this chapter, I argued that the complexity of the work that led to the powerful outcomes in the chapters of this book needs to be named, and one promising framework has emerged that highlights the core sets of practices for successfully designing, implementing, and monitoring clinically based teacher education. If teacher education is truly to be flipped upside down or turned inside out to center clinical practice as educational reform suggests (AACTE, 2010; NCATE, 2010), then understanding more deeply how to create, resource, and research clinically based education programs is imperative. The field of teacher education must not only focus on teacher candidate preparation, but it must also pay attention to the education of teacher educators to develop teacher education scholars who have the knowledge, skills, and dispositions to conduct engaged scholarship and work collaboratively with school partners and other faculty to create clinical environments that foster learning for candidates, teachers, and K–12 students. By naming the nature of the complex work occurring in clinically based teacher education programs, teacher educators can advocate for adequate resources and for recognizing the role and importance of engaged scholarship in the academy. Those engaged in clinically based teacher education programs recognize the complexity and the value of the work, but now it is time to explain through common terms the difficult but essential work of working across school-university borders to create meaningful clinical education.

REFERENCES

American Association of Colleges of Teacher Education. (2010). *The clinical preparation of teachers: A policy brief.* Washington, DC. Retrieved from https://coe.uni.edu/sites/default/files/wysiwyg/AACTE_-_Clinical_Prep_Paper.pdf

Bates, A. J., Drits, D., & Ramirez, L. A. (2011). Self-awareness and enactment of supervisory stance: Influences on responsiveness toward student teacher learning. *Teacher Education Quarterly, 38*(3), 69–87.

Boyer, E. L. (1990). *Scholarship reconsidered: Priorities of the professoriate.* New York, NY: Carnegie Foundation for the Advancement of Teaching.

Bullough, R. V., Jr., & Draper, R. J. (2004). Making sense of a failed triad: Mentors, university supervisors, and positioning theory. *Journal of Teacher Education, 55*(5), 407–420.

Burns, R. W., & Badiali, B. (2016). Unearthing the complexities of clinical pedagogy in supervision: Identifying pedagogical skills of supervisors. *Action in Teacher Education, 38*(2), 156–174.

Butler, B. M., Burns, R. W., & Willey, C. J. (2016, October). *Supervision as an endangered or emerging field of study? A duoethnography of supervision practice and scholarship in teacher education.* Paper presented at the annual meeting of the Council of Professors of Instructional Supervision, Tampa, FL.

Butler, B. M., Burns, R. W., Willey, C. J., McIntyre, J., Badiali, B., Diacopoulos, M., . . . & Davis, S. (2017, February). *Supervision as a field of study—Endangered or emerging? Scholars share their stories and perspectives.* Symposium at the annual meeting of the Association of Teacher Educators, Orlando, FL.

Cogan, M. (1973). *Clinical supervision.* Boston, MA: Houghton Mifflin.

Gimbert, B., & Nolan, J. F., Jr. (2003). The influence of the professional development school context on supervisory practice: A university supervisor's and interns' perspectives. *Journal of Curriculum & Supervision, 18*(4), 353–379.

Glickman, C., Gordon, S. P., & Ross-Gordon, J. M. (2014). *Supervision and instructional leadership: A developmental approach* (9th ed.). Boston, MA: Allyn and Bacon.

Loughran, J. J. (2006). *Developing a pedagogy of teacher education: Understanding teaching and learning about teaching.* London, England: Routledge.

National Council for the Accreditation of Teacher Education. (2010). *Transforming teacher education through clinical practice: A national strategy to prepare effective teachers. A report of the Blue Ribbon Panel on Clinical Preparation and Partnership for Improved Student Learning.* Washington, DC: NCATE.

Rodgers, A., & Keil, V. L. (2007). Restructuring a traditional student teacher supervision model: Fostering enhanced professional development and mentoring within a professional development school context. *Teaching & Teacher Education: An International Journal of Research and Studies, 23*(1), 63–80.

Yendol-Hoppey, D. (2013, November). *Teacher Education in the United States: Possibilities and Problems.* Invited Keynote at ISATT 2013 Conference, Uberaba, Brazil.

Yendol-Hoppey, D., Hoppey, D., Jacobs, J., Burns, R. W., Allsopp, D., & Ellerbrock, C. (2017, March). *Defining university-based clinically-rich teacher education practices and understanding the implications for university-based teacher educators.* Presentation at the 2017 annual American Association of Colleges of Teacher Education meeting, Tampa, FL.

Zeichner, K. (2005). A research agenda for teacher education. In M. Cochran-Smith & K. M. Zeichner (Eds.), *Studying teacher education: The report of the AERA panel on research and teacher education* (pp. 737–760). Washington, DC: American Education Research Association.

Zeichner, K. (2010). Rethinking the connections between campus courses and field experiences in college- and university-based teacher education. *Journal of Teacher Education, 61*(1–2), 89–99.

ABOUT THE EDITORS

David Hoppey, PhD, is an associate professor and director of the doctoral program in educational leadership at the University of North Florida. He received his PhD from the University of Florida. Prior to arriving at UNF, David held faculty positions at West Virginia University and the University of South Florida. Previously, he worked as an inclusion specialist and district administrator for Alachua County Public Schools in Gainesville, FL and started his career as a middle school special educator in Orlando, FL. David has taught courses to both special education and elementary education majors on best inclusive practices to meet the needs of students with disabilities as well as doctoral seminars on teacher education and special education. He also has worked extensively redesigning undergraduate and doctoral programs to include more clinically rich teacher preparation components. David's scholarship examines inclusive teacher education, special education policy, and school university partnerships, including providing quality preservice teacher education, and ongoing in-service teacher professional development. Dr. Hoppey's research has been published in *The Journal of Special Education, Teachers College Record,* and *Learning Disabilities Research and Practice,* as well as in book and handbook chapters.

Diane Yendol-Hoppey, PhD, is a professor and the dean of the College of Education and Human Services at the University of North Florida. Diane's research specifically focuses on understanding practice-based teacher education, preservice and in-service job-embedded teacher learning (e.g., teacher inquiry, coaching, mentoring, PLCs), and teacher leadership. Prior to her current position at the University of South Florida, she held positions

Outcomes of High-Quality Clinical Practice in Teacher Education, pages 263–264
Copyright © 2018 by Information Age Publishing
All rights of reproduction in any form reserved.

at the University of Florida and West Virginia University. Her leadership, related to working with schools, has helped develop and sustain several nationally recognized school/university partnerships. Diane has co-authored four books as well as published over 50 studies which have appeared in such journals as *Educational Researcher, Teachers College Record,* and *Journal of Teacher Education.* During Diane's first 13 years in education, she taught PK–5 in Pennsylvania and Maryland.

ABOUT THE CONTRIBUTORS

David H. Allsopp, PhD, as assistant dean, oversees all preservice programs in the college including accreditation and state approval processes, the college's Office of Continuing Information Services, and Student Academic Services. As director of the David C. Anchin Center, David oversees all center activities and works closely with school partners to address educator professional development needs to improve outcomes for struggling students. As a faculty member, David teaches undergraduate and doctoral level coursework including supervising preservice students in their clinical experiences. His scholarly interests include teacher education in special education and effective instructional methods for students with disabilities and other struggling learners, particularly in mathematics. David is widely published in peer reviewed journals, and has co-authored books, book chapters, and online professional development resources.

Yukari Takimoto Amos, PhD, is a professor in the Department of Education, Development, Teaching, and Learning at Central Washington University where she teaches multicultural education and TESL-related classes. Her research interests include teachers of color's experiences, studies of immigrant students' English language learning, international students at American universities, studies of Japanese as a second language among immigrants in Japan, and the dispositions of preservice teachers in the United States towards cultural and linguistic diversity.

Johnna Bolyard, PhD, is currently an associate professor in mathematics education at West Virginia University. She teaches content and pedagogy

Outcomes of High-Quality Clinical Practice in Teacher Education, pages 265–271
Copyright © 2018 by Information Age Publishing
265

courses for prospective and current teachers of mathematics. Her ongoing research interests focus on the development of teachers and teacher leaders of elementary and middle school mathematics.

Michael P. Brady, PhD, is a professor and chair of the Department of Exceptional Student Education at Florida Atlantic University. His research interests in teacher preparation include instructional and coaching applications for teachers, and the impact of policies that affect teacher preparation. He also has an active research agenda on practices and policies that promote community inclusion of people with developmental disabilities including behavioral teaching strategies, community-based instruction, interventions that promote social development and relationships, and post-secondary education programs for adults with intellectual disabilities.

Jamey Burns, EdD, is an educational consultant who specializes in professional learning. Most recently Dr. Burns' work has focused on improving teaching and learning in high-poverty schools and districts throughout the Southeastern United States. She leads professional development including teacher inquiry, instructional coaching, teacher lesson study, and student engagement/collaboration. She has co-authored a book on teacher inquiry and written articles on the Lastinger coaching model, which captures the work she completed with turnaround schools in the state of Florida. Her current research centers on K–12 professional development systems in the state of Florida, early learning coaching, instructional coaching, leadership coaching, and inquiry.

Rebecca West Burns, PhD, is an associate professor in the Department of Teaching and Learning at the University of South Florida where she studies supervision, clinically rich teacher education, and school–university partnerships. In particular, her research examines the clinical pedagogy used in clinical experiences, the hybrid roles needed to enact clinically rich teacher education in school–university partnerships, and how supervision in school–university partnerships can develop teacher leadership capacity to renew schools and colleges of education.

William (Will) A. Butler, EdD, has been in education for 16 years. His classroom teaching experience includes working with students with disabilities in a resource setting as well as working with students with behavior disorders in a self-contained classroom. Will spent two years at the district level working as a staff development coach and helping to establish a teacher induction program for first year teachers. He has been a site coordinator for the iTeach program since 2011.

Diana V. Cantu, PhD, currently teaches with the Monarch Teach Program at Old Dominion University. She has recently worked as a master teacher in the program where she actively recruited and trained potential STEM teachers. Her research focus is on furthering technology and engineering education, particularly at an elementary level. She is the field editor for *The Children's Technology and Engineering Journal.*

Jessica A. DeBiase, MEd, has served in the education field for approximately 20 years in both the P–12 and Higher Education sectors. She received a Bachelor of Arts in Special Education degree from Arizona State University and a Master in Bilingual Multicultural Education degree from Northern Arizona University. In her early career, Jessica supported students with disabilities in resource and inclusion settings and taught second language learners. In the area of teacher preparation, Jessica has taught a variety of courses, assisted with course development, contributed to program projects, and supervised preservice teachers. In her current role as a program specialist, Jessica is responsible for supporting site coordinators in their roles, hosting professional development, assisting with grant initiatives and program reform, and presenting at national conferences. She is currently completing her Doctor of Education in Educational Leadership degree from Northern Arizona University and she is expected to graduate in 2017. Her research interests lie in preservice teacher dispositions and professionalism.

Gail K. Dickinson, PhD, is the associate dean for Graduate Studies and Research in the Darden College of Education at Old Dominion University. She has published extensively in the field of school librarianship, focusing on curriculum issues and school library management. Previous to her work at ODU, she was an assistant professor at UNC-Greensboro, a library supervisor for Union-Endicott School District in Endicott, NY, and a school librarian at various schools on the Eastern Shore of Virginia. She earned her PhD from the University of Virginia, and a master's in library science from the University of North Carolina at Chapel Hill.

Penelope A. Dyer, PhD, has over 30 years of experience in the field of education. Penny earned a PhD in Education in Curriculum and Instruction at the University of California, Berkeley. As a clinical assistant professor in the role of site coordinator at Central High School for Arizona State University, she instructs, coaches, and supervises a senior year residency program focusing on teacher candidate development in the high school setting. Dyer's duties also include designing and delivering professional development and individual coaching for mentor teachers. on-site. Recently, Dyer authored the Education and Career Action Plan (ECAP) pilot program curriculum, sponsored by community-based Experience Matters, the ASU Global Pathways Institute, and the Arizona Department of Education. The program is in its second pilot year at Central High School and she is supporting its statewide expansion, which is a goal set by the ECAP division of the Arizona State Department of Education.

Aimee Frier, MA, NBCT, is a doctoral candidate in Special Education and Literacy Studies at the University of South Florida. She teaches preservice teacher methods courses in literacy and special education. Her research interests include preservice teacher education in evidence-based literacy practices for all students and the inclusion of technology within traditional literacy practices.

Lauren Gibbs, EdD, currently works as the associate director at The University of North Florida's Center for Urban Education and Policy. Her research interests include instructional coaching, teacher leadership as professional development, social justice, and instructional leadership. Dr. Gibbs develops and implements differentiated professional development for K–12 educators, administrators, and district leaders in Northeast Florida, and conducts research on instructional leadership coaching as a form of job-embedded professional development. She has publications relating to instructional coaching, teacher leadership development, and literacy development in teacher preparation programs.

Darcey J. Gray, EdD, has worked in education for the past 14 years in Duval County Public Schools. Currently, she works for both Duval County and the University of North Florida as resident clinical faculty. Dr. Gray supervises teacher candidates at one of the UNF Urban Professional Development Partnership Schools.

Stacy A. Hahn, PhD, is the director of Professional Development Pathway Initiatives and Partnerships for the College of Education Anchin Center and the associate director of the David C. Anchin Center. Her work revolves around creating strategic partnerships focused on the development of quality and relevant teacher preparation and support programs. In this role, Dr. Hahn works with USF faculty, multiple school districts, community leaders, and other education related agencies to create teacher education pathways and continuing education courses that will increase the responsiveness to the needs of school districts and the University of South Florida. Prior to working in the Anchin Center, Dr. Hahn was a faculty member in the USF-COEDU Department of Teaching & Learning and the program coordinator for the Undergraduate Special Education Program. Dr. Hahn also engages in teacher education research related to how teacher educators can most effectively prepare teachers to address the needs of students with disabilities and other struggling learners. Dr. Hahn began her career in education as an elementary school teacher for students with learning disabilities. Dr. Hahn earned her PhD in Special Education from the University of Florida. Her career is comprised of a spectrum of roles such as a public school teacher, student advocate, grant facilitator, program coordinator, educational researcher, and university professor. She understands the effect quality schools have on our community and she continues to follow a path, which she hopes will have a positive impact on the education system.

Sharon B. Hayes, PhD, is currently an associate professor in elementary education at West Virginia University and teaches courses in curriculum, instructional design, teacher leadership, practitioner inquiry, and qualitative research. Her ongoing research interests focus on the purposes and possibilities for qualitative inquiry; practitioner inquiry as a space for the transformation of personal, local, and global views of teaching, learning, and the ways we do school; and the construction and reconstruction of identity in prospective and practicing teachers. This work provides opportunities to cross boundaries and explore the borderlands between the university and K–12 schools.

Emily Headrick-Hall, MS, is a doctoral student at the University of Tennessee, Knoxville, studying teacher perceptions of language development in children with hearing loss. Holding degrees in secondary education language arts and deaf education, she is a certified reading specialist and has been teaching high school English language arts at the Tennessee School for the Deaf for 10 years. Her research interests include the potential impact of hearing loss on the development and usage of language as well as ways teacher preparation aligns with the demands of the field.

Ruhi Khan, EdD, is an 18-year veteran in education. As a clinical assistant professor, she supports educational efficacy by ensuring a successful learning environment for all interns and teacher candidates. This is accomplished by her instructional competencies in clinically embedded coursework and professional development opportunities that are focused on student achievement, research-based practices, and data-driven decision-making. As a site coordinator for Arizona State University, Ruhi works with teacher candidates in the Deer Valley Unified School District to support effective instructional practices and professionalism in order to prepare future teachers for their careers in education.

Jennifer Renée Kilpatrick, PhD, is an assistant professor of Deaf Education at University of North Florida. Her research focuses on deaf education teacher preparation and the language and literacy development, assessment, and instruction of deaf and hard of hearing students. She also conducts program evaluation and professional development for several schools for the deaf in Haiti.

Kelly M. Mark, PhD, is a third grade teacher in the State College Area School District where she also serves as a mentor to interns in a yearlong professional development school (PDS) program. She previously worked as a professional development associate in the PDS program (2011–2015). Her research interests are in mentoring practices, their development, and change over time. She is also interested in mentors' beliefs and how they emerge in practice.

Katie M. Miller, PhD, is an assistant professor in the Department of Exceptional Student Education at Florida Atlantic University. She is passionate about teacher and leader preparation in special education including finding best practices that increase special education teacher efficacy. Dr. Miller also has a research focus that examines research-based interventions that infuse technology to increase academic performance for students with disabilities. She has a particular interest in self-regulated strategy development (SRSD) in writing.

James F. Nolan, PhD, is a former elementary and secondary teacher and guidance counselor. Dr. Nolan also served as a faculty member (1987–2015) and the Hermanowicz Professor of Education (2005–2015) at Penn State University. At Penn State, he coordinated the Elementary Professional Development School Partnership with the State College Area School district for 15 years. His research interests are in teacher supervision and evaluation, teacher education and professional development, educational change and classroom learning environments.

Deborah (Debbie) S. Reed, EdD, has worked in higher education for the past ten years at the University of North Florida as an instructor in the Exceptional, Deaf, and Interpreter Education Department in the College of Education. She is currently the Professional Development School coordinator and works closely with teacher candidates, P–12 students, faculty, the local school district and individual schools to help develop and refine clinically rich partnerships. Dr. Reed has worked at a local middle school PDS for the past 5 years as professor in residence.

Michael W. Riley, PhD, is an adjunct instructor in Special Education at the University of South Florida and a full-time classroom teacher in the Pasco (Florida) County School District. His research centers on issues in teacher education and school–family–community partnerships.

Mary Kay Rodgers, PhD, is an adjunct faculty member, researcher, and professional development coordinator at the University of Florida who currently teaches online graduate and doctoral level education courses in the School of Teaching and Learning, as well as researches and coordinates Lastinger Center for Learning professional development efforts nationwide. Her research interests are in inquiry-based professional learning within teacher education for PreK–12 teachers, and she has publications centering on early childhood professional development systems, instructional coaching, critical pedagogy, instructional supervision, and teacher leadership within preK–12 classrooms.

Janice Bell Underwood, PhD, currently serves as the lead science educator at Old Dominion University in Norfolk Virginia. She is also the program director for the Teacher Immersion Residency Program, a collaboration between the Darden School of Education and Norfolk Public Schools, where she actively prepares preservice science and mathematics teachers at the secondary level to work in diverse settings. Additionally, she has in the past served as a Monarch Teach instructor. Her passion and research focus is culturally relevant teaching in all subjects, but particularly in STEM fields. For 16 years prior to joining ODU, Dr. Underwood taught high school students with and without exceptionalities a love for biology as a nationally board certified teacher.

Vicki Vescio, PhD, is an assistant clinical professor at the University of Florida School of Teaching and Learning whose research interests are focused in the areas of equity and social justice as well as pre- and in-service teacher professional development. Dr. Vescio has been involved in research projects to examine preservice teachers' work in high poverty schools, and transformation in the perspectives of teacher educators toward a social justice standpoint. Her publications include a seminally cited article on professional learning communities, as well articles on multicultural education strategies and pedagogy, and clinical supervision with a social justice focus.

Kimberly A. Wolbers, PhD, CI/CT, is an associate professor and coordinator of the Education of the Deaf and Hard of Hearing program at the University of Tennessee in Knoxville. Her research primarily centers on language and literacy instruction of deaf children and adolescents. She conceptualized an approach for teaching writing to deaf students called Strategic and Interactive Writing Instruction.

CPSIA information can be obtained
at www.ICGtesting.com
Printed in the USA
BVHW081958220219
540969BV00006B/32/P